（含 2014 年修正案）

2006 年海事劳工公约

MARITIME LABOUR CONVENTION，2006

（中英对照）

张　铎　校译

U0962835

大连海事大学出版社

图书在版编目(CIP)数据

2006年海事劳工公约=Maritime labour convention, 2006：汉英对照/张铎校译.—大连：大连海事大学出版社，2013.7
(2014.8重印)
ISBN 978-7-5632-2891-1

Ⅰ.①2… Ⅱ.①张… Ⅲ.①海员—国际劳动公约—2006—汉、英
Ⅳ.①D998.2

中国版本图书馆CIP数据核字(2013)第172306号

大连海事大学出版社出版
地址:大连市凌海路1号 邮编:116026 电话:0411-84728394 传真:0411-84727996
http://www.dmupress.com E-mail:cbs@dmupress.com
大连住友彩色印刷有限公司印装 大连海事大学出版社发行
2013年7月第1版 2014年8月第2次印刷
幅面尺寸:144 mm×210 mm 印张:13.375
字数:301千 印数:1001～2000册
出版人:徐华东
责任编辑:陆 梅 版式设计:小 月
封面设计:王 艳 责任校对:何 乔
ISBN 978-7-5632-2891-1 定价:58.00元

前　言

国际劳工组织(ILO),作为国际联盟的附属机构,于1919年根据《凡尔赛和约》设立,1946年转为联合国专门机构。国际劳工组织以公约、议定书和建议书的形式,制定和推动国际劳工标准,促进全世界劳动者的体面工作及其基本权益的保护。迄今为止,国际劳工组织已通过了189项公约、5项公约议定书和202项建议书。

中国为该组织的创始成员国之一,于1944年成为其理事会常任政府理事。1971年,中华人民共和国在该组织的合法席位得以恢复,并于1983年正式恢复在该组织的活动。迄今中国共批准了25项国际劳工公约,其中包括承认由当时的民国政府批准的14项公约。目前,这25项公约中有22项对中国有效,其余3项有关最低年龄的公约因相关新公约的生效而被取代,中国因此自动退出。

《2006年海事劳工公约》是国际劳工组织在综合和修订了其先前通过的68个相关公约和建议书的基础上制定的新的综合性海事劳工公约,被喻为海员的"人权法案",同时又被称作与IMO通过的SOLAS公约、MARPOL公约和STCW公约共同支撑国际海事法律体系的第四根支柱。但是,与前述三个IMO海事公约相比,《2006年海事劳工公约》具有突出的特点:除技术性和行政管理的公法属性外,还兼有私法属性,直接涉及海员与船东等不同主体之间的劳动和民事法律关系。这就要求对《2006年海事劳工公约》的理解更要全面和准确。

在《2006年海事劳工公约》于2006年2月23日通过后,国际劳工组织官方网站(http://www.ilo.org)登载了该公约的中文译文("ILO中文译文")。该ILO中文译文对及早认识和理解《2006年海事劳工公约》以及我国的履约准备起到了重要和积极的作用,但相对于该公约内容的繁杂性和重要性以及我国现有履约法规体系而言,还存在诸多疏漏。此外,《2006年海事劳工公约》的官方英文文本此后进行了多处修饰性的修改。基于以上原因,现依据国际劳工组织最新官方英文文本,在ILO中文译文的基础上,对《2006年海事劳工公约》的中文译文进行全面校译。此次校译遵循以下原则：

一、改正原译文中的错译和误译，补译原译文中漏译的短语和词语，注重公约翻译中源语言和目标语言的对应性；

二、规范和统一词语的译法，使相同词语的译法通篇保持统一和一致；

三、规范航海、造船和海事管理等专业的技术术语的译法，与IMO海事公约中的译法统一，也与实践中的表述方式一致；

四、规范和统一法律术语的译法，与我国法律体系中的表述方式统一；

五、改正原译文中的文字输入和数字编号等编辑性错误；

六、对于英文原文中可能的文字错误以及该公约中的个别概念，以“校译者注”的方式在脚注中予以说明，便于参考和理解。

通过以上几个方面的工作，此次校译共涉及了原ILO中文译文中一半以上的条款，使校译后的中文译文整体连贯统一，也与我国现行的法律、航海技术、海事管理等体系相贯通，便于对该公约的理解和实施。鉴于校译者的学识有限，错误和疏漏在所难免，敬请读者批评指正。

此校译文本可作为我国相关主管部门、船东协会和海员工会、船员服务机构和有关学者研究和实施《2006年海事劳工公约》时参考，也可以供船东、海员以及其他参与实施和执行该公约的人员参考。

张 铎

2013年2月

国际劳工大会
INTERNATIONAL LABOUR CONFERENCE

2006 年海事劳工公约
MARITIME LABOUR CONVENTION, 2006

INTERNATIONAL LABOUR CONFERENCE

Contents

国际劳工大会

目　录

MARITIME LABOUR CONVENTION, 2006

PREAMBLE

The General Conference of the International Labour Organization,

Having been convened at Geneva by the Governing Body of the International Labour Office, and having met in its Ninety-fourth Session on 7 February 2006, and

Desiring to create a single, coherent instrument embodying as far as possible all up-to-date standards of existing international maritime labour Conventions and Recommendations, as well as the fundamental principles to be found in other international labour Conventions, in particular:

—the Forced Labour Convention, 1930 (No. 29);

—the Freedom of Association and Protection of the Right to Organise Convention, 1948 (No. 87);

—the Right to Organise and Collective Bargaining Convention, 1949 (No. 98);

—the Equal Remuneration Convention, 1951 (No. 100);

—the Abolition of Forced Labour Convention, 1957 (No. 105);

2006年海事劳工公约

序　言

国际劳工组织大会，

经国际劳工局理事会召集，于2006年2月7日在日内瓦举行了其第94届会议，并

希望制定一项条理统一的单一文件，尽可能体现现有国际海事劳工公约和建议书中的所有最新标准以及其他国际劳工公约，特别是以下公约❶中的基本原则：

—《1930年强迫劳动公约》(第29号)；

—《1948年自由结社和保护组织权利公约》(第87号)；

—《1949年组织权利和集体谈判公约》(第98号)；

—《1951年同酬公约》(第100号)；

—《1957年废除强迫劳动公约》(第105号)；

---

❶ 以下所列是ILO的全部八项"基本公约"，又称"核心公约"，其中第100、111、138和182号公约我国已批准。这八项基本公约所体现的四项基本原则和权利列于公约正文第三条。——校译者注

此书中凡是原文脚注用阳圈码标识，校译者注用阴圈码标识。

—the Discrimination (Employment and Occupation) Convention, 1958 (No. 111);

—the Minimum Age Convention, 1973 (No. 138);

—the Worst Forms of Child Labour Convention, 1999 (No. 182); and

Mindful of the core mandate of the Organization, which is to promote decent conditions of work, and

Recalling the ILO Declaration on Fundamental Principles and Rights at Work, 1998, and

Mindful also that seafarers are covered by the provisions of other ILO instruments and have other rights which are established as fundamental rights and freedoms applicable to all persons, and

Considering that, given the global nature of the shipping industry, seafarers need special protection, and

Mindful also of the international standards on ship safety, human security and quality ship management in the International Convention for the Safety of Life at Sea, 1974, as amended, the Convention on the International Regulations for Preventing Collisions at Sea, 1972, as amended, and the seafarer training and competency requirements in the International Convention on Standards of Training, Certification and Watchkeeping for Seafarers, 1978, as amended, and

Recalling that the United Nations Convention on the Law of the Sea, 1982, sets out a general legal framework within which all activities in the oceans and seas must be carried out and is of strategic importance as the basis for national, regional and global action and cooperation in the marine sector, and that its integrity needs to be

—《1958年(就业和职业)歧视公约》(第111号);

—《1973年最低年龄公约》(第138号);

—《1999年最恶劣形式的童工公约》(第182号);并

意识到本组织倡导体面工作条件的核心使命,并

忆及《1998年国际劳工组织工作中的基本原则和权利宣言》[1],并

还意识到海员受国际劳工组织其他文件[2]的规定所保护,且享有作为适用于所有人基本权利和自由而确立的其他权利,并

考虑到由于航运业的全球性,海员需要特殊保护,并

还意识到经修正的《1974年国际海上人命安全公约》和经修正的《1972年国际海上避碰规则公约》中关于船舶安全、人的保障和优质船舶管理的国际标准,以及经修正的《1978年海员培训、发证和值班标准国际公约》中关于海员培训和适任要求的国际标准,并

忆及《1982年联合国海洋法公约》规定了一个总体法律框架,海洋和海域中的所有活动都必须在此框架下展开,它是海洋部门进行国家、地区和全球性活动和合作的基础,具有战略重要性,其完整性需要得到维持,并

---

[1] 该宣言促使成员国,不论其是否批准了前述八项核心公约,均要尊重并促进该核心公约中所体现的列于公约正文第三条中的四项基本原则和权利,并进一步明确,这些权利适用于所有国家中的所有人员,单凭经济的发展不足以确保平等、社会进步和根除贫困。为此在该宣言中设立了一项跟踪程序,要求没有全部批准前述八项核心公约的成员国每年对于其境内的相关原则和权利的状况做出报告,说明批准公约的障碍以及可能需要协助的方面,并由独立专家咨询委员会对报告进行审查。其审查的评述再由ILO理事会进行审议。——校译者注

[2] 国际劳工组织的“文件(instrument)”是指国际劳工组织的“公约(Convention)”、“议定书(Protocol)”和“建议书(Recommendation)”。——校译者注

maintained, and

Recalling that Article 94 of the United Nations Convention on the Law of the Sea, 1982, establishes the duties and obligations of a flag State with regard to, inter alia, labour conditions, crewing and social matters on ships that fly its flag, and

Recalling paragraph 8 of article 19 of the Constitution of the International Labour Organisation which provides that in no case shall the adoption of any Convention or Recommendation by the Conference or the ratification of any Convention by any Member be deemed to affect any law, award, custom or agreement which ensures more favourable conditions to the workers concerned than those provided for in the Convention or Recommendation, and

Determined that this new instrument should be designed to secure the widest possible acceptability among governments, shipowners and seafarers committed to the principles of decent work, that it should be readily updateable and that it should lend itself to effective implementation and enforcement, and

Having decided upon the adoption of certain proposals for the realization of such an instrument, which is the only item on the agenda of the session, and

Having determined that these proposals shall take the form of an international Convention;

adopts this twenty-third day of February of the year two thousand and six the following Convention, which may be cited as the Maritime Labour Convention, 2006.

忆及《1982年联合国海洋法公约》第九十四条确立了船旗国对悬挂其旗帜的船舶上的尤其是劳动条件、船员配备和社会事务的职责和义务，并

忆及《国际劳工组织章程》第十九条第8款规定，无论在何种情况下，大会通过任何公约或建议书或任何成员国批准任何公约都不得被视为影响到那些确保有关工人得到优于公约或建议书所规定条件的任何法律、裁决、惯例或协议，并

决定此新文件的制定应保证得到致力于体面工作原则的政府、船东和海员尽可能最广泛的接受，且应易于更新并有助于有效的实施和执行，并

决定通过某些提案，以完成作为本届会议议程唯一项目的这一文件，并且

决定这些提案须采用一项国际公约的形式；

于二○○六年二月二十三日通过以下公约，可引用为《2006年海事劳工公约》。

GENERAL OBLIGATIONS

Article I

1. Each Member which ratifies this Convention undertakes to give complete effect to its provisions in the manner set out in Article VI in order to secure the right of all seafarers to decent employment.

2. Members shall cooperate with each other for the purpose of ensuring the effective implementation and enforcement of this Convention.

DEFINITIONS AND SCOPE OF APPLICATION

Article II

1. For the purpose of this Convention and unless provided otherwise in particular provisions, the term:

(a) *competent authority* means the minister, government department or other authority having power to issue and enforce regulations, orders or other instructions having the force of law in respect of the subject matter of the provision concerned;

(b) *declaration of maritime labour compliance* means the declaration referred to in Regulation 5.1.3;

(c) *gross tonnage* means the gross tonnage calculated in accordance with the tonnage measurement regulations contained in Annex I to the International Convention on Tonnage Measurement of Ships, 1969, or any successor Convention; for ships covered by

一般义务

第一条

1. 批准本公约的各成员国[1]承诺按第六条规定的方式全面履行公约的规定，以确保所有海员体面就业的权利。

2. 成员国须为确保有效实施和执行本公约之目的而相互合作。

定义和适用范围

第二条

1. 除非具体条款另行规定，就本公约而言：

(a)“主管当局”一词系指有权就相关规定的主题颁布和实施具有法律效力的条例、命令或其他指令的部长、政府部门或其他当局；

(b)“海事劳工符合声明”一词系指规则 5.1.3 所述之声明；

(c)“总吨位”一词系指根据《1969 年船舶吨位丈量国际公约》附则一或任何后继公约中载明的吨位丈量条款所计算出的总吨位；对于国际海事组织通过的临时吨位丈量表所涵盖的船舶，总吨位为填写在“国际吨位证书(1969)”的“备注”栏中的总吨位；

---

[1] 在本公约中，“成员国(member)”一词，即使其前面没有“已批准本公约”的限定，也是指已批准本公约的 ILO 成员国。如果特别指明为 ILO 的“任何”成员国，如在第十五条第 2 款中，则包括 ILO 的全部成员国，无论其是否已批准本公约。——校译者注

the tonnage measurement interim scheme adopted by the International Maritime Organization, the gross tonnage is that which is included in the REMARKS column of the International Tonnage Certificate (1969);

(d) *maritime labour certificate* means the certificate referred to in Regulation 5. 1. 3;

(e) *requirements of this Convention* refers to the requirements in these Articles and in the Regulations and Part A of the Code of this Convention;

(f) *seafarer* means any person who is employed or engaged[1] or works in any capacity on board a ship to which this Convention applies;

(g) *seafarers' employment agreement* includes both a contract of employment and articles of agreement;

(h) *seafarer recruitment and placement service* means any person, company, institution, agency or other organization, in the public or the private sector, which is engaged in recruiting seafarers on behalf of shipowners or placing seafarers with shipowners;

(i) *ship* means a ship other than one which navigates exclusively in inland waters or waters within, or closely adjacent to, sheltered waters or areas where port regulations apply;

---

[1] 在 ILO 的所有公约中,主要使用 employ 一词(包括其派生词)表示劳资双方之间的关系。一直到第 7 号公约(《1920 年海员安置公约》)才首次出现 engage(包括其派生词),用以表示这种劳资关系。其中,engage 较为正式,偏重于与人建立劳资关系,而 employ 偏重于人的职业资格。在本公约中,两者没有明显的区分,以 employ 为主,间或混用。但在翻译时,仍做了严格对应:将 engage 译成“聘用”,将 employ 译成“雇用”。另,employ 依上下文还译成“就业”。——校译者注

(d)“海事劳工证书”一词系指规则5.1.3中所述之证书；

(e)“本公约的要求”一词指本公约的正文条款和规则及守则A部分中的要求；

(f)“海员”一词系指在本公约所适用的船舶上以任何职务受雇或受聘或工作的任何人员；

(g)“海员就业协议”一词包括就业合同和协议条款；

(h)“海员招募和安置服务机构”一词系指公共或私营部门中从事代表船东招募海员或向船东安置海员的任何人员、公司、机构、代理处或其他组织；

(i)“船舶”一词系指除专门在内陆水域或在遮蔽水域之内或其紧邻水域或在适用港章的区域航行的船舶以外的船舶；

(j) *shipowner* means the owner of the ship or another organization or person, such as the manager, agent or bareboat charterer, who has assumed the responsibility for the operation of the ship from the owner and who, on assuming such responsibility, has agreed to take over the duties and responsibilities imposed on shipowners in accordance with this Convention, regardless of whether any other organization or persons fulfil certain of the duties or responsibilities on behalf of the shipowner.

2. Except as expressly provided otherwise, this Convention applies to all seafarers.

3. In the event of doubt as to whether any categories of persons are to be regarded as seafarers for the purpose of this Convention, the question shall be determined by the competent authority in each Member after consultation with the shipowners' and seafarers' organizations concerned with this question.

4. Except as expressly provided otherwise, this Convention applies to all ships, whether publicly or privately owned, ordinarily engaged in commercial activities, other than ships engaged in fishing or in similar pursuits and ships of traditional build such as dhows and junks. This Convention does not apply to warships or naval auxiliaries.

5. In the event of doubt as to whether this Convention applies to a ship or particular category of ships, the question shall be determined by the competent authority in each Member after consultation with the shipowners' and seafarers' organizations concerned.

6. Where the competent authority determines that it would not be reasonable or practicable at the present time to apply certain de-

(j)“船东”一词系指船舶所有人或从船舶所有人那里承担了船舶经营责任并在承担这种责任时已同意接受船东根据本公约所承担的职责和责任的另一组织或个人,如管理人、代理人或光船承租人,无论是否有任何其他组织或个人代表船东履行了某些职责或责任。

2. 除非另有明文规定,本公约适用于所有海员。

3. 如果就某类人员是否将被视为本公约意义上的海员存在疑问,该问题须由各成员国的主管当局在与此问题所涉及的船东组织和海员组织进行协商后决定。

4. 除非另有明文规定,本公约适用于通常从事商业活动的所有船舶,无论其为公有或私有,但不包括从事捕鱼或类似捕捞的船舶以及传统构造的船舶,例如独桅三角帆船和舢板。本公约不适用于军用船舶和军事辅助船。

5. 如果就本公约是否适用于某一船或特定类别船舶存在疑问,该问题须由各成员国的主管当局在与有关船东组织和海员组织进行协商后决定。

6. Where the competent authority determines that it would not be reasonable or practicable at the present time to apply certain details of the Code referred to in Article VI, paragraph 1, to a ship or particular categories of ships flying the flag of the Member, the relevant provisions of the Code shall not apply to the extent that the subject matter is dealt with differently by national laws or regulations or collective bargaining agreements or other measures. Such a determination may only be made in consultation with the shipowners' and seafarers' organizations concerned and may only be made with respect to ships of less than 200 gross tonnage not engaged in international voyages.

7. Any determinations made by a Member under paragraph 3 or 5 or 6 of this Article shall be communicated to the Director-General of the International Labour Office, who shall notify the Members of the Organization.

8. Unless expressly provided otherwise, a reference to this Convention constitutes at the same time a reference to the Regulations and the Code.

FUNDAMENTAL RIGHTS AND PRINCIPLES

Article III

Each Member shall satisfy itself that the provisions of its law and regulations respect, in the context of this Convention, the fundamental rights to:

(a) freedom of association and the effective recognition of the right to collective bargaining;

6. 如果主管当局决定目前对悬挂该成员国旗帜的一艘船或特定类别船舶适用第六条第1款中所述守则的某些细节不合理或不可行，在国内法律或条例或集体谈判协议或其他措施对该主题有不同处理的范围内，守则的有关规定将不适用。此决定只能与有关船东组织和海员组织协商做出，且只能针对那些不从事国际航行的200总吨以下的船舶。

7. 一成员国根据本条第3或5或6款所做的任何决定均须通报国际劳工局局长[1]，局长须通知本组织成员国。

8. 除非另有明文规定，提及本公约构成了同时提及规则和守则。

基本权利和原则

第三条

就本公约所涉事项，各成员国须自行确认其法律和条例的规定尊重以下基本权利：

(a) 结社自由和有效承认集体谈判权利；

[1] 国际劳工局是国际劳工组织的常设工作机构，是国际劳工大会、理事会和其他会议的秘书处，受理事会管理。国际劳工局局长（Director-General）由理事会任命，是国际劳工组织的主要负责人，相当于国际海事组织的秘书长。鉴于 Director-General（局长）在中文中可译成“总干事”，且其为国际劳工组织的主要负责人，故国际劳工局局长现也译成“国际劳工组织总干事”。——校译者注

(b) the elimination of all forms of forced or compulsory labour;

(c) the effective abolition of child labour; and

(d) the elimination of discrimination in respect of employment and occupation.

SEAFARERS' EMPLOYMENT AND SOCIAL RIGHTS

Article IV

1. Every seafarer has the right to a safe and secure workplace that complies with safety standards.

2. Every seafarer has a right to fair terms of employment.

3. Every seafarer has a right to decent working and living conditions on board ship.

4. Every seafarer has a right to health protection, medical care, welfare measures and other forms of social protection.

5. Each Member shall ensure, within the limits of its jurisdiction, that the seafarers' employment and social rights set out in the preceding paragraphs of this Article are fully implemented in accordance with the requirements of this Convention. Unless specified otherwise in the Convention, such implementation may be achieved through national laws or regulations, through applicable collective bargaining agreements or through other measures or in practice.

(b) 消除所有形式的强迫或强制劳动；

(c) 有效废除童工；以及

(d) 消除就业和职业方面的歧视。

海员的就业和社会权利

第四条

1. 每一海员均有权获得符合安全标准的安全且可靠的工作场所。

2. 每一海员均有权获得公平的就业条款。

3. 每一海员均有权获得体面的船上工作和生活条件。

4. 每一海员均有权享有健康保护、医护、福利措施及其他形式的社会保护。

5. 各成员国在其管辖范围内须确保本条上述各款所规定的海员就业和社会权利根据本公约的要求得以充分实施。除非公约中另有具体规定，此种实施可通过国内法律或条例、通过适用的集体谈判协议或通过其他措施或在实践中得以实现。

IMPLEMENTATION AND ENFORCEMENT RESPONSIBILITIES

Article V

1. Each Member shall implement and enforce laws or regulations or other measures that it has adopted to fulfil its commitments under this Convention with respect to ships and seafarers under its jurisdiction.

2. Each Member shall effectively exercise its jurisdiction and control over ships that fly its flag by establishing a system for ensuring compliance with the requirements of this Convention, including regular inspections, reporting, monitoring and legal proceedings under the applicable laws.

3. Each Member shall ensure that ships that fly its flag carry a maritime labour certificate and a declaration of maritime labour compliance as required by this Convention.

4. A ship to which this Convention applies may, in accordance with international law, be inspected by a Member other than the flag State, when the ship is in one of its ports, to determine whether the ship is in compliance with the requirements of this Convention.

5. Each Member shall effectively exercise its jurisdiction and control over seafarer recruitment and placement services, if these are established in its territory.

6. Each Member shall prohibit violations of the requirements of this Convention and shall, in accordance with international law, establish sanctions or require the adoption of corrective measures under

实施和执行责任

第五条

1．各成员国须对其管辖下的船舶和海员实施和执行其为履行本公约之下的承诺而通过的法律或条例或其他措施。

2．各成员国须通过建立确保遵守本公约要求的制度，对悬挂其旗帜的船舶有效行使其管辖和控制，包括依据适用法律的定期检查、报告、监控和法律程序。

3．各成员国须确保悬挂其旗帜的船舶按本公约的要求持有海事劳工证书和海事劳工符合声明。

4．本公约适用的船舶，当位于除船旗国以外的成员国的某港口时，可根据国际法受到该成员国的检查以确定其是否符合本公约的要求。[1]

5．各成员国须对在其领土内设立的海员招募和安置服务机构有效行使其管辖和控制。

6．各成员国须对违反本公约要求的行为予以禁止，并须根据国际法，在其法律中规定或要求采取足以阻止此种违反行为的制裁或改正措施。

---

[1] 本款确立了将本公约纳入港口国检查范围的原则。——校译者注

its laws which are adequate to discourage such violations.

7. Each Member shall implement its responsibilities under this Convention in such a way as to ensure that the ships that fly the flag of any State that has not ratified this Convention do not receive more favourable treatment than the ships that fly the flag of any State that has ratified it.

REGULATIONS AND PARTS A AND B OF THE CODE

Article VI

1. The Regulations and the provisions of Part A of the Code are mandatory. The provisions of Part B of the Code are not mandatory.

2. Each Member undertakes to respect the rights and principles set out in the Regulations and to implement each Regulation in the manner set out in the corresponding provisions of Part A of the Code. In addition, the Member shall give due consideration to implementing its responsibilities in the manner provided for in Part B of the Code.

3. A Member which is not in a position to implement the rights and principles in the manner set out in Part A of the Code may, unless expressly provided otherwise in this Convention, implement Part A through provisions in its laws and regulations or other measures which are substantially equivalent to the provisions of Part A.

4. For the sole purpose of paragraph 3 of this Article, any law, regulation, collective agreement or other implementing measure shall be considered to be substantially equivalent, in the context of this Convention, if the Member satisfies itself that:

7. 各成员国须以确保悬挂未批准本公约之任何国家旗帜的船舶得不到比悬挂已批准本公约之任何国家旗帜的船舶更优惠待遇的方式履行其在本公约之下的责任。[1]

规则以及守则之A部分和B部分

第六条

1. 规则和守则A部分的条款具有强制性。守则B部分的条款为非强制性。

2. 各成员国保证尊重规则中规定的权利和原则，并按守则A部分的对应条款所规定的方式实施每条规则。此外，成员国须充分考虑到按守则B部分给出的方式履行其责任。

3. 除非本公约另有明文规定，不能按守则A部分规定的方式实施权利和原则的成员国，可以通过实质上等效于A部分规定的法律和条例的规定或其他措施来实施A部分。

4. 仅就本条第3款而言，对于本公约所涉事项，任何法律、条例、集体协议或其他履约措施只有在成员国自行确认以下情况时才须被视为实质上等效：

---

[1] 本款确立了“非更优惠待遇”原则，对于本公约的非批约国，仍以公约规定的标准对其船舶进行检查，不使其从不批约中得到益处。——校译者注

(a) it is conducive to the full achievement of the general object and purpose of the provision or provisions of Part A of the Code concerned; and

(b) it gives effect to the provision or provisions of Part A of the Code concerned.

CONSULTATION WITH SHIPOWNERS' AND SEAFARERS' ORGANIZATIONS

Article VII

Any derogation, exemption or other flexible application of this Convention for which the Convention requires consultation with shipowners' and seafarers' organizations may, in cases where representative organizations of shipowners or of seafarers do not exist within a Member, only be decided by that Member through consultation with the Committee referred to in Article XIII.

ENTRY INTO FORCE

Article VIII

1. The formal ratifications of this Convention shall be communicated to the Director-General of the International Labour Office for registration.

2. This Convention shall be binding only upon those Members of the International Labour Organization whose ratifications have been registered by the Director-General.

3. This Convention shall come into force 12 months after the

(a) 它有助于充分实现守则A部分有关规定的总体目标和目的;且

(b) 它落实了守则A部分的有关规定。

与船东组织和海员组织协商

第七条

如果在一成员国内不存在船东的或海员的代表性组织,公约中要求与船东组织和海员组织进行协商的任何对本公约的减损、免除或其他灵活适用,只能由该成员国通过与第十三条所述之委员会协商决定。

生　效

第八条

1. 对本公约的正式批准书须送请国际劳工局局长登记。

2. 本公约只对其批准书已由局长登记的国际劳工组织成员国具有约束力。

3. 本公约须在合计占世界船舶总吨位33%的至少30个成员国的批准书[1]已经登记之日12个月后生效。

---

[1] 本款仅规定了以较为严格的"批准"方式使公约生效,未规定"接受、核准或加入"等方式。依据我国《缔结条约程序法》第七条的规定,本公约在我国的批准由我国人大常委会决定。——校译者注

date on which there have been registered ratifications by at least 30 Members with a total share in the world gross tonnage of ships of 33 per cent.

4. Thereafter, this Convention shall come into force for any Member 12 months after the date on which its ratification has been registered.

DENUNCIATION

Article IX

1. A Member which has ratified this Convention may denounce it after the expiration of ten years from the date on which the Convention first comes into force, by an act communicated to the Director-General of the International Labour Office for registration. Such denunciation shall not take effect until one year after the date on which it is registered.

2. Each Member which does not, within the year following the expiration of the period of ten years mentioned in paragraph 1 of this Article, exercise the right of denunciation provided for in this Article, shall be bound for another period of ten years and, thereafter, may denounce this Convention at the expiration of each new period of ten years under the terms provided for in this Article.

4. 此后，对于任何成员国，本公约须在其批准书经登记之日 12 个月后对其生效。

退 出

第九条

1. 已批准本公约的成员国，自公约初次生效之日起满十年后，可通过向国际劳工局局长送请登记决议书来退出本公约。此项退出须自登记之日起一年后发生效力。

2. 在本条第 1 款所述十年期满后的一年内未行使本条所规定之退出权利的各成员国，即需再遵守十年，此后每当新的十年期满，可依本条规定的条款退出本公约。

EFFECT OF ENTRY INTO FORCE

Article X

This Convention revises the following Conventions:

Minimum Age (Sea) Convention, 1920 (No. 7)

Unemployment Indemnity (Shipwreck) Convention, 1920 (No. 8)

Placing of Seamen Convention, 1920 (No. 9)

Medical Examination of Young Persons (Sea) Convention, 1921 (No. 16)

Seamen's Articles of Agreement Convention, 1926 (No. 22)

Repatriation of Seamen Convention, 1926 (No. 23)

Officers' Competency Certificates Convention, 1936 (No. 53)

Holidays with Pay (Sea) Convention, 1936 (No. 54)

Shipowners' Liability (Sick and Injured Seamen) Convention, 1936 (No. 55)

Sickness Insurance (Sea) Convention, 1936 (No. 56)

Hours of Work and Manning (Sea) Convention, 1936 (No. 57)

Minimum Age (Sea) Convention (Revised), 1936 (No. 58)

Food and Catering (Ships' Crews) Convention, 1946 (No. 68)

Certification of Ships' Cooks Convention, 1946 (No. 69)

Social Security (Seafarers) Convention, 1946 (No. 70)

生效的影响

第十条

本公约修订以下公约[1]：

《1920年(海上)最低年龄公约》(第7号)[2]

《1920年(海难)失业赔偿公约》(第8号)

《1920年海员安置公约》(第9号)

《1921年(海上)未成年人体检公约》(第16号)[3]

《1926年海员协议条款公约》(第22号)[3]

《1926年海员遣返公约》(第23号)[3]

《1936年高级船员适任证书公约》(第53号)

《1936年(海上)带薪假期公约》(第54号)

《1936年船东(对病、伤海员)责任公约》(第55号)

《1936年(海上)疾病保险公约》(第56号)

《1936年(海上)工时和配员公约》(第57号)

《1936年(海上)最低年龄公约(修订)》(第58号)

《1946年(船员)食品和膳食服务公约》(第68号)

《1946年船上厨师发证公约》(第69号)

《1946年(海员)社会保障公约》(第70号)

---

[1] 下列公约，无脚注说明者，为我国未批准的公约。——校译者注

[2] 该公约于1936年12月2日由当时的中华民国政府批准，1984年我国政府予以承认；但在1999年4月28日因被第138号公约取代，我国自动退出。——校译者注

[3] 该公约于1936年12月2日由当时的中华民国政府批准，1984年我国政府予以承认，现仍有效。——校译者注

Paid Vacations (Seafarers) Convention, 1946 (No. 72)

Medical Examination (Seafarers) Convention, 1946 (No. 73)

Certification of Able Seamen Convention, 1946 (No. 74)

Accommodation of Crews Convention, 1946 (No. 75)

Wages, Hours of Work and Manning (Sea) Convention, 1946 (No. 76)

Paid Vacations (Seafarers) Convention (Revised), 1949 (No. 91)

Accommodation of Crews Convention (Revised), 1949 (No. 92)

Wages, Hours of Work and Manning (Sea) Convention (Revised), 1949 (No. 93)

Wages, Hours of Work and Manning (Sea) Convention (Revised), 1958 (No. 109)

Accommodation of Crews (Supplementary Provisions) Convention, 1970 (No. 133)

Prevention of Accidents (Seafarers) Convention, 1970 (No. 134)

Continuity of Employment (Seafarers) Convention, 1976 (No. 145)

Seafarers' Annual Leave with Pay Convention, 1976 (No. 146)

Merchant Shipping (Minimum Standards) Convention, 1976 (No. 147)

Protocol of 1996 to the Merchant Shipping (Minimum Standards) Convention, 1976 (No. 147)

《1946年(海员)带薪休假公约》(第72号)

《1946年(海员)体检公约》(第73号)

《1946年一等水手证书公约》(第74号)

《1946年船员起居舱室公约》(第75号)

《1946年(海上)工资、工时和配员公约》(第76号)

《1949年(海员)带薪休假公约(修订)》(第91号)

《1949年船员起居舱室公约(修订)》(第92号)

《1949年(海上)工资、工时和配员公约(修订)》(第93号)

《1958年(海上)工资、工时和配员公约(修订)》(第109号)

《1970年船员起居舱室(补充规定)公约》(第133号)

《1970年(海员)事故预防公约》(第134号)

《1976年(海员)连续就业公约》(第145号)

《1976年海员带薪年休假公约》(第146号)

《1976年商船(最低标准)公约》(第147号)

《1976年商船(最低标准)公约》(第147号)的1996年议定书

Seafarers' Welfare Convention, 1987 (No. 163)

Health Protection and Medical Care (Seafarers) Convention, 1987 (No. 164)

Social Security (Seafarers) Convention (Revised), 1987 (No. 165)

Repatriation of Seafarers Convention (Revised), 1987 (No. 166)

Labour Inspection (Seafarers) Convention, 1996 (No. 178)

Recruitment and Placement of Seafarers Convention, 1996 (No. 179)

Seafarers' Hours of Work and the Manning of Ships Convention, 1996 (No. 180).

DEPOSITARY FUNCTIONS

Article XI

1. The Director-General of the International Labour Office shall notify all Members of the International Labour Organization of the registration of all ratifications, acceptances and denunciations under this Convention.

2. When the conditions provided for in paragraph 3 of Article VIII have been fulfilled, the Director-General shall draw the attention of the Members of the Organization to the date upon which the Convention will come into force.

《1987 年海员福利公约》(第 163 号)

《1987 年(海员)健康保护和医护公约》(第 164 号)

《1987 年(海员)社会保障公约(修订)》(第 165 号)

《1987 年海员遣返公约(修订)》(第 166 号)

《1996 年(海员)劳动监察公约》(第 178 号)

《1996 年海员招募和安置公约》(第 179 号)

《1996 年海员工时和船舶配员公约》(第 180 号)。

保存人职责

第十一条

1. 国际劳工局局长须将本公约之下的所有批准书、接受书和退出书的登记情况通报国际劳工组织的全体成员国。

2. 在第八条第 3 款规定的条件得到满足时,局长须提请本组织成员国注意公约将生效的日期。

Article XII

The Director-General of the International Labour Office shall communicate to the Secretary-General of the United Nations for registration in accordance with Article 102 of the Charter of the United Nations full particulars of all ratifications, acceptances and denunciations registered under this Convention.

SPECIAL TRIPARTITE COMMITTEE

Article XIII

1. The Governing Body of the International Labour Office shall keep the working of this Convention under continuous review through a committee established by it with special competence in the area of maritime labour standards.

2. For matters dealt with in accordance with this Convention, the Committee shall consist of two representatives nominated by the Government of each Member which has ratified this Convention, and the representatives of Shipowners and Seafarers appointed by the Governing Body after consultation with the Joint Maritime Commission.

3. The Government representatives of Members which have not yet ratified this Convention may participate in the Committee but shall have no right to vote on any matter dealt with in accordance with this Convention. The Governing Body may invite other organizations or entities to be represented on the Committee by observers.

4. The votes of each Shipowner and Seafarer representative in

第十二条

国际劳工局局长须按照《联合国宪章》第一百〇二条，将根据本公约登记的所有批准、接受和退出的全部细节送请联合国秘书长进行登记。

特别三方委员会

第十三条

1. 国际劳工局理事会须通过其所设立的一个在海事劳工标准领域有专长的委员会保持对本公约的作用进行持续审核。

2. 就根据本公约处理的事项而言，委员会须由已批准本公约的每个成员国政府指派的两名代表和理事会经与联合海事委员会[1]协商后指定的船东和海员代表组成。

3. 尚未批准本公约的成员国的政府代表可以参加委员会，但对根据本公约处理的任何事项无表决权。理事会可以邀请其他组织或实体通过观察员来代表出席委员会。

4. 须对委员会中每个船东和海员代表的票数予以加权，以保证船东组和海员组各自拥有出席有关会议并有表决权的政府总数投票权的一半。

---

[1] 联合海事委员会(JMC)是国际劳工组织内的一个三方常设机构，就航运业标准的设定等海事问题向国际劳工局理事会提供建议。JMC依据《1996年海员工资、工时和船舶配员建议书》(第187号)更新了一等水手最低基本工资的数额，并设立了海员工资分委会对该工资数额进行定期更新。本公约导则B2.2.4第1款和导则B2.5.1第2款还提及了该委员会。——校译者注

the Committee shall be weighted so as to ensure that the Shipowners' group and the Seafarers' group each have half the voting power of the total number of governments which are represented at the meeting concerned and entitled to vote.

AMENDMENT OF THIS CONVENTION

Article XIV

1. Amendments to any of the provisions of this Convention may be adopted by the General Conference of the International Labour Organization in the framework of article 19 of the Constitution of the International Labour Organisation and the rules and procedures of the Organization for the adoption of Conventions. Amendments to the Code may also be adopted following the procedures in Article XV.

2. In the case of Members whose ratifications of this Convention were registered before the adoption of the amendment, the text of the amendment shall be communicated to them for ratification.

3. In the case of other Members of the Organization, the text of the Convention as amended shall be communicated to them for ratification in accordance with article 19 of the Constitution.

4. An amendment shall be deemed to have been accepted on the date when there have been registered ratifications, of the amendment or of the Convention as amended, as the case may be, by at least 30 Members with a total share in the world gross tonnage of ships of at least 33 per cent.

5. An amendment adopted in the framework of article 19 of the

本公约的修正案

第十四条

1. 对本公约任何规定的修正案均可由国际劳工组织大会在《国际劳工组织章程》第十九条和本组织通过公约的议事规则的框架内予以通过。对守则的修正案还可按第十五条的程序通过。

2. 对于在修正案通过前登记了其对本公约的批准书的成员国,须将修正案的文本送交他们以供批准。

3. 对于本组织的其他成员国,须根据《章程》第十九条将经修正的公约文本送交他们以供批准。

4. 修正案须在合计占世界船舶总吨位至少33%的至少30个成员国视情况对修正案的或对经修正公约的批准书已经登记之日视为已被接受。

5. 在《章程》第十九条框架内通过的修正案须只对那些批准书已交国际劳工局局长登记的本组织成员国具有约束力。

Constitution shall be binding only upon those Members of the Organization whose ratifications have been registered by the Director-General of the International Labour Office.

6. For any Member referred to in paragraph 2 of this Article, an amendment shall come into force 12 months after the date of acceptance referred to in paragraph 4 of this Article or 12 months after the date on which its ratification of the amendment has been registered, whichever date is later.

7. Subject to paragraph 9 of this Article, for Members referred to in paragraph 3 of this Article, the Convention as amended shall come into force 12 months after the date of acceptance referred to in paragraph 4 of this Article or 12 months after the date on which their ratifications of the Convention have been registered, whichever date is later.

8. For those Members whose ratification of this Convention was registered before the adoption of an amendment but which have not ratified the amendment, this Convention shall remain in force without the amendment concerned.

9. Any Member whose ratification of this Convention is registered after the adoption of the amendment but before the date referred to in paragraph 4 of this Article may, in a declaration accompanying the instrument of ratification, specify that its ratification relates to the Convention without the amendment concerned. In the case of a ratification with such a declaration, the Convention shall come into force for the Member concerned 12 months after the date on which the ratification was registered. Where an instrument of ratification is not accompanied by such a declaration, or where the ratification is registered on or after the date referred to in paragraph

6. 对于本条第 2 款所述的任何成员国，修正案须于本条第 4 款中所述的接受之日起 12 个月后生效，或于其对修正案的批准书登记之日起 12 个月后生效，以较晚者为准。

7. 在本条第 9 款的限制下，对于本条第 3 款所述的成员国，经修正的公约须于本条第 4 款中所述的接受之日起 12 个月后生效，或于其对公约的批准书登记之日起 12 个月后生效，以较晚者为准。

8. 对于其对本公约的批准书在某一修正案通过之前登记但并没有批准该修正案的成员国，未作该相关修正的本公约须继续有效。

9. 在修正案通过以后但在本条第 4 款所述日期之前登记了对本公约的批准书的任何成员国，可在批准书上随附一份声明，明确其批准书涉及的是未经相关修正的公约。对于批准书附有这样一份声明的情况，公约将在批准书登记之日 12 个月后对该有关成员国生效。如果批准书未附有这样一份声明，或者批准书于第 4 款所述日期或之后登记，公约将在批准书登记之日 12 个月以后对该有关成员国生效，并且，在修正案根据本条第 7 款生效后，该修正案须对该有关成员国有约束力，除非修正案另有规定。

4, the Convention shall come into force for the Member concerned 12 months after the date on which the ratification was registered and, upon its entry into force in accordance with paragraph 7 of this Article, the amendment shall be binding on the Member concerned unless the amendment provides otherwise.

AMENDMENTS TO THE CODE

Article XV

1. The Code may be amended either by the procedure set out in Article XIV or, unless expressly provided otherwise, in accordance with the procedure set out in the present Article.

2. An amendment to the Code may be proposed to the Director-General of the International Labour Office by the government of any Member of the Organization or by the group of Shipowner representatives or the group of Seafarer representatives who have been appointed to the Committee referred to in Article XIII. An amendment proposed by a government must have been proposed by, or be supported by, at least five governments of Members that have ratified the Convention or by the group of Shipowner or Seafarer representatives referred to in this paragraph.

3. Having verified that the proposal for amendment meets the requirements of paragraph 2 of this Article, the Director-General shall promptly communicate the proposal, accompanied by any comments or suggestions deemed appropriate, to all Members of the Organization, with an invitation to them to transmit their observations or suggestions concerning the proposal within a period of six months

对守则的修正案

第十五条

1. 守则既可以按第十四条规定的程序修正，或者，除非另有明文规定，也可以根据本条规定的程序修正。

2. 本组织的任何成员国政府或被指定参加第十三条所述委员会的船东代表组或海员代表组可向国际劳工局局长提出对守则的修正案。由一国政府提出的修正案必须得到至少五个已批准公约的成员国政府的共同提议或支持，或者得到本款所述船东代表组或海员代表组的共同提议或支持。

3. 经核实关于修正案的提案满足本条第 2 款的要求后，局长须立即将此提案连同任何被视为适当的评论或建议通知给本组织的所有成员国，并请成员国在六个月内或理事会规定的其他期限（不得少于三个月但不超过九个月）内提交其对该提案的评述或建议。

or such other period (which shall not be less than three months nor more than nine months) prescribed by the Governing Body.

4. At the end of the period referred to in paragraph 3 of this Article, the proposal, accompanied by a summary of any observations or suggestions made under that paragraph, shall be transmitted to the Committee for consideration at a meeting. An amendment shall be considered adopted by the Committee if:

(a) at least half the governments of Members that have ratified this Convention are represented in the meeting at which the proposal is considered; and

(b) a majority of at least two-thirds of the Committee members vote in favour of the amendment; and

(c) this majority comprises the votes in favour of at least half the government voting power, half the Shipowner voting power and half the Seafarer voting power of the Committee members registered at the meeting when the proposal is put to the vote.

5. Amendments adopted in accordance with paragraph 4 of this Article shall be submitted to the next session of the Conference for approval. Such approval shall require a majority of two-thirds of the votes cast by the delegates present. If such majority is not obtained, the proposed amendment shall be referred back to the Committee for reconsideration should the Committee so wish.

6. Amendments approved by the Conference shall be notified by the Director-General to each of the Members whose ratifications of this Convention were registered before the date of such approval by the Conference. These Members are referred to below as "the ratifying Members". The notification shall contain a reference to the present Article and shall prescribe the period for the communication

4. 在本条第3款所述的期限届满时，须将该提案连同根据该款所提出的评述或建议的要点提交给委员会召开会议审议。在下述情况下须认为修正案已获得了委员会的通过：

(a) 至少有半数已批准本公约的成员国政府出席审议该提案之会议；且

(b) 委员会成员中至少有三分之二多数投票支持修正案；且

(c) 此多数票中至少包含了对提案付诸表决时在会议注册的委员会成员中政府表决权半数的支持票、船东表决权半数的支持票和海员表决权半数的支持票。

5. 根据本条第4款通过的修正案须提交下一届大会批准。这种批准须要求出席代表所投票的三分之二多数。如果没有获得这种多数，若委员会有此意愿，须将建议修正案发回委员会重新审议。

6. 局长须将经大会批准的修正案通知给其对本公约的批准书在大会批准修正案前业经登记的每一成员国。下文称此类成员国为“批约成员国”。该通知须援引本条，并须规定提出任何正式异议的期限。除非大会在批准时确定了不同期限(须至少为一年)，此期限须为自通知之日起两年。通知的副本须送本组织的其他成员国供其知晓。

of any formal disagreement. This period shall be two years from the date of the notification unless, at the time of approval, the Conference has set a different period, which shall be a period of at least one year. A copy of the notification shall be communicated to the other Members of the Organization for their information.

7. An amendment approved by the Conference shall be deemed to have been accepted unless, by the end of the prescribed period, formal expressions of disagreement have been received by the Director-General from more than 40 per cent of the Members which have ratified the Convention and which represent not less than 40 per cent of the gross tonnage of the ships of the Members which have ratified the Convention.

8. An amendment deemed to have been accepted shall come into force six months after the end of the prescribed period for all the ratifying Members except those which had formally expressed their disagreement in accordance with paragraph 7 of this Article and have not withdrawn such disagreement in accordance with paragraph 11. However:

(a) before the end of the prescribed period, any ratifying Member may give notice to the Director-General that it shall be bound by the amendment only after a subsequent express notification of its acceptance; and

(b) before the date of entry into force of the amendment, any ratifying Member may give notice to the Director-General that it will not give effect to that amendment for a specified period.

9. An amendment which is the subject of a notice referred to in paragraph 8(a) of this Article shall enter into force for the Member giving such notice six months after the Member has notified the

7. 除非局长在规定的期限结束时收到超过40%的已批准公约成员国的正式异议，并且他们代表着不少于已批准公约成员国船舶总吨位的40%，大会批准的修正案须视为已被接受。[1]

8. 视为已被接受的修正案须于规定期限届满六个月后对所有批约成员国生效，根据本条第7款正式表示了异议且没有根据第11款撤销该异议的批约成员国除外。但是：

(a) 任何批约成员国可在规定的期限届满前通知局长，只有其随后明确通知其接受后，才受修正案的约束；以及

(b) 任何批约成员国可在修正案生效之日前通知局长，其在一段具体规定的期间内将不执行该修正案。

9. 本条第8(a)款所述通知中所指的修正案对于做出该通知的成员国来说，须于该成员国通知局长其接受修正案起六个月后对其生效，或于修正案初次生效之日对其生效，以较晚者为准。

---

[1] 本款确立了对守则修正案的"默认接受"程序。——校译者注

Director-General of its acceptance of the amendment or on the date on which the amendment first comes into force, whichever date is later.

10. The period referred to in paragraph 8(b) of this Article shall not go beyond one year from the date of entry into force of the amendment or beyond any longer period determined by the Conference at the time of approval of the amendment.

11. A Member that has formally expressed disagreement with an amendment may withdraw its disagreement at any time. If notice of such withdrawal is received by the Director-General after the amendment has entered into force, the amendment shall enter into force for the Member six months after the date on which the notice was registered.

12. After entry into force of an amendment, the Convention may only be ratified in its amended form.

13. To the extent that a maritime labour certificate relates to matters covered by an amendment to the Convention which has entered into force:

(a) a Member that has accepted that amendment shall not be obliged to extend the benefit of the Convention in respect of the maritime labour certificates issued to ships flying the flag of another Member which:

(i) pursuant to paragraph 7 of this Article, has formally expressed disagreement to the amendment and has not withdrawn such disagreement; or

(ii) pursuant to paragraph 8(a) of this Article, has given notice that its acceptance is subject to its subsequent express notifi-

10. 本条第8(b)款所述期间自修正案生效之日起不得超过一年或超过大会批准修正案时确定的任何更长期限。

11. 对一项修正案正式表示过异议的成员国可以随时撤销其异议。如果局长在修正案生效以后收到此种撤销通知,修正案须于该通知登记之日六个月后对该成员国生效。

12. 一项修正案生效后,只能批准经修正的公约。

13. 在海事劳工证书与已生效的公约修正案所涉及事项有关的范围内:

(a) 接受了该修正案的成员国没有义务在签发的海事劳工证书方面将公约的益处扩展到悬挂另一成员国旗帜的船舶,如果该另一成员国:

(i) 根据本条第7款,对修正案正式表示了异议且未撤销该异议;或

(ii) 根据本条第8(a)款,通知了其对修正案的接受取决于随后的明确通知且尚未接受该修正案;以及

cation and has not accepted the amendment; and

(b) a Member that has accepted the amendment shall extend the benefit of the Convention in respect of the maritime labour certificates issued to ships flying the flag of another Member that has given notice, pursuant to paragraph 8(b) of this Article, that it will not give effect to that amendment for the period specified in accordance with paragraph 10 of this Article.

AUTHORITATIVE LANGUAGES

Article XVI

The English and French versions of the text of this Convention are equally authoritative.

(b) 如果某成员国根据本条第 8(b)款做出了在依据本条第 10 款具体规定的期间内其将不执行修正案的通知，接受了该修正案的另一成员国在签发的海事劳工证书方面须将公约的益处扩展到悬挂上述成员国旗帜的船舶。

作准语言

第十六条

本公约文本的英文本和法文本同等作准。

EXPLANATORY NOTE TO THE REGULATIONS AND CODE OF THE MARITIME LABOUR CONVENTION

1. This explanatory note, which does not form part of the Maritime Labour Convention, is intended as a general guide to the Convention.

2. The Convention comprises three different but related parts: the Articles, the Regulations and the Code.

3. The Articles and Regulations set out the core rights and principles and the basic obligations of Members ratifying the Convention. The Articles and Regulations can only be changed by the Conference in the framework of article 19 of the Constitution of the International Labour Organisation (see Article XIV of the Convention).

4. The Code contains the details for the implementation of the Regulations. It comprises Part A (mandatory Standards) and Part B (non-mandatory Guidelines). The Code can be amended through the simplified procedure set out in Article XV of the Convention. Since the Code relates to detailed implementation, amendments to it must remain within the general scope of the Articles and Regulations.

5. The Regulations and the Code are organized into general areas under five Titles:

Title 1: Minimum requirements for seafarers to work on a ship

Title 2: Conditions of employment

Title 3: Accommodation, recreational facilities, food and catering

Title 4: Health protection, medical care, welfare and social security protection

Title 5: Compliance and enforcement

海事劳工公约的规则和守则的解注

1. 本解注旨在作为对《海事劳工公约》的一般性指导，不构成公约的组成部分。

2. 公约由三个不同但相关的部分构成：正文条款、规则和守则。

3. 正文条款和规则规定了核心权利和原则以及批准公约成员国的基本义务。正文条款和规则只能由大会在《国际劳工组织章程》第十九条的框架内修改(见公约第十四条)。

4. 守则载明了规则的实施细节。它由A部分(强制性标准)和B部分(非强制性导则)组成。守则可以通过公约第十五条规定的简化程序来修正。由于守则涉及具体实施，对守则的修正必须仍放在正文条款和规则的总体范畴内。

5. 规则和守则编排成五个标题下的多个一般领域：

标题一：海员上船工作的最低要求

标题二：就业条件

标题三：起居舱室、娱乐设施、食品和膳食服务

标题四：健康保护、医护、福利和社会保障保护

标题五：遵守与执行

6. Each Title contains groups of provisions relating to a particular right or principle (or enforcement measure in Title 5), with connected numbering. The first group in Title 1, for example, consists of Regulation 1. 1, Standard A1. 1 and Guideline B1. 1, relating to minimum age.

7. The Convention has three underlying purposes:

(a) to lay down, in its Articles and Regulations, a firm set of rights and principles;

(b) to allow, through the Code, a considerable degree of flexibility in the way Members implement those rights and principles; and

(c) to ensure, through Title 5, that the rights and principles are properly complied with and enforced.

8. There are two main areas for flexibility in implementation: one is the possibility for a Member, where necessary (see Article VI, paragraph 3), to give effect to the detailed requirements of Part A of the Code through substantial equivalence (as defined in Article VI, paragraph 4).

9. The second area of flexibility in implementation is provided by formulating the mandatory requirements of many provisions in Part A in a more general way, thus leaving a wider scope for discretion as to the precise action to be provided for at the national level. In such cases, guidance on implementation is given in the non-mandatory Part B of the Code. In this way, Members which have ratified this Convention can ascertain the kind of action that might be expected of them under the corresponding general obligation in Part A, as well as action that would not necessarily be required. For example, Standard A4. 1 requires all ships to provide prompt access to the necessary medicines for medical care on board ship (paragraph 1(b))

6. 每一标题载明了关于具体权利或原则(或标题五中的执行措施)的几组规定,其编号相关联。例如,标题一的第一组包括关于最低年龄的规则 1.1、标准 A1.1 和导则 B1.1。

7. 公约有三个根本宗旨[1]:

(a) 在其正文条款和规则中规定一套确定的权利和原则;

(b) 通过守则允许成员国在实施这些权利和原则的方式上有相当程度的灵活性;以及

(c) 通过标题五确保这些权利和原则得以妥善遵守和执行。

8. 在实施中有两个主要方面的灵活性:其一是成员国在必要时(见第六条第 3 款)通过实质上等效(如第六条第 4 款所界定)来执行守则 A 部分的具体要求的可能性。

9. 实施中灵活性的第二个方面是通过将 A 部分许多条款的强制性要求表述得更加宽泛来实现的,这样就为在本国层面上规定确切的行动留出了更广泛的自主权。在这种情况下,守则中非强制性的 B 部分给出了实施指导。这样,已批准本公约的成员国能够确定在 A 部分相应的一般性义务下他们会被期望采取什么样的行动,以及未必会被要求的行动。例如,标准 A4.1 要求在所有船舶上能够迅速获得用于船上医护所必需的药品(第 1(b)款)并"携带一个医药箱"(第 4(a)款)。善意履行后者的义务明显意味着不仅仅是简单地在每艘船上配备一个医药箱。在对应的导则 B4.1.1(第 4 款)中对于所涉问题给出了更为准确的指示,以便确保妥善地存放、使用和维护医药箱内的物品。

---

[1] 这三个宗旨体现了本公约"在权利上坚定,在实施上灵活,在执行上强制"的总体立法原则。——校译者注

and to "carry a medicine chest" (paragraph 4(a)). The fulfilment in good faith of this latter obligation clearly means something more than simply having a medicine chest on board each ship. A more precise indication of what is involved is provided in the corresponding Guideline B4. 1. 1 (paragraph 4) so as to ensure that the contents of the chest are properly stored, used and maintained.

10. Members which have ratified this Convention are not bound by the guidance concerned and, as indicated in the provisions in Title 5 on port State control, inspections would deal only with the relevant requirements of this Convention (Articles, Regulations and the Standards in Part A). However, Members are required under paragraph 2 of Article VI to give due consideration to implementing their responsibilities under Part A of the Code in the manner provided for in Part B. If, having duly considered the relevant Guidelines, a Member decides to provide for different arrangements which ensure the proper storage, use and maintenance of the contents of the medicine chest, to take the example given above, as required by the Standard in Part A, then that is acceptable. On the other hand, by following the guidance provided in Part B, the Member concerned, as well as the ILO bodies responsible for reviewing implementation of international labour Conventions, can be sure without further consideration that the arrangements the Member has provided for are adequate to implement the responsibilities under Part A to which the Guideline relates.

10. 已批准本公约的成员国不受相关导则的约束，而且，正如标题五中关于港口国监督的规定所指出，检查只针对本公约(正文条款、规则和A部分标准)的有关要求。但是，第六条第2款要求成员国充分考虑以B部分提供的方式履行其在守则A部分下的责任。用上文所举的例子，如果在充分考虑到相关导则后，成员国决定做出不同的安排来确保按A部分标准的要求对医药箱中的物品进行妥善存放、使用和维护，则是可以接受的。另一方面，通过遵循B部分给出的指南，有关成员国以及国际劳工组织负责审核国际劳工公约实施的机构就能够确定，成员国做出的安排足以履行导则所涉及的A部分下的责任，而无须作进一步审议。

THE REGULATIONS AND THE CODE

规则和守则

TITLE 1. MINIMUM REQUIREMENTS FOR SEAFARERS TO WORK ON A SHIP

Regulation 1.1—Minimum age

Purpose: To ensure that no under-age persons work on a ship

1. No person below the minimum age shall be employed or engaged or work on a ship.

2. The minimum age at the time of the initial entry into force of this Convention is 16 years.

3. A higher minimum age shall be required in the circumstances set out in the Code.

Standard A1.1—Minimum age

1. The employment, engagement or work on board a ship of any person under the age of 16 shall be prohibited.

2. Night work of seafarers under the age of 18 shall be prohibited. For the purposes of this Standard, "night" shall be defined in accordance with national law and practice. It shall cover a period of at least nine hours starting no later than midnight and ending no earlier than 5 a.m.

3. An exception to strict compliance with the night work restriction may be made by the competent authority when:

(a) the effective training of the seafarers concerned, in accordance with established programmes and schedules, would be impaired; or

标题一　海员上船工作的最低要求

规则 1.1—最低年龄

目的：确保无未成年人上船工作

1. 低于最低年龄的人不得在船上受雇或受聘或工作。

2. 在本公约生效伊始，最低年龄为 16 岁。

3. 在守则规定的情形中须要求更高的最低年龄。

标准 A1.1—最低年龄

1. 须禁止任何 16 岁以下的人员在船上受雇、受聘或工作。

2. 须禁止 18 岁以下的海员在夜间工作。就本标准而言，"夜间"须根据国内法律和惯例来界定。它须包括从不晚于午夜开始至不早于上午 5 点钟结束的一个至少九个小时的时段。

3. 在下列情况下主管当局可以对严格遵守夜间工作的限制做出例外：

(a) 有关海员根据既定计划和安排的有效培训会受到妨害；或

(b) the specific nature of the duty or a recognized training programme requires that the seafarers covered by the exception perform duties at night and the authority determines, after consultation with the shipowners' and seafarers' organizations concerned, that the work will not be detrimental to their health or well-being.

4. The employment, engagement or work of seafarers under the age of 18 shall be prohibited where the work is likely to jeopardize their health or safety. The types of such work shall be determined by national laws or regulations or by the competent authority, after consultation with the shipowners' and seafarers' organizations concerned, in accordance with relevant international standards.

Guideline B1.1—Minimum age

1. When regulating working and living conditions, Members should give special attention to the needs of young persons under the age of 18.

Regulation 1.2—Medical certificate

Purpose: To ensure that all seafarers are medically fit to perform their duties at sea

1. Seafarers shall not work on a ship unless they are certified as medically fit to perform their duties.

2. Exceptions can only be permitted as prescribed in the Code.

Standard A1.2—Medical certificate

1. The competent authority shall require that, prior to begin-

(b) 职责的具体性质或认可的培训计划要求例外中所涉及的海员在夜间履行职责，且当局在与有关船东组织和海员组织协商后确定，该工作不会对他们的健康或幸福[1]产生有害影响。

4. 如果工作可能损害18岁以下海员的健康或安全，则须禁止其受雇、受聘或工作。这些工作的类型须由国内法律或条例确定，或由主管当局根据相关国际标准与有关船东组织和海员组织协商后确定。

导则 B1.1—最低年龄

1. 在对工作和生活条件进行规范时，成员国应特别注意18岁以下未成年人的需要。

规则 1.2—健康证书

目的：确保所有海员的健康状况适合履行其海上职责

1. 除非海员的健康状况经证明适合履行其职责，否则不得上船工作。

2. 只有在守则规定的情况下才允许有例外。

标准 A1.2—健康证书

1. 主管当局须要求，海员在上船开始工作之前持有有效的健康证书，证明其健康状况适合履行其将在海上履行的职责。

[1] 其英文 well-being 在此是指日常工作和生活中的“舒适、健康和开心”，在中文中没有一个现成对应的词，现译成“幸福”。——校译者注

ning work on a ship, seafarers hold a valid medical certificate attesting that they are medically fit to perform the duties they are to carry out at sea.

2. In order to ensure that medical certificates genuinely reflect seafarers' state of health, in light of the duties they are to perform, the competent authority shall, after consultation with the shipowners' and seafarers' organizations concerned, and giving due consideration to applicable international guidelines referred to in Part B of this Code, prescribe the nature of the medical examination and certificate.

3. This Standard is without prejudice to the International Convention on Standards of Training, Certification and Watchkeeping for Seafarers, 1978, as amended ("STCW"). A medical certificate issued in accordance with the requirements of STCW shall be accepted by the competent authority, for the purpose of Regulation 1. 2. A medical certificate meeting the substance of those requirements, in the case of seafarers not covered by STCW, shall similarly be accepted.

4. The medical certificate shall be issued by a duly qualified medical practitioner or, in the case of a certificate solely concerning eyesight, by a person recognized by the competent authority as qualified to issue such a certificate. Practitioners must enjoy full professional independence in exercising their medical judgement in undertaking medical examination procedures.

5. Seafarers that have been refused a certificate or have had a limitation imposed on their ability to work, in particular with respect to time, field of work or trading area, shall be given the opportunity to have a further examination by another independent medical practi-

2. 为了确保健康证书真实地反映海员的健康状况，主管当局须根据其将要履行的职责，并充分考虑到本守则 B 部分所述的适用国际性导则，与有关船东组织和海员组织协商后规定体检和证书的性质。

3. 本标准并不损害经修正的《1978 年海员培训、发证和值班标准国际公约》（“《STCW 公约》”）。就规则 1.2 而言，主管当局须接受根据《STCW 公约》的要求签发的健康证书。对于《STCW 公约》未涵盖的海员，满足那些要求的实质性内容的健康证书须同样予以接受。

4. 健康证书须由有正规资格的从业医生签发，或者，对于只涉及视力的证书而言，由经主管当局认可的具备签发此类证书资格的人员签发。从业医生在执行体检程序中进行医学判断时，必须享有完全的专业独立性。

5. 对于被拒绝发证的海员或在其工作能力方面，特别是关于时间、工作范围或航行区域方面，被施加了限制的海员，须给予他们由另一位独立的从业医生或独立的医学鉴定人做进一步检查的机会。

tioner or by an independent medical referee.

6. Each medical certificate shall state in particular that:

(a) the hearing and sight of the seafarer concerned, and the colour vision in the case of a seafarer to be employed in capacities where fitness for the work to be performed is liable to be affected by defective colour vision, are all satisfactory; and

(b) the seafarer concerned is not suffering from any medical condition likely to be aggravated by service at sea or to render the seafarer unfit for such service or to endanger the health of other persons on board.

7. Unless a shorter period is required by reason of the specific duties to be performed by the seafarer concerned or is required under STCW:

(a) a medical certificate shall be valid for a maximum period of two years unless the seafarer is under the age of 18, in which case the maximum period of validity shall be one year;

(b) a certification of colour vision shall be valid for a maximum period of six years.

8. In urgent cases the competent authority may permit a seafarer to work without a valid medical certificate until the next port of call where the seafarer can obtain a medical certificate from a qualified medical practitioner, provided that:

(a) the period of such permission does not exceed three months; and

(b) the seafarer concerned is in possession of an expired medical certificate of recent date.

9. If the period of validity of a certificate expires in the course of a voyage, the certificate shall continue in force until the next port of

6. 每份健康证书须特别申明：

(a) 该有关海员的听力和视力，以及在受雇职位上所从事工作的适任性易于受到缺陷辨色力影响的海员的辨色力，全部符合要求；以及

(b) 该有关海员未患有任何由于在海上工作而可能会加重或使其变得不适合从事此种工作或危及船上其他人员健康的疾患。

7. 除非由于该有关海员将履行的特定职责或《STCW公约》要求更短的期间：

(a) 健康证书的最长有效期须为两年，除非海员低于18岁，在这种情况下最长有效期须为一年；

(b) 辨色力证书的最长有效期须为六年。

8. 在紧急情况下，主管当局可以允许没有有效健康证书的海员工作，直至该海员能够从合格的从业医生那里取得一份健康证书的下一停靠港，条件是：

(a) 该允许的期间不超过三个月；且

(b) 该相关海员持有近日过期的健康证书。

9. 如果在航行途中证书的有效期届满，该证书须继续有效至该海员能够从合格的从业医生那里取得一份健康证书的下一停靠港，条件是这段时间不得超过三个月。

call where the seafarer can obtain a medical certificate from a qualified medical practitioner, provided that the period shall not exceed three months.

10. The medical certificates for seafarers working on ships ordinarily engaged on international voyages must as a minimum be provided in English.

Guideline B1.2—Medical certificate

Guideline B1.2.1—International guidelines

1. The competent authority, medical practitioners, examiners, shipowners, seafarers' representatives and all other persons concerned with the conduct of medical fitness examinations of seafarer candidates and serving seafarers should follow the ILO/WHO *Guidelines for Conducting Pre-sea and Periodic Medical Fitness Examinations for Seafarers*, including any subsequent❶ versions, and any other applicable international guidelines published by the International Labour Organization, the International Maritime Organization or the World Health Organization.

Regulation 1.3—Training and qualifications

Purpose: To ensure that seafarers are trained or qualified to carry out their duties on board ship

1. Seafarers shall not work on a ship unless they are trained or

❶ 在最初公布的公约正式英文文本中，此处为 revised，现修订为 subsequent。此修订主要是考虑到新的《海员体检导则》不是本款所述指南的"修订"版本，而是其"后续"版本。——校译者注

10. 在通常从事国际航行的船舶上工作的海员，其健康证书必须至少用英文写成。

导则 B1.2—健康证书

导则 B1.2.1—国际性导则

1. 主管当局、从业医生、体检人员、船东、海员的代表和所有其他对求职海员和在职海员实施健康检查的有关人员，应遵循 ILO/WHO《海员上船前和定期健康检查指南》[1]，包括任何后续版本以及国际劳工组织、国际海事组织或世界卫生组织出版的任何其他适用的国际性导则。

规则 1.3—培训和资格

目的：确保海员经过培训或具备履行其船上职责的资格

1. 除非海员经过培训或经证明适任或者以其他方式具备履行其职责的资格，否则不得在船上工作。

---

[1] 该指南已被 ILO 和 IMO 于 2011 年联合公布的《海员体检导则（Guidelines on the Medical Examinations of Seafarers）》所代替。——校译者注

certified as competent or otherwise qualified to perform their duties.

2. Seafarers shall not be permitted to work on a ship unless they have successfully completed training for personal safety on board ship.

3. Training and certification in accordance with the mandatory instruments adopted by the International Maritime Organization shall be considered as meeting the requirements of paragraphs 1 and 2 of this Regulation.

4. Any Member which, at the time of its ratification of this Convention, was bound by the Certification of Able Seamen Convention, 1946 (No. 74), shall continue to carry out the obligations under that Convention unless and until mandatory provisions covering its subject matter have been adopted by the International Maritime Organization and entered into force, or until five years have elapsed since the entry into force of this Convention in accordance with paragraph 3 of Article VIII, whichever date is earlier.

Regulation 1.4—Recruitment and placement

Purpose: To ensure that seafarers have access to an efficient and well-regulated seafarer recruitment and placement system

1. All seafarers shall have access to an efficient, adequate and accountable system for finding employment on board ship without charge to the seafarer.

2. Seafarer recruitment and placement services operating in a Member's territory shall conform to the standards set out in the Code.

2. 除非海员成功地完成了船上个人安全培训，否则不得允许其在船上工作。

3. 按国际海事组织通过的强制性文件进行的培训和发证须被认为满足本规则第1和2款的要求。

4. 任何在批准本公约时受《1946年一等水手证书公约》(第74号)约束的成员国，须继续履行该公约下的义务，除非并且直到国际海事组织通过了覆盖该公约主题的强制性规定并已生效，或者直到本公约根据第八条第3款生效后已经过去了五年，以较早的日期为准。

规则1.4—招募和安置

目的：确保海员有机会利用高效和良好规范的海员招募和安置机制

1. 所有海员须能够利用不向海员收费的高效、充分和负责的机制寻找船上就业。

2. 在成员国领土内开办的海员招募和安置服务机构须符合守则所规定的标准。

3. Each Member shall require, in respect of seafarers who work on ships that fly its flag, that shipowners who use seafarer recruitment and placement services that are based in countries or territories in which this Convention does not apply, ensure that those services conform to the requirements set out in the Code.

Standard A1.4—Recruitment and placement

1. Each Member that operates a public seafarer recruitment and placement service shall ensure that the service is operated in an orderly manner that protects and promotes seafarers' employment rights as provided in this Convention.

2. Where a Member has private seafarer recruitment and placement services operating in its territory whose primary purpose is the recruitment and placement of seafarers or which recruit and place a significant number of seafarers, they shall be operated only in conformity with a standardized system of licensing or certification or other form of regulation. This system shall be established, modified or changed only after consultation with the shipowners' and seafarers' organizations concerned. In the event of doubt as to whether this Convention applies to a private recruitment and placement service, the question shall be determined by the competent authority in each Member after consultation with the shipowners' and seafarers' organizations concerned. Undue proliferation of private seafarer recruitment and placement services shall not be encouraged.

3. The provisions of paragraph 2 of this Standard shall also apply — to the extent that they are determined by the competent authority, in consultation with the shipowners' and seafarers' organizations concerned, to be appropriate — in the context of recruitment

3. 对于在悬挂其旗帜的船舶上工作的海员，各成员国须要求船东，若其利用那些在本公约不适用的国家或领土内设立的海员招募和安置服务机构，则保证这些服务机构符合守则中规定的要求。

标准 A1.4—招募和安置

1. 开办公共海员招募和安置服务机构的各成员国须确保，该服务机构以保护和促进本公约所规定的海员就业权利的方式有序运作。

2. 如果某成员国有以招募和安置海员为主要目的或招募和安置相当数量海员的私营海员招募和安置服务机构在其领土内运营，这些服务机构须依照一种标准化的发放许可证或发证或其他规范形式的机制来运营。这种机制须在与有关船东组织和海员组织协商后才能建立、修改或改变。在对本公约是否适用于某一私营招募和安置服务机构存有疑问时，该问题须由各成员国的主管当局在与有关船东组织和海员组织协商后决定。不得鼓励私营海员招募和安置服务机构过度扩散。

3. 本标准第 2 款的规定还须适用于——在该规定由主管当局与有关船东组织和海员组织协商确定为合适的范围内——在成员国领土内由海员组织运营的招募和安置服务机构向悬挂该成员国旗帜的船舶提供本国海员的情况。本款所包括的服务机构为满足以下条件者：

and placement services operated by a seafarers' organization in the territory of the Member for the supply of seafarers who are nationals of that Member to ships which fly its flag. The services covered by this paragraph are those fulfilling the following conditions:

(a) the recruitment and placement service is operated pursuant to a collective bargaining agreement between that organization and a shipowner;

(b) both the seafarers' organization and the shipowner are based in the territory of the Member;

(c) The Member has national laws or regulations or a procedure to authorize or register the collective bargaining agreement permitting the operation of the recruitment and placement service; and

(d) the recruitment and placement service is operated in an orderly manner and measures are in place to protect and promote seafarers' employment rights comparable to those provided in paragraph 5 of this Standard.

4. Nothing in this Standard or Regulation 1.4 shall be deemed to:

(a) prevent a Member from maintaining a free public seafarer recruitment and placement service for seafarers in the framework of a policy to meet the needs of seafarers and shipowners, whether the service forms part of or is coordinated with a public employment service for all workers and employers; or

(b) impose on a Member the obligation to establish a system for the operation of private seafarer recruitment or placement services in its territory.

5. A Member adopting a system referred to in paragraph 2 of

(a) 该招募和安置服务机构根据该组织与船东之间的集体谈判协议运营;

(b) 海员组织和船东均设立于该成员国的领土之内;

(c) 该成员国有国内法律或条例或程序,对允许运营招募和安置服务机构的集体谈判协议进行授权或登记;且

(d) 招募和安置服务机构以有序的方式运营,并具备与本标准第5款所规定者相当的保护和促进海员就业权利的措施。

4. 本标准或规则1.4中的任何规定都不得被视为:

(a) 阻止一成员国在满足海员和船东需要的政策框架内为海员保持一个免费的公共海员招募和安置服务机构,无论该服务机构是作为面向所有工人和雇主的公共就业服务机构的一部分还是与之相协调;或

(b) 向成员国施加在其领土内建立一个运作私营海员招募或安置服务机构机制的义务。

5. 采用了本标准第2款所述机制的成员国,在其法律和条例或其他措施中须至少:

this Standard shall, in its laws and regulations or other measures, at a minimum:

(a) prohibit seafarer recruitment and placement services from using means, mechanisms or lists intended to prevent or deter seafarers from gaining employment for which they are qualified;

(b) require that no fees or other charges for seafarer recruitment or placement or for providing employment to seafarers are borne directly or indirectly, in whole or in part, by the seafarer, other than the cost of the seafarer obtaining a national statutory medical certificate, the national seafarer's book and a passport or other similar personal travel documents, not including, however, the cost of visas, which shall be borne by the shipowner; and

(c) ensure that seafarer recruitment and placement services operating in its territory:

(i) maintain an up-to-date register of all seafarers recruited or placed through them, to be available for inspection by the competent authority;

(ii) make sure that seafarers are informed of their rights and duties under their employment agreements prior to or in the process of engagement and that proper arrangements are made for seafarers to examine their employment agreements before and after they are signed and for them to receive a copy of the agreements;

(iii) verify that seafarers recruited or placed by them are qualified and hold the documents necessary for the job concerned, and that the seafarers' employment agreements are in accordance with applicable laws and regulations and any

(a) 禁止海员招募和安置服务机构利用各种手段、机制或清单来阻止或阻挠海员获得其有资格的就业；

(b) 要求海员招募或安置的或者为海员提供就业的费用或其他收费不得直接或间接、全部或部分地由该海员承担，海员取得国家法定健康证书、本国海员证和护照或其他类似个人旅行证件的费用除外，但签证费不除外，须由船东负担；以及

(c) 确保其领土内运营的海员招募和安置服务机构：

(i) 维持一份通过其招募或安置的所有海员的最新登记册，以备主管当局检查；

(ii) 保证海员在受聘前或受聘过程中被告知其在就业协议下的权利和职责，并为海员做出适当安排，使其在签署就业协议之前和之后对之进行核阅且收到一份该协议；

(iii) 核实被其招募或安置的海员具备资格并持有相关工作所必需的证书，而且海员就业协议符合适用的法律和条例和构成就业协议一部分的任何集体谈判协议；

collective bargaining agreement that forms part of the employment agreement;

(iv) make sure, as far as practicable, that the shipowner has the means to protect seafarers from being stranded in a foreign port;

(v) examine and respond to any complaint concerning their activities and advise the competent authority of any unresolved complaint;

(vi) establish a system of protection, by way of insurance or an equivalent appropriate measure, to compensate seafarers for monetary loss that they may incur as a result of the failure of a recruitment and placement service or the relevant shipowner under the seafarers' employment agreement to meet its obligations to them.

6. The competent authority shall closely supervise and control all seafarer recruitment and placement services operating in the territory of the Member concerned. Any licences or certificates or similar authorizations for the operation of private services in the territory are granted or renewed only after verification that the seafarer recruitment and placement service concerned meets the requirements of national laws and regulations.

7. The competent authority shall ensure that adequate machinery and procedures exist for the investigation, if necessary, of complaints concerning the activities of seafarer recruitment and placement services, involving, as appropriate, representatives of shipowners and seafarers.

8. Each Member which has ratified this Convention shall, in so far as practicable, advise its nationals on the possible problems of

(iv) 尽实际可行地保证船东有保护海员免于受困在国外港口的手段；

(v) 对有关其活动的任何投诉进行核查并做出反应，并将任何未解决的投诉报告主管当局；

(vi) 建立一个保护机制，通过保险或适当的等效措施，赔偿由于招募和安置服务机构或者海员就业协议之下的有关船东未能履行其对海员的义务而使海员可能遭受的金钱损失。

6. 主管当局须密切监督和控制在该有关成员国领土内运营的所有海员招募和安置服务机构。只有经过核实有关海员招募和安置服务机构符合国内法律和条例的要求后，才为在该领土内的私营服务机构的运营核发或换新任何许可证或证书或类似授权。

7. 主管当局须确保存在适当的机制和程序，在必要时对关于海员招募和安置服务机构活动的投诉开展调查，并视情况请船东的和海员的代表参与。

8. 批准了本公约的各成员国，就签约登上一艘悬挂未批准公约国家的旗帜的船可能引起的问题，须尽实际可行地告知其本国国民，直至其认为与本公约所确定的标准等效的标准得以实施。已批准本公约的成员国为此而采取的措施不得与相关的两个国家可能都已参加的条约所规定的工人自由流动原则相冲突。

signing on a ship that flies the flag of a State which has not ratified the Convention, until it is satisfied that standards equivalent to those fixed by this Convention are being applied. Measures taken to this effect by the Member that has ratified this Convention shall not be in contradiction with the principle of free movement of workers stipulated by the treaties to which the two States concerned may be parties.

9. Each Member which has ratified this Convention shall require that shipowners of ships that fly its flag, who use seafarer recruitment and placement services based in countries or territories in which this Convention does not apply, ensure, as far as practicable, that those services meet the requirements of this Standard.

10. Nothing in this Standard shall be understood as diminishing the obligations and responsibilities of shipowners or of a Member with respect to ships that fly its flag.

Guideline B1.4—Recruitment and placement

Guideline B1.4.1—Organizational and operational guidelines

1. When fulfilling its obligations under Standard A1.4, paragraph 1, the competent authority should consider:

(a) taking the necessary measures to promote effective cooperation among seafarer recruitment and placement services, whether public or private;

(b) the needs of the maritime industry at both the national and international levels, when developing training programmes for seafarers that form the part of the ship's crew that is responsible for the ship's safe navigation and pollution prevention operations, with the participation of shipowners, seafarers and the

9. 已批准本公约的各成员国须要求悬挂其旗帜船舶的船东，如果使用了在本公约不适用的国家或领土内设立的海员招募和安置服务机构，尽实际可行地确保这些服务机构符合本标准的要求。

10. 本标准的任何规定都不得被理解为减少了船东的或成员国对悬挂本国旗帜船舶的义务和责任。

导则 B1.4—招募和安置

导则 B1.4.1—组织和操作导则

1. 在履行其在标准 A1.4 第 1 款下的义务时，主管当局应：

(a) 考虑采取必要的措施促进海员招募和安置服务机构间的有效合作，无论其为公共或私营；

(b) 在船东、海员和相关培训机构的参与下，为那些参与负责船舶安全航行和防污染操作的海员制订培训计划时，考虑海运业在国家层面和国际层面上的需求；

relevant training institutions;

(c) making suitable arrangements for the cooperation of representative shipowners' and seafarers' organizations in the organization and operation of the public seafarer recruitment and placement services, where they exist;

(d) determining, with due regard to the right to privacy and the need to protect confidentiality, the conditions under which seafarers' personal data may be processed by seafarer recruitment and placement services, including the collection, storage, combination and communication of such data to third parties;

(e) maintaining an arrangement for the collection and analysis of all relevant information on the maritime labour market, including the current and prospective supply of seafarers that work as crew classified by age, sex, rank and qualifications, and the industry's requirements, the collection of data on age or sex being admissible only for statistical purposes or if used in the framework of a programme to prevent discrimination based on age or sex;

(f) ensuring that the staff responsible for the supervision of public and private seafarer recruitment and placement services for ship's crew with responsibility for the ship's safe navigation and pollution prevention operations have had adequate training, including approved sea-service experience, and have relevant knowledge of the maritime industry, including the relevant maritime international instruments on training, certification and labour standards;

(g) prescribing operational standards and adopting codes of conduct and ethical practices for seafarer recruitment and placement ser-

(c) 如果存在公共海员招募和安置服务机构，为有代表性的船东组织和海员组织在这些机构的组织和运作方面的合作，考虑做出适当的安排；

(d) 充分顾及隐私权和保密需要，考虑确定可由海员招募和安置服务机构来处理海员个人资料的条件，包括这些资料的收集、存储、合并以及向第三方传送；

(e) 考虑保持一种安排来收集和分析海运劳动力市场的所有相关信息，其中包括根据年龄、性别、级别和资格分类的作为船员工作的海员目前和预期供应情况，以及行业的需求，有关年龄或性别数据的收集只能纳入统计目的或者，如果使用，用于防止基于年龄或性别歧视的计划框架中；

(f) 考虑确保负责监督那些为承担船舶安全航行和防污染操作职责的船员服务的公共和私营海员招募和安置服务机构的职员获得了适当的培训，包括认可的海上服务资历，并具有海运业的相关知识，其中包括关于培训、发证和劳工标准的相关国际海事文件的知识；

(g) 考虑为海员招募和安置服务机构规定经营标准并通过行为准则和道德规范；以及

vices; and

(h) exercising supervision of the licensing or certification system on the basis of a system of quality standards.

2. In establishing the system referred to in Standard A1. 4, paragraph 2, each Member should consider requiring seafarer recruitment and placement services, established in its territory, to develop and maintain verifiable operational practices. These operational practices for private seafarer recruitment and placement services and, to the extent that they are applicable, for public seafarer recruitment and placement services should address the following matters:

(a) medical examinations, seafarers' identity documents and such other items as may be required for the seafarer to gain employment;

(b) maintaining, with due regard to the right to privacy and the need to protect confidentiality, full and complete records of the seafarers covered by their recruitment and placement system, which should include but not be limited to:

(i) the seafarers' qualifications;

(ii) record of employment;

(iii) personal data relevant to employment; and

(iv) medical data relevant to employment;

(c) maintaining up-to-date lists of the ships for which the seafarer recruitment and placement services provide seafarers and ensuring that there is a means by which the services can be contacted in an emergency at all hours;

(d) procedures to ensure that seafarers are not subject to exploitation by the seafarer recruitment and placement services or their per-

(h) 考虑基于质量标准体系对许可证或证书的发放机制实施监督。

2. 在建立标准 A1.4 第 2 款所述的机制时，各成员国应考虑要求在其领土内设立的海员招募和安置服务机构制定并维持可以核实的经营规范。私营海员招募和安置服务机构的以及在适用的限度内公共海员招募和安置机构的这些经营规范应处理以下事项：

(a) 体检、海员身份证件以及海员为获得就业可能被要求的这类其他项目；

(b) 充分顾及隐私权和保密需要，保持其招募和安置机制涉及的对海员的全面和完整的记录。此类记录应包括但不限于：

(i) 海员的资格；

(ii) 就业记录；

(iii) 与就业有关的个人资料；和

(iv) 与就业有关的健康资料；

(c) 保持由该海员招募和安置服务机构提供海员的船舶的最新名单，并确保存在一种在紧急情况下能够随时与该服务机构进行联络的手段；

(d) 有程序确保海员，在得以受聘到特定船舶或特定公司方面，不受海员招募和安置服务机构或其人员的盘剥；

sonnel with regard to the offer of engagement on particular ships or by particular companies;

(e) procedures to prevent the opportunities for exploitation of seafarers arising from the issue of joining advances or any other financial transaction between the shipowner and the seafarers which are handled by the seafarer recruitment and placement services;

(f) clearly publicizing costs, if any, which the seafarer will be expected to bear in the recruitment process;

(g) ensuring that seafarers are advised of any particular conditions applicable to the job for which they are to be engaged and of the particular shipowner's policies relating to their employment;

(h) procedures which are in accordance with the principles of natural justice for dealing with cases of incompetence or indiscipline consistent with national laws and practice and, where applicable, with collective agreements;

(i) procedures to ensure, as far as practicable, that all mandatory certificates and documents submitted for employment are up to date and have not been fraudulently obtained and that employment references are verified;

(j) procedures to ensure that requests for information or advice by families of seafarers while the seafarers are at sea are dealt with promptly and sympathetically and at no cost; and

(k) verifying that labour conditions on ships where seafarers are placed are in conformity with applicable collective bargaining agreements concluded between a shipowner and a representative seafarers' organization and, as a matter of policy, supplying seafarers only to shipowners that offer terms and conditions of

(e) 有程序防止因海员招募和安置服务机构经办船东与海员之间上船预付款的发放或任何其他财务转账而产生的盘剥海员的机会；

(f) 清楚地公布在招募过程中预期由海员承担的费用，如有任何费用；

(g) 确保海员被告知适用于其即将受聘工作的任何特定条件以及与其就业相关的特定船东的政策；

(h) 有根据自然公正的原则处理不适任或不守纪律情况的程序，此类程序符合国内法律和惯例并，在适用时，符合集体协议；

(i) 有程序尽实际可行地确保为就业所提交的所有强制性证书和文件都是最新的，不是通过欺骗获得，而且其就业证明情况经过核实；

(j) 有程序确保海员在海上期间其家属获得信息或消息的要求得到迅速和富有同情的处理，且不收取费用；以及

(k) 核实海员所被安置的船舶上的劳动条件符合船东与有代表性的海员组织所达成的适用集体谈判协议，并作为一项方针，只向那些为海员提供的就业条款和条件符合适用的法律或条例或集体协议的船东提供海员。

employment to seafarers which comply with applicable laws or regulations or collective agreements.

3. Consideration should be given to encouraging international cooperation between Members and relevant organizations, such as:

(a) the systematic exchange of information on the maritime industry and labour market on a bilateral, regional and multilateral basis;

(b) the exchange of information on maritime labour legislation;

(c) the harmonization of policies, working methods and legislation governing recruitment and placement of seafarers;

(d) the improvement of procedures and conditions for the international recruitment and placement of seafarers; and

(e) workforce planning, taking account of the supply of and demand for seafarers and the requirements of the maritime industry.

3. 应考虑鼓励成员国和相关组织之间的国际合作，例如：

(a) 在双边、区域和多边基础上系统地交换关于海运业和海运劳动力市场的信息；

(b) 交换关于海事劳工立法的信息；

(c) 协调管辖招募和安置海员的政策、工作方法和立法；

(d) 改善海员国际招募和安置的程序和条件；以及

(e) 考虑海员的供求情况和海运业的要求制订劳动力规划。

TITLE 2. CONDITIONS OF EMPLOYMENT

Regulation 2.1—Seafarers' employment agreements

Purpose: To ensure that seafarers have a fair employment agreement

1. The terms and conditions for employment of a seafarer shall be set out or referred to in a clear written legally enforceable agreement and shall be consistent with the standards set out in the Code.

2. Seafarers' employment agreements shall be agreed to by the seafarer under conditions which ensure that the seafarer has an opportunity to review and seek advice on the terms and conditions in the agreement and freely accepts them before signing.

3. To the extent compatible with the Member's national law and practice, seafarers' employment agreements shall be understood to incorporate any applicable collective bargaining agreements.

Standard A2.1—Seafarers' employment agreements

1. Each Member shall adopt laws or regulations requiring that ships that fly its flag comply with the following requirements:

(a) seafarers working on ships that fly its flag shall have a seafarers' employment agreement signed by both the seafarer and the shipowner or a representative of the shipowner (or, where they are not employees, evidence of contractual or similar arrangements) providing them with decent working and living conditions on board the ship as required by this Convention;

(b) seafarers signing a seafarers' employment agreement shall be

标题二　就业条件

规则 2.1—海员就业协议

目的：确保海员取得公平的就业协议

1. 海员的就业条款和条件须在一份明确的法律上可执行的书面协议中加以规定或提及并须与守则中规定的标准一致。

2. 海员就业协议须在确保海员有机会对协议中的条款和条件进行审阅和征求意见并在签字前对其自由接受的条件下，取得海员的同意。

3. 在与成员国国内法律和惯例不冲突的范围内，海员就业协议须被理解为并入了任何适用的集体谈判协议。

标准 A2.1—海员就业协议

1. 各成员国须通过法律或条例，要求悬挂其旗帜的船舶符合下述要求：

(a) 在悬挂其旗帜的船舶上工作的海员须持有一份由海员和船东或船东代表双方签署的海员就业协议（或者，如果他们不是雇员，契约性或类似约定的证明），为其提供本公约所要求的体面的船上工作和生活条件；

(b) 签署海员就业协议的海员在签字前须有机会对协议进行审查和征询意见，还要为海员提供其他必要的便利确保其在充分理解了其权利和责任后自由达成协议；

given an opportunity to examine and seek advice on the agreement before signing, as well as such other facilities as are necessary to ensure that they have freely entered into an agreement with a sufficient understanding of their rights and responsibilities;

(c) the shipowner and seafarer concerned shall each have a signed original of the seafarers' employment agreement;

(d) measures shall be taken to ensure that clear information as to the conditions of their employment can be easily obtained on board by seafarers, including the ship's master, and that such information, including a copy of the seafarers' employment agreement, is also accessible for review by officers of a competent authority, including those in ports to be visited; and

(e) seafarers shall be given a document containing a record of their employment on board the ship.

2. Where a collective bargaining agreement forms all or part of a seafarers' employment agreement, a copy of that agreement shall be available on board. Where the language of the seafarers' employment agreement and any applicable collective bargaining agreement is not in English, the following shall also be available in English (except for ships engaged only in domestic voyages):

(a) a copy of a standard form of the agreement; and

(b) the portions of the collective bargaining agreement that are subject to a port State inspection under Regulation 5.2.

3. The document referred to in paragraph 1(e) of this Standard shall not contain any statement as to the quality of the seafarers' work or as to their wages. The form of the document, the particulars

(c) 有关船东和海员须各持有一份经签字的海员就业协议原件；

(d) 须采取措施确保包括船长在内的海员在船上可以容易地获得关于其就业条件的明确信息，并且这些信息，包括一份海员就业协议的副本，还能够供主管当局的官员，包括所停靠港口的官员查验；以及

(e) 须发给海员一份载有其船上就业记录的文件。

2. 如果集体谈判协议构成海员就业协议的全部或一部分，该协议的一份副本须能够在船上提供。如果海员就业协议和任何适用的集体谈判协议的语言不是英语，以下内容还须用英语提供（仅从事国内航行的船舶除外）：

(a) 一份协议的标准格式；以及

(b) 根据规则5.2，集体谈判协议中要受港口国检查的部分。

3. 本标准第1(e)款中所述的文件不得载有关于海员工作的质量或关于其工资的任何陈述。该文件的格式、将要记录的细节和这些细节将被记录的方式须由国内法律确定。

to be recorded and the manner in which such particulars are to be entered, shall be determined by national law.

4. Each Member shall adopt laws and regulations specifying the matters that are to be included in all seafarers' employment agreements governed by its national law. Seafarers' employment agreements shall in all cases contain the following particulars:

(a) the seafarer's full name, date of birth or age, and birthplace;

(b) the shipowner's name and address;

(c) the place where and date when the seafarers' employment agreement is entered into;

(d) the capacity in which the seafarer is to be employed;

(e) the amount of the seafarer's wages or, where applicable, the formula used for calculating them;

(f) the amount of paid annual leave or, where applicable, the formula used for calculating it;

(g) the termination of the agreement and the conditions thereof, including:

(i) if the agreement has been made for an indefinite period, the conditions entitling either party to terminate it, as well as the required notice period, which shall not be less for the shipowner than for the seafarer;

(ii) if the agreement has been made for a definite period, the date fixed for its expiry; and

(iii) if the agreement has been made for a voyage, the port of destination and the time which has to expire after arrival before the seafarer should be discharged;

(h) the health and social security protection benefits to be provided

4. 各成员国须通过法律和条例，具体规定受其国内法律管辖的所有海员就业协议中将要包括的事项。在所有情况下海员就业协议均须载明以下细节：

(a) 海员的全名、出生日期或年龄及出生地；

(b) 船东的名称和地址；

(c) 订立海员就业协议的地点及日期；

(d) 海员将受雇的职务；

(e) 海员的工资数额或者，如果适用，用于计算工资的公式；

(f) 带薪年休假的天数或者，如果适用，用于计算天数的公式；

(g) 协议的终止及其终止条件，包括：

(i) 如果协议签订为无固定期限，各方有权终止协议的条件，以及所要求的提前通知期，船东的提前通知期不得短于海员的提前通知期；

(ii) 如果协议签订为固定期限，其确定的期满日期；和

(iii) 如果协议签订为一个航程，目的港以及到达后海员应被解职前需经历的时间；

(h) 将由船东提供给海员的健康和社会保障保护津贴；

to the seafarer by the shipowner;

(i) the seafarer's entitlement to repatriation;

(j) reference to the collective bargaining agreement, if applicable; and

(k) any other particulars which national law may require.

5. Each Member shall adopt laws or[1] regulations establishing minimum notice periods to be given by the seafarers and shipowners for the early termination of a seafarers' employment agreement. The duration of these minimum periods shall be determined after consultation with the shipowners' and seafarers' organizations concerned, but shall not be shorter than seven days.

6. A notice period shorter than the minimum may be given in circumstances which are recognized under national law or regulations or applicable collective bargaining agreements as justifying termination of the employment agreement at shorter notice or without notice. In determining those circumstances, each Member shall ensure that the need of the seafarer to terminate, without penalty, the employment agreement on shorter notice or without notice for compassionate or other urgent reasons is taken into account.

Guideline B2.1—Seafarers' employment agreements

Guideline B2.1.1—Record of employment

1. In determining the particulars to be recorded in the record of employment referred to in Standard A2.1, paragraph 1(e), each Member should ensure that this document contains sufficient information, with a translation in English, to facilitate the acquisition of

[1] 在最初公布的公约正式英文文本中，此处为 and，现修订为 or。——校译者注

(i) 海员遣返的权利；

(j) 提及集体谈判协议，如适用；以及

(k) 国内法律可能要求的任何其他细节。

5. 各成员国须通过法律或条例，确定海员和船东为提前终止海员就业协议而发出的最短提前通知期限。最短期限的长度须在与有关船东组织和海员组织协商后确定，但不得短于七天。

6. 在国内法律或条例或适用的集体谈判协议认可以更短时间通知或不经通知即为合理地终止就业协议的情形下，发出的提前通知期可以比最短期限更短。在确定这些情形时，各成员国须保证考虑到，出于值得同情的或其他紧急的原因，海员需要在不受处罚的情况下以更短的时间通知或不经通知即终止就业协议。

导则 B2.1—海员就业协议

导则 B2.1.1—就业记录

1. 在确定标准 A2.1 第 1(e)款所述的就业记录中将记录的细节时，各成员国应确保该文件包含足够的信息并有英语译文，以便于将来找到工作或满足升级或升迁的海上服务资历要求。海员履职书[1]可满足该标准第 1(e)款的要求。

[1] 该词对应的英文是 seafarers' discharge book，也可译成"海员离职簿"，用于在离职时记录海员在船的工作资历，相当于我国《船员条例》中规定的船员服务簿。——校译者注

further work or to satisfy the sea-service requirements for upgrading or promotion. A seafarers' discharge book may satisfy the requirements of paragraph 1(e) of that Standard.

Regulation 2.2—Wages

Purpose: To ensure that seafarers are paid for their services

1. All seafarers shall be paid for their work regularly and in full in accordance with their employment agreements.

Standard A2.2—Wages

1. Each Member shall require that payments due to seafarers working on ships that fly its flag are made at no greater than monthly intervals and in accordance with any applicable collective agreement.

2. Seafarers shall be given a monthly account of the payments due and the amounts paid, including wages, additional payments and the rate of exchange used where payment has been made in a currency or at a rate different from the one agreed to.

3. Each Member shall require that shipowners take measures, such as those set out in paragraph 4 of this Standard, to provide seafarers with a means to transmit all or part of their earnings to their families or dependants or legal beneficiaries.

4. Measures to ensure that seafarers are able to transmit their earnings to their families include:

(a) a system for enabling seafarers, at the time of their entering employment or during it, to allot, if they so desire, a proportion of their wages for remittance at regular intervals to their families by bank transfers or similar means; and

规则 2.2—工资

目的：确保海员得到其服务报酬

1. 所有海员均须根据其就业协议定期获得全额工作报酬。

标准 A2.2—工资

1. 各成员国须要求，按不超过一个月的间隔并根据任何适用的集体协议，向在悬挂其旗帜的船舶上工作的海员支付其应得的报酬。

2. 须给海员一个应得报酬和实付数额的月份账目，包括工资、额外报酬，以及在支付报酬的货币或兑换率不同于约定时所用的兑换率。

3. 各成员国须要求船东采取措施，例如本标准第 4 款中规定的措施，为海员提供一种将其收入的全部或部分转给其家人或受扶养人[1]或法定受益人的方式。

4. 确保海员能够将其收入转给其家人的措施包括：

(a) 如果其本人愿意，在海员开始就业时或在就业期间使其能够通过银行转账或类似方式拨出其工资的一定比例用于定期汇款的一种机制；以及

[1] 对应的英文为 dependant，指依赖海员生活的人，即需要海员赡养的长辈、抚养的晚辈和扶养的平辈。此处中文译文中的“扶养”取其广义，包括狭义的赡养、抚养和扶养。——校译者注

(b) a requirement that allotments should be remitted in due time and directly to the person or persons nominated by the seafarers.

5. Any charge for the service under paragraphs 3 and 4 of this Standard shall be reasonable in amount, and the rate of currency exchange, unless otherwise provided, shall, in accordance with national laws or regulations, be at the prevailing market rate or the official published rate and not unfavourable to the seafarer.

6. Each Member that adopts national laws or regulations governing seafarers' wages shall give due consideration to the guidance provided in Part B of the Code.

Guideline B2.2—Wages

Guideline B2.2.1—Specific definitions

1. For the purpose of this Guideline, the term:

(a) *able seafarer* means any seafarer who is deemed competent to perform any duty which may be required of a rating serving in the deck department, other than the duties of a supervisory or specialist rating, or who is defined as such by national laws, regulations or practice, or by collective agreement;

(b) *basic pay or wages* means the pay, however composed, for normal hours of work; it does not include payments for overtime worked, bonuses, allowances, paid leave or any other additional remuneration;

(c) *consolidated wage* means a wage or salary which includes the basic pay and other pay-related benefits; a consolidated wage may include compensation for all overtime hours which are worked and all other pay-related benefits, or it may include only certain benefits in a partial consolidation;

(b) 应按时将拨出数额直接汇给海员指定的一人或多人的要求。

5. 本标准第3和4款下之服务的任何收费须在数额上合理，且除非另行规定，货币兑换率须根据国内法律或条例采用主要市场汇率或官方公布的汇率，且不得对海员不利。

6. 各成员国在通过管理海员工资的国内法律或条例时，须充分考虑到守则B部分提供的指导。

导则 B2.2—工资

导则 B2.2.1—具体定义

1. 就本导则而言：

(a) “一等水手”[1]一词系指任何被认为胜任可能要求在甲板部服务的一名普通船员从事的除普通船员的监督性或专门性职责以外的任何职责的海员，或根据国内法律、条例或惯例或根据集体协议被如此界定的任何海员；

(b) “基本报酬或工资”系指正常工作时间的报酬，无论其如何构成；它不包括所做加班的报酬、奖金、补贴、带薪休假或任何其他额外薪酬；

(c) “合并工资”一词系指包括基本报酬和其他与报酬有关的津贴在内的工资或薪资；合并工资可包括对所有所做加班时间给予的补偿和所有其他与报酬相关的津贴，或者，它可以仅包括部分合并工资内的某些津贴；

---

[1] 该定义中普通船员的“监督性职责”和“专门性职责”主要指水手长和木匠的职责。除上述两方面的特殊职责外，一等水手应当能够胜任甲板部普通船员的所有其他职责，包括值班职责。从这一点来看，一等水手相当于《STCW 公约》中的高级值班水手(able seafarer deck)，两者的英文名称也类似。在船舶配员实践中，一级水手(able-bodied seaman)通常指具有参与航行值班资格的甲板部普通船员，应包括值班水手和高级值班水手，因此不同于一等水手。——校译者注

(d) *hours of work* means time during which seafarers are required to do work on account of the ship;

(e) *overtime* means time worked in excess of the normal hours of work.

Guideline B2.2.2—Calculation and payment

1. For seafarers whose remuneration includes separate compensation for overtime worked:

(a) for the purpose of calculating wages, the normal hours of work at sea and in port should not exceed eight hours per day;

(b) for the purpose of calculating overtime, the number of normal hours per week covered by the basic pay or wages should be prescribed by national laws or regulations, if not determined by collective agreements, but should not exceed 48 hours per week; collective agreements may provide for a different but not less favourable treatment;

(c) the rate or rates of compensation for overtime, which should be not less than one and one-quarter times the basic pay or wages per hour, should be prescribed by national laws or regulations or by collective agreements, if applicable; and

(d) records of all overtime worked should be maintained by the master, or a person assigned by the master, and endorsed by the seafarer at no greater than monthly intervals.

2. For seafarers whose wages are fully or partially consolidated:

(a) the seafarers' employment agreement should specify clearly, where appropriate, the number of hours of work expected of the seafarer in return for this remuneration, and any additional allowances which might be due in addition to the consolidated

(d)“工作时间”一词系指海员因船舶而被要求工作的时间；

(e)“加班”一词系指超出正常工作时间之外工作的时间。

导则 B2.2.2—计算和支付

1. 对于其薪酬包括了另计的所做加班补偿的海员：

(a) 出于计算工资之目的，在海上和港口的正常工作时间每天不应超过八小时；

(b) 出于计算加班之目的，对于由基本报酬或工资所涵盖的每周正常时间长度，如果集体协议未予确定，应由国内法律或条例规定，但每周不应超过 48 小时；集体协议可以规定不同的但不能较之不利的待遇；

(c) 加班补偿率应由国内法律或条例或由集体协议（如适用）予以规定，但不应低于每小时基本报酬或工资的 1.25 倍；以及

(d) 所做的所有加班应由船长或船长指派的人员进行记录，并以不超过一个月的间隔由海员签字。

2. 对于其工资系全部或部分合并的海员：

(a) 适当时，海员就业协议应明确订明为换取这一薪酬而期望海员工作的时间长度，以及除了合并工资外可能应支付的任何额外补贴及在何种情况下应支付；

wage, and in which circumstances;

(b) where hourly overtime is payable for hours worked in excess of those covered by the consolidated wage, the hourly rate should be not less than one and one-quarter times the basic rate corresponding to the normal hours of work as defined in paragraph 1 of this Guideline; the same principle should be applied to the overtime hours included in the consolidated wage;

(c) remuneration for that portion of the fully or partially consolidated wage representing the normal hours of work as defined in paragraph 1(a) of this Guideline should be no less than the applicable minimum wage; and

(d) for seafarers whose wages are partially consolidated, records of all overtime worked should be maintained and endorsed as provided for in paragraph 1(d) of this Guideline.

3. National laws or regulations or collective agreements may provide for compensation for overtime or for work performed on the weekly day of rest and on public holidays by at least equivalent time off duty and off the ship or additional leave in lieu of remuneration or any other compensation so provided.

4. National laws and regulations adopted after consulting the representative shipowners' and seafarers' organizations or, as appropriate, collective agreements should take into account the following principles:

(a) equal remuneration for work of equal value should apply to all seafarers employed on the same ship without discrimination based upon race, colour, sex, religion, political opinion, national extraction or social origin;

(b) the seafarers' employment agreement specifying the applicable

(b) 凡对超出合并工资所涵盖的工作时间之外的工作时间按每小时加班支付的，该小时报酬率不应低于与本导则第1款所界定的正常工作时间相对应的基本报酬率的1.25倍；同样的原则应适用于包括在合并工资内的加班时间；

(c) 全部和部分合并工资中代表本导则第1(a)款所界定的正常工作时间的那一部分薪酬不应低于适用的最低工资；以及

(d) 对于其工资为部分合并的海员，应按本导则第1(d)款的规定保持并签署所有所做加班的记录。

3. 国内法律或条例或集体协议可以规定，对加班或在每周一天休息日和公共节假日工作的补偿，至少以相当的不值班时间和离船时间或是以追加休假，来代替薪酬或为此规定的任何其他补偿。

4. 在与有代表性的船东组织和海员组织协商后通过的国内法律和条例或者适当时的集体协议应考虑到以下原则：

(a) 同工同酬应适用于受雇于同一船舶的所有海员，而不基于种族、肤色、性别、宗教、政治观点、民族血统或社会出身加以歧视；

(b) 具体订明适用的工资或工资率的海员就业协议应随船携带；应通过用海员懂得的语言向其提供至少一份业已签字的有关信息，或通过在海员能够进入的地点张贴一份协议，或通过其他一些适宜的手段，使每名海员都能得到有关工资额或工资率的信息；

wages or wage rates should be carried on board the ship; information on the amount of wages or wage rates should be made available to each seafarer, either by providing at least one signed copy of the relevant information to the seafarer in a language which the seafarer understands, or by posting a copy of the agreement in a place accessible to seafarers or by some other appropriate means;

(c) wages should be paid in legal tender; where appropriate, they may be paid by bank transfer, bank cheque, postal cheque or money order;

(d) on termination of engagement all remuneration due should be paid without undue delay;

(e) adequate penalties or other appropriate remedies should be imposed by the competent authority where shipowners unduly delay, or fail to make, payment of all remuneration due;

(f) wages should be paid directly to seafarers' designated bank accounts unless they request otherwise in writing;

(g) subject to subparagraph (h) of this paragraph, the shipowner should impose no limit on seafarers' freedom to dispose of their remuneration;

(h) deduction from remuneration should be permitted only if:

(i) there is an express provision in national laws or regulations or in an applicable collective agreement and the seafarer has been informed, in the manner deemed most appropriate by the competent authority, of the conditions for such deductions; and

(ii) the deductions do not in total exceed the limit that may have been established by national laws or regulations or collective

(c) 工资应以法定货币支付；适宜时，可以通过银行转账、银行支票、邮政支票或汇票支付工资；

(d) 在终止聘用时，所有应付薪酬的支付不应出现不正当的拖延；

(e) 如果船东不正当地拖延支付或未能支付所有应付薪酬，主管当局应对其适当处罚或强制其他适当补救措施；

(f) 工资应直接支付给海员指定的银行账户，除非其以书面形式另行要求；

(g) 除依照本款(h)项规定者，船东不应对海员支配其薪酬的自由施加限制；

(h) 只有在下列情况下，才允许在薪酬中做出扣减：

(i) 国内法律或条例或适用的集体协议有明确规定且已通过主管当局认为最合适的方式向海员通知了此种扣减的条件；和

(ii) 扣减总额不超过国内法律或条例或集体协议或法院裁决可能已为此种扣减确定的限制；

agreements or court decisions for making such deductions;

(i) no deductions should be made from a seafarer's remuneration in respect of obtaining or retaining employment;

(j) monetary fines against seafarers other than those authorized by national laws or regulations, collective agreements or other measures should be prohibited;

(k) the competent authority should have the power to inspect stores and services provided on board ship to ensure that fair and reasonable prices are applied for the benefit of the seafarers concerned; and

(l) to the extent that seafarers' claims for wages and other sums due in respect of their employment are not secured in accordance with the provisions of the International Convention on Maritime Liens and Mortgages, 1993, such claims should be protected in accordance with the Protection of Workers' Claims (Employer's Insolvency) Convention, 1992 (No. 173).

5. Each Member should, after consulting with representative shipowners' and seafarers' organizations, have procedures to investigate complaints relating to any matter contained in this Guideline.

Guideline B2.2.3—Minimum wages

1. Without prejudice to the principle of free collective bargaining, each Member should, after consulting representative shipowners' and seafarers' organizations, establish procedures for determining minimum wages for seafarers. Representative shipowners' and seafarers' organizations should participate in the operation of such procedures.

2. When establishing such procedures and in fixing minimum

(i) 不应为获得或保持就业而在海员的薪酬中做出扣减；

(j) 除国内法律或条例、集体协议或其他措施授权者外，应禁止对海员罚款；

(k) 主管当局应有权检查船上提供的物品和服务，以确保为了相关海员的利益实行了公平合理的价格；以及

(l) 在海员的工资和与其就业有关的其他应付款项之请求根据《1993年船舶优先权和抵押权国际公约》❶的规定无法获得担保的范围内，此类请求应根据《1992年(雇主破产)保护工人债权公约》❷(第173号)予以保护。

5. 各成员国应在与有代表性的船东组织和海员组织协商后，对相关于本导则所载任何事项的投诉，制定调查的程序。

导则 B2.2.3—最低工资

1. 在不损害自由集体谈判原则的前提下，各成员国应在与有代表性的船东组织和海员组织协商后，建立确定海员最低工资的程序。有代表性的船东组织和海员组织应参与此类程序的运作。

2. 在建立此类程序和确定最低工资时，应充分顾及有关确定最低工资的国际劳工标准以及以下原则：

---

❶ 我国于1994年8月18日签署该公约。该公约目前尚未生效。我国1992年公布的《海商法》中有关船舶优先权的规定即参照该公约，将5类债权设定为船舶优先权。——校译者注

❷ 该公约已于1995年6月8日生效。我国未批准该公约。——校译者注

wages, due regard should be given to international labour standards concerning minimum wage fixing, as well as the following principles:

(a) the level of minimum wages should take into account the nature of maritime employment, crewing levels of ships, and seafarers' normal hours of work; and

(b) the level of minimum wages should be adjusted to take into account changes in the cost of living and in the needs of seafarers.

3. The competent authority should ensure:

(a) by means of a system of supervision and sanctions, that wages are paid at not less than the rate or rates fixed; and

(b) that any seafarers who have been paid at a rate lower than the minimum wage are enabled to recover, by an inexpensive and expeditious judicial or other procedure, the amount by which they have been underpaid.

Guideline B2.2.4—Minimum monthly basic pay or wage figure for able seafarers

1. The basic pay or wages for a calendar month of service for an able seafarer should be no less than the amount periodically set by the Joint Maritime Commission or another body authorized by the Governing Body of the International Labour Office. Upon a decision of the Governing Body, the Director-General shall notify any revised amount to the Members of the Organization.

2. Nothing in this Guideline should be deemed to prejudice arrangements agreed between shipowners or their organizations and seafarers' organizations with regard to the regulation of standard minimum terms and conditions of employment, provided such terms

(a) 最低工资的水平应考虑到海上就业的性质、船舶的配员水平和海员的正常工作时间；以及

(b) 最低工资的水平应考虑生活成本的变化和海员需求的变化而予以调整。

3. 主管当局应保证：

(a) 通过监督和制裁制度，使所支付的工资不低于所确定的工资率；以及

(b) 已按低于最低工资的工资率领取了工资的任何海员，能够通过一种花费不多且迅速的司法或其他程序，追偿对其少付的数额。

导则 B2.2.4——一等水手的月最低基本报酬或工资数额

1. 一等水手一个日历月工作的基本报酬或工资不应低于联合海事委员会或国际劳工局理事会授权的另一机构所定期确定的数额。理事会一旦做出决定，局长须向本组织的成员国通知任何修订的数额。

2. 本导则的任何条款都不应被视为有损船东或其组织和海员组织之间就标准的最低就业条款和条件的规范所达成的协议，条件是此种条款和条件得到主管当局的认可。

and conditions are recognized by the competent authority.

Regulation 2.3—Hours of work and hours of rest

Purpose: To ensure that seafarers have regulated hours of work or hours of rest

1. Each Member shall ensure that the hours of work or hours of rest for seafarers are regulated.

2. Each Member shall establish maximum hours of work or minimum hours of rest over given periods that are consistent with the provisions in the Code.

Standard A2.3—Hours of work and hours of rest

1. For the purpose of this Standard, the term:

(a) *hours of work* means time during which seafarers are required to do work on account of the ship;

(b) *hours of rest* means time outside hours of work; this term does not include short breaks.

2. Each Member shall within the limits set out in paragraphs 5 to 8 of this Standard fix either a maximum number of hours of work which shall not be exceeded in a given period of time, or a minimum number of hours of rest which shall be provided in a given period of time.

3. Each Member acknowledges that the normal working hours' standard for seafarers, like that for other workers, shall be based on an eight-hour day with one day of rest per week and rest on public holidays. However, this shall not prevent the Member from having

规则 2.3—工作时间和休息时间

目的：确保海员享有规范的工作时间或休息时间

1. 各成员国须确保对海员的工作时间或休息时间加以规范。

2. 各成员国须确立符合守则规定的特定时间内的最长工作时间或最短休息时间。

标准 A2.3—工作时间和休息时间

1. 就本标准而言：

(a)“工作时间”一词系指海员因船舶而被要求工作的时间；

(b)“休息时间”一词系指工作时间以外的时间；该词不包括暂短的休息。

2. 各成员国须在本标准第 5 至 8 款规定的限制内，确定在一段给定的时间内不得超过的最长工作时间，或是在一段给定时间内须提供的最短休息时间。

3. 各成员国承认，同对其他工人的标准一样，海员的正常工时标准须以每天八小时、每周休息一天和公共节假日休息为基础。然而，这不得妨碍成员国制定程序，批准或登记在不低于这一标准的基础上确定海员正常工时的集体协议。

procedures to authorize or register a collective agreement which determines seafarers' normal working hours on a basis no less favourable than this standard.

4. In determining the national standards, each Member shall take account of the danger posed by the fatigue of seafarers, especially those whose duties involve navigational safety and the safe and secure operation of the ship.

5. The limits on hours of work or rest shall be as follows:

(a) maximum hours of work shall not exceed:

(i) 14 hours in any 24-hour period; and

(ii) 72 hours in any seven-day period;

or

(b) minimum hours of rest shall not be less than:

(i) ten hours in any 24-hour period; and

(ii) 77 hours in any seven-day period.

6. Hours of rest may be divided into no more than two periods, one of which shall be at least six hours in length, and the interval between consecutive periods of rest shall not exceed 14 hours.

7. Musters, fire-fighting and lifeboat drills, and drills prescribed by national laws and regulations and by international instruments, shall be conducted in a manner that minimizes the disturbance of rest periods and does not induce fatigue.

8. When a seafarer is on call, such as when a machinery space is unattended, the seafarer shall have an adequate compensatory rest period if the normal period of rest is disturbed by call-outs to work.

9. If no collective agreement or arbitration award exists or if the

4. 在确定本国标准时，各成员国须考虑到海员的疲劳，特别是其职责涉及船舶航行安全以及安全和安保操作的那些海员的疲劳所带来的危险。

5. 工作或休息时间须作如下限制：

(a) 最长工作时间：

(i) 在任何 24 小时时段内不得超过 14 小时；且

(ii) 在任何七天时段内不得超过 72 小时；

或者

(b) 最短休息时间：

(i) 在任何 24 小时时段内不得少于十小时；且

(ii) 在任何七天时段内不得少于 77 小时。

6. 休息时间至多可分为两段，其中一段的长度须至少有六小时，且相连的两段休息时间的间隔不得超过 14 小时。

7. 应变部署、消防和救生艇演习以及国内法律和条例及国际文件规定的演习须以对休息时间的影响最小和不会造成疲劳的方式进行。

8. 在某一海员处于随时待命时，例如机器处所处于无人值守时，如果海员因被召去工作而打扰了正常的休息时间，则须给予充分的补休时间。

9. 如果没有集体协议或仲裁裁决中，或如果主管当局确定协议或裁决中关于本标准第 7 或 8 款的规定不适当，则主管当局须确定此类规定，以确保有关海员得到充分的休息。

competent authority determines that the provisions in the agreement or award in respect of paragraph 7 or 8 of this Standard are inadequate, the competent authority shall determine such provisions to ensure the seafarers concerned have sufficient rest.

10. Each Member shall require the posting, in an easily accessible place, of a table with the shipboard working arrangements, which shall contain for every position at least:

(a) the schedule of service at sea and service in port; and

(b) the maximum hours of work or the minimum hours of rest required by national laws or regulations or applicable collective agreements.

11. The table referred to in paragraph 10 of this Standard shall be established in a standardized format in the working language or languages of the ship and in English.

12. Each Member shall require that records of seafarers' daily hours of work or of their daily hours of rest be maintained to allow monitoring of compliance with paragraphs 5 to 11 inclusive of this Standard. The records shall be in a standardized format established by the competent authority taking into account any available guidelines of the International Labour Organization or shall be in any standard format prepared by the Organization. They shall be in the languages required by paragraph 11 of this Standard. The seafarers shall receive a copy of the records pertaining to them which shall be endorsed by the master, or a person authorized by the master, and by the seafarers.

13. Nothing in paragraphs 5 and 6 of this Standard shall prevent a Member from having national laws or regulations or a procedure for

10. 各成员国须要求在容易进入的地点张贴一份船上工作安排表，该表格须至少载明每一岗位的下列内容：

(a) 在海上和在港口的工作安排表；以及

(b) 国内法律或条例或适用的集体协议所要求的最长工作时间或最短休息时间。

11. 本标准第 10 款所述的表格须按标准化的格式以船上的一种或多种工作语言和英文制定。

12. 各成员国须要求保持对海员的日工作时间或其日休息时间进行记录，以便监控对本标准第 5 至 11 款的遵守情况。记录须采用主管当局考虑到国际劳工组织的任何可用导则而确定的标准格式，或者须采用本组织制定的任何标准格式。它们须使用本标准第 11 款所要求的语言。海员须得到一份由船长或船长授权人员以及海员本人签字认可的有关其本人的记录。

13. 本标准第 5 和 6 款的任何规定不得妨碍成员国为主管当局制定国内法律或条例或程序来批准或登记对规定的限制允许有例外情况的集体协议。此类例外须尽可能遵循本标准的规定，但可考虑给予值班海员或在短途航程船舶上工作的海员更经常或更长时间的休假或准予补休。

the competent authority to authorize or register collective agreements permitting exceptions to the limits set out. Such exceptions shall, as far as possible, follow the provisions of this Standard but may take account of more frequent or longer leave periods or the granting of compensatory leave for watchkeeping seafarers or seafarers working on board ships on short voyages.

14. Nothing in this Standard shall be deemed to impair the right of the master of a ship to require a seafarer to perform any hours of work necessary for the immediate safety of the ship, persons on board or cargo, or for the purpose of giving assistance to other ships or persons in distress at sea. Accordingly, the master may suspend the schedule of hours of work or hours of rest and require a seafarer to perform any hours of work necessary until the normal situation has been restored. As soon as practicable after the normal situation has been restored, the master shall ensure that any seafarers who have performed work in a scheduled rest period are provided with an adequate period of rest.

Guideline B2.3—Hours of work and hours of rest

Guideline B2.3.1—Young seafarers

1. At sea and in port the following provisions should apply to all young seafarers under the age of 18:

(a) working hours should not exceed eight hours per day and 40 hours per week and overtime should be worked only where unavoidable for safety reasons;

(b) sufficient time should be allowed for all meals, and a break of at least one hour for the main meal of the day should be assured; and

14. 本标准的任何规定不得妨碍船长出于船舶、船上人员或货物的直接安全需要,或为了帮助海上遇险的其他船舶或人员的需要而要求一名海员从事任何时间工作的权利。为此,船长可中止工作时间或休息时间安排,要求一名海员从事任何时间的必要工作,直至情况恢复正常。一旦情况恢复正常,船长须尽实际可行地及早确保在计划的休息时间内从事工作的任何海员获得充足的休息时间。

导则 B2.3—工作时间和休息时间

导则 B2.3.1—未成年海员

1. 在海上和港口,下述规定应适用于所有 18 岁以下的未成年海员:

(a) 工作时间不应超过每日八小时和每周 40 小时,只有出于安全原因无法避免才应加班;

(b) 各餐都应留有充分的时间,并应保证在日间正餐有至少一个小时的休息时间;以及

(c) a 15-minute rest period as soon as possible following each two hours of continuous work should be allowed.

2. Exceptionally, the provisions of paragraph 1 of this Guideline need not be applied if:

(a) they are impracticable for young seafarers in the deck, engine room and catering departments assigned to watchkeeping duties or working on a rostered shiftwork system; or

(b) the effective training of young seafarers in accordance with established programmes and schedules would be impaired.

3. Such exceptional situations should be recorded, with reasons, and signed by the master.

4. Paragraph 1 of this Guideline does not exempt young seafarers from the general obligation on all seafarers to work during any emergency as provided for in Standard A2. 3, paragraph 14.

Regulation 2.4—Entitlement to leave

Purpose: To ensure that seafarers have adequate leave

1. Each Member shall require that seafarers employed on ships that fly its flag are given paid annual leave under appropriate conditions, in accordance with the provisions in the Code.

2. Seafarers shall be granted shore leave to benefit their health and well-being and consistent with the operational requirements of their positions.

Standard A2.4—Entitlement to leave

1. Each Member shall adopt laws and regulations determining

(c) 每连续工作两小时后应尽可能早地准予15分钟的休息时间。

2. 作为例外，不必适用本导则第1款的规定，如果：

(a) 对于在甲板部、轮机部和膳食部被分派担任值班职责或按班组轮班制工作的未成年海员，这些规定不可行；或者

(b) 未成年海员根据既定计划和安排的有效培训会受到妨害。

3. 这类例外情况应予记录，说明原因，且由船长签字。

4. 本导则第1款对未成年海员不免除标准A2.3第14款规定的对所有海员在任何紧急情况时工作的一般义务。

规则2.4—休假的权利

目的：确保海员享有充分的休假

1. 各成员国须要求在悬挂其旗帜船舶上受雇的海员，在适当的条件下根据守则的规定享受带薪年休假。

2. 须准许海员上岸休假以利于海员的健康和幸福并顺应其职位上的操作要求。

标准A2.4—休假的权利

1. 各成员国须通过法律和条例，确定在悬挂其旗帜的船舶上工作的海员的最低年休假标准，并适当考虑到海员对这种休假的特殊需要。

the minimum standards for annual leave for seafarers serving on ships that fly its flag, taking proper account of the special needs of seafarers with respect to such leave.

2. Subject to any collective agreement or laws or regulations providing for an appropriate method of calculation that takes account of the special needs of seafarers in this respect, the annual leave with pay entitlement shall be calculated on the basis of a minimum of 2.5 calendar days per month of employment. The manner in which the length of service is calculated shall be determined by the competent authority or through the appropriate machinery in each country. Justified absences from work shall not be considered as annual leave.

3. Any agreement to forgo the minimum annual leave with pay prescribed in this Standard, except in cases provided for by the competent authority, shall be prohibited.

Guideline B2.4—Entitlement to leave

Guideline B2.4.1—Calculation of entitlement

1. Under conditions as determined by the competent authority or through the appropriate machinery in each country, service off-articles should be counted as part of the period of service.

2. Under conditions as determined by the competent authority or in an applicable collective agreement, absence from work to attend an approved maritime vocational training course or for such reasons as illness or injury or for maternity should be counted as part of the period of service.

3. The level of pay during annual leave should be at the seafarer's normal level of remuneration provided for by national laws or regulations or in the applicable seafarers' employment agreement.

2. 带薪年休假的权利须以每工作一个月最低2.5日历天为基础加以计算，但受限于任何集体协议或法律或条例所规定的考虑了海员在此方面特殊需要的适当计算方法。计算服务期长度的方法须在各国由主管当局或通过适当的机制来确定。合理的缺勤不得被视作年休假。

3. 除非属于主管当局规定的情况，否则禁止达成放弃本标准规定的最低带薪年休假的任何协议。

导则B2.4—休假的权利

导则B2.4.1—权利的计算

1. 根据各国由主管当局或通过适当机制确定的条件，协议服务中断的期间[1]应被算作服务期的一部分。

2. 根据由主管当局或适用的集体协议确定的条件，参加认可的海事职业培训课程或出于诸如患病或受伤的原因或因生育造成的缺勤，应算作服务期的一部分。

3. 在年休假期间的报酬水平应为国内法律或条例或适用的海员就业协议中规定的海员正常薪酬水平。对于受雇期短于一年的海员，或在雇用关系终止的情况下，休假的权利应按比例计算。

---

[1] 对应的英文为service off-articles，是指海员在服务期间短暂离船的时间，例如某海员在其船舶靠港期间离船回家几天。在中文中，没有现成的对应译法。现依据其含义，译成"协议服务中断的期间"。——校译者注

For seafarers employed for periods shorter than one year or in the event of termination of the employment relationship, entitlement to leave should be calculated on a pro-rata basis.

4. The following should not be counted as part of annual leave with pay:

(a) public and customary holidays recognized as such in the flag State, whether or not they fall during the annual leave with pay;

(b) periods of incapacity for work resulting from illness or injury or from maternity, under conditions as determined by the competent authority or through the appropriate machinery in each country;

(c) temporary shore leave granted to a seafarer while under an employment agreement; and

(d) compensatory leave of any kind, under conditions as determined by the competent authority or through the appropriate machinery in each country.

Guideline B2.4.2—Taking of annual leave

1. The time at which annual leave is to be taken should, unless it is fixed by regulation, collective agreement, arbitration award or other means consistent with national practice, be determined by the shipowner after consultation and, as far as possible, in agreement with the seafarers concerned or their representatives.

2. Seafarers should in principle have the right to take annual leave in the place with which they have a substantial connection, which would normally be the same as the place to which they are entitled to be repatriated. Seafarers should not be required without

4. 下述情况不应算作带薪年休假的一部分：

(a) 船旗国认可的公共和传统节假日，不论其是否出现在带薪年休假内；

(b) 在各国由主管当局或通过适当机制确定的条件下，因患病或受伤或因生育而不能工作的期间；

(c) 在履行就业协议期间准许海员的短暂上岸休假；以及

(d) 在各国由主管当局或通过适当机制确定的条件下，任何类型的补休。

导则 B2.4.2—年休假的使用

1. 除非由条例、集体协议、仲裁裁决或其他符合国内惯例的方式确定，年休假的休假时间应由船东在与有关海员或其代表协商并尽可能达成一致后确定。

2. 原则上海员应有权在其具有实质性联系的地点休年休假，该地点通常应与其有权获得遣返去往之地点相同。除非在海员就业协议或国内法律或条例规定的情况下，未经海员同意，不应要求海员在另一地点休其应享的年休假。

their consent to take annual leave due to them in another place except under the provisions of a seafarers' employment agreement or of national laws or regulations.

3. If seafarers are required to take their annual leave from a place other than that permitted by paragraph 2 of this Guideline, they should be entitled to free transportation to the place where they were engaged or recruited, whichever is nearer their home; subsistence and other costs directly involved should be for the account of the shipowner; the travel time involved should not be deducted from the annual leave with pay due to the seafarer.

4. A seafarer taking annual leave should be recalled only in cases of extreme emergency and with the seafarer's consent.

Guideline B2.4.3—Division and accumulation

1. The division of the annual leave with pay into parts, or the accumulation of such annual leave due in respect of one year together with a subsequent period of leave, may be authorized by the competent authority or through the appropriate machinery in each country.

2. Subject to paragraph 1 of this Guideline and unless otherwise provided in an agreement applicable to the shipowner and the seafarer concerned, the annual leave with pay recommended in this Guideline should consist of an uninterrupted period.

Guideline B2.4.4—Young seafarers

1. Special measures should be considered with respect to young seafarers under the age of 18 who have served six months or any other shorter period of time under a collective agreement or seafarers' employment agreement without leave on a foreign-going ship which has not returned to their country of residence in that time, and

3. 如果要求海员在本导则第 2 款所允许地点以外的地点休其年休假，他们应有权免费旅行到其受聘或被招募的地点，以离其家较近者为准；生活费用以及其他直接发生的费用应由船东承担；旅行所花费的时间不应从海员应享的带薪年休假中扣减。

4. 只有在极端紧急的情况下并取得海员的同意后才能将休年休假的海员召回。

导则 B2.4.3—分段和累积

1. 在各国由主管当局或通过适当的机制可批准将带薪年休假分成几个部分，或将一年应享的此种年休假与后来的一段休假累积在一起。

2. 在本导则第 1 款的限制下，除非适用于有关船东和海员的协议另有规定，本导则所建议的带薪年休假应由一段不间断的期间构成。

导则 B2.4.4—未成年海员

1. 对于在一艘前往国外的船上未经休假已服务六个月或根据集体协议或海员就业协议已服务任何更短的时间，并在该段时间内没有返回过其居住国，且在该航程之后的三个月中也不会返回的 18 岁以下未成年海员，应考虑特别的措施。此种措施可以包括，将其免费遣返到其居住国原来的受聘地去休其在航行期间所挣得的任何假期。

will not return in the subsequent three months of the voyage. Such measures could consist of their repatriation at no expense to themselves to the place of original engagement in their country of residence for the purpose of taking any leave earned during the voyage.

Regulation 2.5—Repatriation

Purpose: To ensure that seafarers are able to return home

1. Seafarers have a right to be repatriated at no cost to themselves in the circumstances and under the conditions specified in the Code.

2. Each Member shall require ships that fly its flag to provide financial security to ensure that seafarers are duly repatriated in accordance with the Code.

Standard A2.5—Repatriation

1. Each Member shall ensure that seafarers on ships that fly its flag are entitled to repatriation in the following circumstances:

(a) if the seafarers' employment agreement expires while they are abroad;

(b) when the seafarers' employment agreement is terminated:

  (i) by the shipowner; or

  (ii) by the seafarer for justified reasons; and also

(c) when the seafarers are no longer able to carry out their duties under their employment agreement or cannot be expected to carry them out in the specific circumstances.

2. Each Member shall ensure that there are appropriate provi-

规则 2.5—遣返

目的：确保海员能够回家

1. 在守则具体规定的情形和条件下，海员有权利得到遣返而自己不承担费用。

2. 各成员国须要求悬挂其旗帜的船舶提供财务担保以确保海员根据守则得以及时遣返。

标准 A2.5—遣返

1. 各成员国须确保悬挂其旗帜船舶上的海员在以下情形有权得到遣返：

(a) 如果海员在国外时海员就业协议到期；

(b) 如果海员就业协议：

(i) 被船东终止；或

(ii) 被海员出于合理的理由终止；以及

(c) 如果海员不再具备履行其就业协议中职责的能力或在具体情形下不能指望其履行这些职责。

2. 各成员国须确保在其法律和条例或其他措施中或在集体谈判协议中有相应的条款，规定：

sions in its laws and regulations or other measures or in collective bargaining agreements, prescribing:

(a) the circumstances in which seafarers are entitled to repatriation in accordance with paragraph 1(b) and (c) of this Standard;

(b) the maximum duration of service periods on board following which a seafarer is entitled to repatriation—such periods to be less than 12 months; and

(c) the precise entitlements to be accorded by shipowners for repatriation, including those relating to the destinations of repatriation, the mode of transport, the items of expense to be covered and other arrangements to be made by shipowners.

3. Each Member shall prohibit shipowners from requiring that seafarers make an advance payment towards the cost of repatriation at the beginning of their employment, and also from recovering the cost of repatriation from the seafarers' wages or other entitlements except where the seafarer has been found, in accordance with national laws or regulations or other measures or applicable collective bargaining agreements, to be in serious default of the seafarer's employment obligations.

4. National laws and regulations shall not prejudice any right of the shipowner to recover the cost of repatriation under third-party contractual arrangements.

5. If a shipowner fails to make arrangements for or to meet the cost of repatriation of seafarers who are entitled to be repatriated:

(a) the competent authority of the Member whose flag the ship flies shall arrange for repatriation of the seafarers concerned; if it fails to do so, the State from which the seafarers are to be repatriated

(a) 海员有权根据本标准第1(b)和(c)款得到遣返的情形；

(b) 海员在有权得到遣返前在船上服务的最长期间——这段时间要少于12个月；以及

(c) 船东将给予的具体遣返权利，包括关于遣返的目的地、旅行方式、船东将负担的费用项目和将做出的其他安排方面的权利。

3. 各成员国须禁止船东要求海员在开始受雇时预付遣返费用，禁止船东从海员的工资或其他收益中扣回遣返费用，除非根据国内法律或条例或其他措施或适用的集体谈判协议，认定海员严重违反了其就业义务。

4. 国内法律和条例不得损害船东根据第三方契约性安排收回遣返费用的任何权利。

5. 如船东未能为有权得到遣返的海员做出安排或支付其遣返费用：

(a) 船舶所悬挂旗帜的成员国的主管当局须安排有关海员的遣返；如果它未能这样做，海员将被遣返起程的国家或海员为其国民的国家可安排该海员的遣返，并向船舶所悬旗帜的成员国收回费用；

or the State of which they are a national may arrange for their repatriation and recover the cost from the Member whose flag the ship flies;

(b) costs incurred in repatriating seafarers shall be recoverable from the shipowner by the Member whose flag the ship flies;

(c) the expenses of repatriation shall in no case be a charge upon the seafarers, except as provided for in paragraph 3 of this Standard.

6. Taking into account applicable international instruments, including the International Convention on Arrest of Ships, 1999, a Member which has paid the cost of repatriation pursuant to this Code may detain, or request the detention of, the ships of the shipowner concerned until the reimbursement has been made in accordance with paragraph 5 of this Standard.

7. Each Member shall facilitate the repatriation of seafarers serving on ships which call at its ports or pass through its territorial or internal waters, as well as their replacement on board.

8. In particular, a Member shall not refuse the right of repatriation to any seafarer because of the financial circumstances of a shipowner or because of the shipowner's inability or unwillingness to replace a seafarer.

9. Each Member shall require that ships that fly its flag carry and make available to seafarers a copy of the applicable national provisions regarding repatriation written in an appropriate language.

Guideline B2.5—Repatriation

Guideline B2.5.1—Entitlement

1. Seafarers should be entitled to repatriation:

(b) 遣返海员发生的费用须能够由船舶所悬挂旗帜的成员国向船东索回；

(c) 不论何种情况，均不得由海员承担遣返的花费，本标准第3款规定的情况除外。

6. 考虑到包括《1999年国际扣船公约》[1]在内的适用国际文件，根据本守则支付了遣返费用的成员国，可滞留或请求滞留有关船东的船舶，直至按本标准第5款做出了偿付。

7. 各成员国，对于工作在停靠于其港口的或通过其领水或内水的船舶上的海员，须为其遣返及其在船上的替换提供便利。

8. 特别是，成员国不得因为船东的财务状况或因船东不能或不愿意替换海员而拒绝任何海员得到遣返的权利。

9. 各成员国须要求悬挂其旗帜的船舶携带并向海员提供一份用适当语言写成的有关遣返的适用国内规定。

导则 B2.5—遣返

导则 B2.5.1—权利

1. 在以下情况下海员应享有遣返的权利：

---

[1] 该公约已于2011年9月14日生效。我国未参加该公约。——校译者注

(a) in the case covered by Standard A2. 5, paragraph 1(a), upon the expiry of the period of notice given in accordance with the provisions of the seafarers' employment agreement;

(b) in the cases covered by Standard A2. 5, paragraph 1(b) and (c):

(i) in the event of illness or injury or other medical condition which requires their repatriation when found medically fit to travel;

(ii) in the event of shipwreck;

(iii) in the event of the shipowner not being able to continue to fulfil their legal or contractual obligations as an employer of the seafarers by reason of insolvency, sale of ship, change of ship's registration or any other similar reason;

(iv) in the event of a ship being bound for a war zone, as defined by national laws or regulations or seafarers' employment agreements, to which the seafarer does not consent to go; and

(v) in the event of termination or interruption of employment in accordance with an industrial award or collective agreement, or termination of employment for any other similar reason.

2. In determining the maximum duration of service periods on board following which a seafarer is entitled to repatriation, in accordance with this Code, account should be taken of factors affecting the seafarers' working environment. Each Member should seek, wherever possible, to reduce these periods in the light of technological changes and developments and might be guided by any recommendations made on the matter by the Joint Maritime Commission.

3. The costs to be borne by the shipowner for repatriation under

(a) 在标准 A2.5 第 1(a)款所覆盖的情况下，根据海员就业协议的规定做出的提前通知期结束；

(b) 在标准 A2.5 第 1(b)和(c)款所覆盖的情况下：

(i) 患病或受伤或其他健康状况需要其遣返，确定身体状况适于旅行；

(ii) 船舶失事；

(iii) 由于破产、出售船舶、变更船舶登记或任何其他类似原因，船东不能继续履行其作为海员雇用者的法律或契约义务；

(iv) 船舶驶往国内法律或条例或海员就业协议所界定的战区而海员不同意前往；和

(v) 根据劳资裁定协议[1]或集体协议而终止或中断雇用或出于任何其他类似原因终止雇用。

2. 在确定海员有权得到遣返前在船上服务的最长时间时，根据本守则，应考虑到影响海员工作环境的多种因素。凡可能时，各成员国应视技术的变化和发展而寻求减少这一时间，并可得到联合海事委员会就此事项所提任何建议的指导。

3. 对于标准 A2.5 下的遣返，船东将承担的费用应至少包括以下项目：

[1] 其英文为 industrial award，是指在西方国家中相关劳资裁判庭做出的裁定，对同一个行业或职业规定相同的最低工资和最低雇用条件。该词语还可以译成“工资裁定协议”或“行业裁定待遇标准”等。——校译者注

Standard A2.5 should include at least the following:

(a) passage to the destination selected for repatriation in accordance with paragraph 6 of this Guideline;

(b) accommodation and food from the moment the seafarers leave the ship until they reach the repatriation destination;

(c) pay and allowances from the moment the seafarers leave the ship until they reach the repatriation destination, if provided for by national laws or regulations or collective agreements;

(d) transportation of 30 kg of the seafarers' personal luggage to the repatriation destination; and

(e) medical treatment when necessary until the seafarers are medically fit to travel to the repatriation destination.

4. Time spent awaiting repatriation and repatriation travel time should not be deducted from paid leave accrued to the seafarers.

5. Shipowners should be required to continue to cover the costs of repatriation until the seafarers concerned are landed at a destination prescribed pursuant to this Code or are provided with suitable employment on board a ship proceeding to one of those destinations.

6. Each Member should require that shipowners take responsibility for repatriation arrangements by appropriate and expeditious means. The normal mode of transport should be by air. The Member should prescribe the destinations to which seafarers may be repatriated. The destinations should include the countries with which seafarers may be deemed to have a substantial connection including:

(a) the place at which the seafarer agreed to enter into the engagement;

(b) the place stipulated by collective agreement;

(a) 到达根据本导则第 6 款选定的遣返目的地的旅程；

(b) 从海员离船时起至抵达遣返目的地时止的食宿；

(c) 如果国内法律或条例或集体协议有规定，从海员离船时起至抵达遣返目的地时止的报酬和补贴；

(d) 将海员个人行李 30 千克运至遣返目的地；以及

(e) 必要时的医疗，直至海员身体状况适合旅行至遣返目的地。

4. 等待遣返所用的时间和遣返旅行时间不应从海员积累的带薪休假中扣减。

5. 应要求船东继续承担遣返的费用，直到有关海员到达依据本守则所规定的一个目的地，或在前往这些目的地之一的船舶上为其提供了合适的就业。

6. 各成员国应要求船东通过适当和迅速的方式负责对遣返做出安排。通常的旅行方式应为乘坐飞机。成员国应规定海员可被遣返的目的地。目的地应包括可视为海员与之存在着实质性联系的国家，包括：

(a) 海员同意接受聘用的地点；

(b) 集体协议规定的地点；

(c) the seafarer's country of residence; or

(d) such other place as may be mutually agreed at the time of engagement.

7. Seafarers should have the right to choose from among the prescribed destinations the place to which they are to be repatriated.

8. The entitlement to repatriation may lapse if the seafarers concerned do not claim it within a reasonable period of time to be defined by national laws or regulations or collective agreements.

Guideline B2.5.2—Implementation by Members

1. Every possible practical assistance should be given to a seafarer stranded in a foreign port pending repatriation and in the event of delay in the repatriation of the seafarer, the competent authority in the foreign port should ensure that the consular or local representative of the flag State and the seafarer's State of nationality or State of residence, as appropriate, is informed immediately.

2. Each Member should have regard to whether proper provision is made:

(a) for the return of seafarers employed on a ship that flies the flag of a foreign country who are put ashore in a foreign port for reasons for which they are not responsible:

(i) to the port at which the seafarer concerned was engaged; or

(ii) to a port in the seafarer's State of nationality or State of residence, as appropriate; or

(iii) to another port agreed upon between the seafarer and the master or shipowner, with the approval of the competent authority or under other appropriate safeguards;

(c) 海员的居住国;或

(d) 在聘用时双方可能约定的其他地点。

7. 海员应有权从规定的目的地中选择其将被遣返的地点。

8. 如果有关海员在国内法律或条例或集体协议界定的合理的时间内未要求遣返,其应享的遣返权利可能丧失。

导则 B2.5.2—成员国的实施

1. 对被困于外国港口等候遣返的海员应给予各种可能的实际援助,对于海员遣返受到延误的情况,外国港口的主管当局应确保视情况立即通知船旗国和海员国籍国或居住国的领事代表或当地代表。

2. 各成员国应关注是否为以下事项做出了适当准备:

(a) 将那些由于非其负责的原因在外国港口被置于岸上的受雇于悬挂外国旗帜船舶的海员送回到:

(i) 有关海员受聘的港口;或

(ii) 海员的国籍国或居住国的一个港口,视情况而定;或

(iii) 经主管当局批准或在其他适当保障下,海员和船长或船东之间约定的另一个港口;

(b) for medical care and maintenance of seafarers employed on a ship that flies the flag of a foreign country who are put ashore in a foreign port in consequence of sickness or injury incurred in the service of the ship and not due to their own wilful misconduct.

3. If, after young seafarers under the age of 18 have served on a ship for at least four months during their first foreign-going voyage, it becomes apparent that they are unsuited to life at sea, they should be given the opportunity of being repatriated at no expense to themselves from the first suitable port of call in which there are consular services of the flag State, or the State of nationality or residence of the young seafarer. Notification of any such repatriation, with the reasons therefor, should be given to the authority which issued the papers enabling the young seafarers concerned to take up seagoing employment.

Regulation 2.6—Seafarer compensation for the ship's loss or foundering

Purpose: To ensure that seafarers are compensated when a ship is lost or has foundered

1. Seafarers are entitled to adequate compensation in the case of injury, loss or unemployment arising from the ship's loss or foundering.

Standard A2.6—Seafarer compensation for the ship's loss or foundering

1. Each Member shall make rules ensuring that, in every case of loss or foundering of any ship, the shipowner shall pay to each sea-

(b) 对在船上服务期间非因其自身故意行为不当而患病或受伤,导致其在外国港口被置于岸上的受雇于悬挂外国旗帜船舶的海员进行医护和照料。

3. 首次出航国外的 18 岁以下未成年海员在船上服务至少四个月后,若显示出不适应海上生活,应给予该未成年海员从设有船旗国或者其国籍国或居住国领事服务的第一个合适的停靠港口被免费遣返的机会。应向签发文件使相关未成年海员能够上船就业的有关当局报告任何此种遣返情况及其原因。

规则 2.6—船舶灭失或沉没时对海员的赔偿

目的:确保在船舶灭失或沉没时对海员进行赔偿

1. 海员有权就由于船舶灭失或沉没所造成的伤害、损失或失业得到充分的赔偿。

标准 A2.6—船舶灭失或沉没时对海员的赔偿

1. 各成员国须制定规章,确保在任何船舶灭失或沉没的各种情况下,船东就这种灭失或沉没所造成的失业须向船上每名海员支付赔偿。

farer on board an indemnity against unemployment resulting from such loss or foundering.

2. The rules referred to in paragraph 1 of this Standard shall be without prejudice to any other rights a seafarer may have under the national law of the Member concerned for losses or injuries arising from a ship's loss or foundering.

Guideline B2.6—Seafarer compensation for the ship's loss or foundering

Guideline B2.6.1—Calculation of indemnity against unemployment

1. The indemnity against unemployment resulting from a ship's foundering or loss should be paid for the days during which the seafarer remains in fact unemployed at the same rate as the wages payable under the employment agreement, but the total indemnity payable to any one seafarer may be limited to two months' wages.

2. Each Member should ensure that seafarers have the same legal remedies for recovering such indemnities as they have for recovering arrears of wages earned during the service.

Regulation 2.7—Manning levels

Purpose: To ensure that seafarers work on board ships with sufficient personnel for the safe, efficient and secure operation of the ship

1. Each Member shall require that all ships that fly its flag have a sufficient number of seafarers employed on board to ensure that ships are operated safely, efficiently and with due regard to security under all conditions, taking into account concerns about seafarer fa-

2. 本标准第1款所述的规章不得损害海员根据有关成员国的国内法律,针对船舶灭失或沉没所造成损失或伤害而可能享有的任何其他权利。

导则 B2.6—船舶灭失或沉没时对海员的赔偿

导则 B2.6.1—失业赔偿的计算

1. 对因船舶沉没或灭失而造成失业的赔偿,应按海员实属失业期间的日数以等同于就业协议中可支付工资的比率进行支付,但向任何一名海员支付的赔偿总额可限于两个月的工资。

2. 各成员国应确保海员享有索赔此种赔偿的法律救济,与其索赔其服务期间挣得但被拖欠的工资所享有的法律救济相同。

规则 2.7—配员水平

目的:为了船舶操作的安全、高效和安保,确保海员在人员充足的船上工作

1. 各成员国须要求悬挂其旗帜的所有船舶,考虑到对海员疲劳的关切以及航程的特殊性质和条件,在船上配有充足数目的海员以确保船舶在各种条件下安全、高效地操作并充分注意到保安。

tigue and the particular nature and conditions of the voyage.

Standard A2. 7—Manning levels

1. Each Member shall require that all ships that fly its flag have a sufficient number of seafarers on board to ensure that ships are operated safely, efficiently and with due regard to security. Every ship shall be manned by a crew that is adequate, in terms of size and qualifications, to ensure the safety and security of the ship and its personnel, under all operating conditions, in accordance with the minimum safe manning document or an equivalent issued by the competent authority, and to comply with the standards of this Convention.

2. When determining, approving or revising manning levels, the competent authority shall take into account the need to avoid or minimize excessive hours of work to ensure sufficient rest and to limit fatigue, as well as the principles in applicable international instruments, especially those of the International Maritime Organization, on manning levels.

3. When determining manning levels, the competent authority shall take into account all the requirements within Regulation 3. 2 and Standard A3. 2 concerning food and catering.

Guideline B2. 7—Manning levels

Guideline B2. 7. 1—Dispute settlement

1. Each Member should maintain, or satisfy itself that there is maintained, efficient machinery for the investigation and settlement of complaints or disputes concerning the manning levels on a ship.

2. Representatives of shipowners' and seafarers' organizations should participate, with or without other persons or authorities, in

标准 A2.7—配员水平

1. 各成员国须要求悬挂其旗帜的所有船舶在船上配有充足数目的海员，以确保船舶安全、高效的操作并充分注意到保安。各船舶须配备在数量和资格方面均为充足的船员，依据最低安全配员证书或主管当局签发的等效文件确保在各种操作情况下船舶及其人员的安全和保安，并符合本公约的标准。

2. 在确定、批准或修订配员水平时，主管当局须考虑到避免或尽量减少超时工作从而确保充分休息和限制疲劳的需要，以及适用的国际文件中，特别是国际海事组织的文件中关于配员水平的原则。

3. 在确定配员水平时，主管当局须考虑到规则 3.2 和标准 A3.2 中关于食品和膳食服务的所有要求。

导则 B2.7—配员水平

导则 B2.7.1—争议解决

1. 各成员国应维持一种调查和解决关于船上配员水平的投诉或争议的高效机制，或自行确认其得以维持。

2. 无论有无其他人员或当局的参与，船东组织和海员组织的代表应参与此种机制的运作。

the operation of such machinery.

Regulation 2.8—Career and skill development and opportunities for seafarers' employment

Purpose: To promote career and skill development and employment opportunities for seafarers

1. Each Member shall have national policies to promote employment in the maritime sector and to encourage career and skill development and greater employment opportunities for seafarers domiciled in its territory.

Standard A2.8—Career and skill development and employment opportunities for seafarers

1. Each Member shall have national policies that encourage career and skill development and employment opportunities for seafarers, in order to provide the maritime sector with a stable and competent workforce.

2. The aim of the policies referred to in paragraph 1 of this Standard shall be to help seafarers strengthen their competencies, qualifications and employment opportunities.

3. Each Member shall, after consulting the shipowners' and seafarers' organizations concerned, establish clear objectives for the vocational guidance, education and training of seafarers whose duties on board ship primarily relate to the safe operation and navigation of the ship, including ongoing training.

规则 2.8—海员职业发展和技能开发及就业机会

目的:促进海员职业发展和技能开发及就业机会

1. 各成员国须有国家政策促进在海运部门中的就业并鼓励在其领土内居住的海员的职业发展和技能开发以及更多的就业机会。

标准 A2.8—海员职业发展和技能开发及就业机会

1. 为了向海运部门提供稳定和胜任的劳动力,各成员国须制定鼓励海员职业发展和技能开发及就业机会的国家政策。

2. 本标准第 1 款所述政策的目标须为帮助海员增强其适任能力、资格和就业机会。

3. 各成员国须在与有关船东组织和海员组织协商后,为那些其船上职责主要涉及船舶的安全操作和航行的海员确定关于职业指导、教育和培训的明确目标,包括持续培训的明确目标。

Guideline B2.8—Career and skill development and employment opportunities for seafarers

Guideline B2.8.1—Measures to promote career and skill development and employment opportunities for seafarers

1. Measures to achieve the objectives set out in Standard A2.8 might include:

(a) agreements providing for career development and skills training with a shipowner or an organization of shipowners; or

(b) arrangements for promoting employment through the establishment and maintenance of registers or lists, by categories, of qualified seafarers; or

(c) promotion of opportunities, both on board and ashore, for further training and education of seafarers to provide for skill development and portable competencies in order to secure and retain decent work, to improve individual employment prospects and to meet the changing technology and labour market conditions of the maritime industry.

Guideline B2.8.2—Register of seafarers

1. Where registers or lists govern the employment of seafarers, these registers or lists should include all occupational categories of seafarers in a manner determined by national law or practice or by collective agreement.

2. Seafarers on such a register or list should have priority of engagement for seafaring.

3. Seafarers on such a register or list should be required to be available for work in a manner to be determined by national law or

导则 B2.8—海员职业发展和技能开发及就业机会

导则 B2.8.1—促进海员职业发展和技能开发及就业机会的措施

1. 实现标准 A2.8 所列目标的措施可以包括：

(a) 与船东或船东组织达成提供职业发展和技能培训的协议；或

(b) 通过建立和维护合格海员的分类登记册或名单的方式做出促进就业的安排；或

(c) 促进海员在船上和岸上进一步培训和教育的机会，提供技能开发和通用的适任能力[1]，从而获得并保持体面工作，改善个人就业前景并适应海运业技术和劳动市场状况的变化。

导则 B2.8.2—海员登记册

1. 如果采用登记册或名单来管理海员就业，则这些登记册或名单应按国内法律或惯例或通过集体协议所确定的方式，包括海员的所有职业类别。

2. 此种登记册或名单上的海员应优先受聘出海工作。

3. 应要求此种登记册或名单上的海员按国内法律或惯例或通过集体协议确定的方式随时准备工作。

---

[1] 其英文为 portable competencies，是指海员的适任能力较为灵活，不拘泥于特定船公司的特定船型，能够适应不同船东的多种船型，也可译成"灵活的适任能力"。——校译者注

practice or by collective agreement.

4. To the extent that national laws or regulations permit, the number of seafarers on such registers or lists should be periodically reviewed so as to achieve levels adapted to the needs of the maritime industry.

5. When a reduction in the number of seafarers on such a register or list becomes necessary, all appropriate measures should be taken to prevent or minimize detrimental effects on seafarers, account being taken of the economic and social situation of the country concerned.

4. 在国内法律或条例许可的范围内，应定期审查海员登记册或名单上的海员人数，使之达到适应海运业需要的水平。

5. 在此登记册或名单的人数需要减少时，应考虑到有关国家的经济和社会状况，采取一切适当的措施，防止或最大限度地减小对海员的不利影响。

TITLE 3. ACCOMMODATION, RECREATIONAL FACILITIES, FOOD AND CATERING

Regulation 3.1—Accommodation and recreational facilities

Purpose: To ensure that seafarers have decent accommodation and recreational facilities on board

1. Each Member shall ensure that ships that fly its flag provide and maintain decent accommodations and recreational facilities for seafarers working or living on board, or both, consistent with promoting the seafarers' health and well-being.

2. The requirements in the Code implementing this Regulation which relate to ship construction and equipment apply only to ships constructed on or after the date when this Convention comes into force for the Member concerned. For ships constructed before that date, the requirements relating to ship construction and equipment that are set out in the Accommodation of Crews Convention (Revised), 1949 (No. 92), and the Accommodation of Crews (Supplementary Provisions) Convention, 1970 (No. 133), shall continue to apply to the extent that they were applicable, prior to that date, under the law or practice of the Member concerned. A ship shall be deemed to have been constructed on the date when its keel is laid or when it is at a similar stage of construction.

3. Unless expressly provided otherwise, any requirement under

标题三　起居舱室、娱乐设施、食品和膳食服务

规则3.1—起居舱室和娱乐设施

目的：确保海员在船上有体面的起居舱室和娱乐设施

1. 各成员国须确保悬挂其旗帜的船舶向工作和(或)生活在船上的海员提供并保持与促进海员的健康和幸福一致的体面起居舱室和娱乐设施。

2. 实施本规则的守则中与船舶建造和设备有关的要求仅适用于本公约对有关成员国生效之日或以后建造的船舶。对于该日之前建造的船舶，《1949年船员起居舱室公约(修订)》(第92号)和《1970年船员起居舱室(补充规定)公约》(第133号)中规定的关于船舶建造和设备的要求，须根据有关成员国的法律或惯例在其在该日之前曾适用的范围内继续适用。一艘船须被视为建造于其龙骨铺设之日或当其处于类似建造阶段之日。

3. 除非另有明文规定，守则修正案中与提供海员起居舱室和娱乐设施有关的任何要求须仅适用于该修正案对有关成员国生效之日或以后建造的船舶。

an amendment to the Code relating to the provision of seafarer accommodation and recreational facilities shall apply only to ships constructed on or after the amendment takes effect for the Member concerned.

Standard A3. 1—Accommodation and recreational facilities

1. Each Member shall adopt laws and regulations requiring that ships that fly its flag:

(a) meet minimum standards to ensure that any accommodation for seafarers, working or living on board, or both, is safe, decent and in accordance with the relevant provisions of this Standard; and

(b) are inspected to ensure initial and ongoing compliance with those standards.

2. In developing and applying the laws and regulations to implement this Standard, the competent authority, after consulting the shipowners' and seafarers' organizations concerned, shall:

(a) take into account Regulation 4. 3 and the associated Code provisions on health and safety protection and accident prevention, in light of the specific needs of seafarers that both live and work on board ship, and

(b) give due consideration to the guidance contained in Part B of this Code.

3. The inspections required under Regulation 5. 1. 4 shall be carried out when:

(a) a ship is registered or re-registered; or

标准 A3.1—起居舱室和娱乐设施

1. 各成员国须通过法律和条例，要求悬挂其旗帜的船舶：

(a) 满足最低标准，以确保在船上工作和(或)生活的海员的任何起居舱室安全、体面并符合本标准的相关规定；以及

(b) 受到检查以确保自始持续符合这些标准。

2. 在制定并适用法律和条例来实施本标准时，主管当局在与有关船东组织和海员组织协商后，须：

(a) 根据在船上生活并工作的海员的具体需要，考虑规则 4.3 及相关守则中对健康和安全保护及事故预防的规定，以及

(b) 充分考虑到本守则 B 部分所载的指导。

3. 在以下情形下须进行规则 5.1.4 所要求的检查：

(a) 一艘船进行登记或重新登记；或

(b) the seafarer accommodation on a ship has been substantially altered.

4. The competent authority shall pay particular attention to ensuring implementation of the requirements of this Convention relating to:

(a) the size of rooms and other accommodation spaces;

(b) heating and ventilation;

(c) noise and vibration and other ambient factors;

(d) sanitary facilities;

(e) lighting; and

(f) hospital accommodation.

5. The competent authority of each Member shall require that ships that fly its flag meet the minimum standards for on-board accommodation and recreational facilities that are set out in paragraphs 6 to 17 of this Standard.

6. With respect to general requirements for accommodation:

(a) there shall be adequate headroom in all seafarer accommodation; the minimum permitted headroom in all seafarer accommodation where full and free movement is necessary shall be not less than 203 centimetres; the competent authority may permit some limited reduction in headroom in any space, or part of any space, in such accommodation where it is satisfied that such reduction:

(i) is reasonable; and

(ii) will not result in discomfort to the seafarers;

(b) the accommodation shall be adequately insulated;

(c) in ships other than passenger ships, as defined in Regulation

(b) 对船上的海员起居舱室做了实质性改装。

4. 主管当局须特别注意确保实施本公约关于以下方面的要求：

(a) 房间和其他起居舱室空间的尺寸；

(b) 取暖和通风；

(c) 噪声和振动及其他环境因素；

(d) 卫生设施；

(e) 照明；以及

(f) 医务室。

5. 各成员国的主管当局须要求悬挂其旗帜的船舶满足本标准第6至17款中规定的船上起居舱室和娱乐设施的最低标准。

6. 关于起居舱室的一般要求：

(a) 所有海员起居舱室须具有充足的净高；所有需要在其中充分和自由走动的海员起居舱室的最低允许净高不得低于203厘米；主管当局可准许在此类起居舱室的任何空间或任何部分空间有限地降低净高，如果主管当局认为该降低：

  (i) 是合理的；且

  (ii) 不会给海员带来不适；

(b) 起居舱室须予充分隔离；

(c) 在经修正的《1974年国际海上人命安全公约》(“《SOLAS公约》”)第2(e)和(f)条所界定的客船以外的船舶上，卧室须位于船舶的中部或后部的载重线以上，但在特殊情况下，因船舶的尺度、类型或其预期的用途使任何其他位置不可行，卧室可设在船的前部，但无论如何不得在防撞舱壁之前；

2(e) and (f) of the International Convention for the Safety of Life at Sea, 1974, as amended (the "SOLAS Convention"), sleeping rooms shall be situated above the load line amidships or aft, except that in exceptional cases, where the size, type or intended service of the ship renders any other location impracticable, sleeping rooms may be located in the fore part of the ship, but in no case forward of the collision bulkhead;

(d) in passenger ships, and in special ships constructed in compliance with the IMO *Code of Safety for Special Purpose Ships*, 1983, and subsequent versions (hereinafter called "special purpose ships"), the competent authority may, on condition that satisfactory arrangements are made for lighting and ventilation, permit the location of sleeping rooms below the load line, but in no case shall they be located immediately beneath working alleyways;

(e) there shall be no direct openings into sleeping rooms from cargo and machinery spaces or from galleys, storerooms, drying rooms or communal sanitary areas; that part of a bulkhead separating such places from sleeping rooms and external bulkheads shall be efficiently constructed of steel or other approved substance and be watertight and gas-tight;

(f) the materials used to construct internal bulkheads, panelling and sheeting, floors and joinings shall be suitable for the purpose and conducive to ensuring a healthy environment;

(g) proper lighting and sufficient drainage shall be provided; and

(h) accommodation and recreational and catering facilities shall meet

(d) 在客船上以及在根据国际海事组织《1983年特殊用途船舶安全规则》[1]及其后续版本而建造的特殊船舶(以下称为“特殊用途船舶”)上,如果对照明和通风状况做出了满意的安排,主管当局可准许将卧室设置在载重线以下,但无论如何不得置于紧贴工作通道之下;

(e) 货物和机器处所或厨房、物料间、烘干房或公共卫生区域不得与卧室直接相通;将上述处所与卧室分开的舱壁部分和外部舱壁须使用钢材或其他经认可的材料有效地建造,并具备水密和气密性;

(f) 用于建造内部舱壁、镶板和护板、地板和连接件的材料须适合于其自身功用并有益于保证健康环境;

(g) 须提供适当的照明和充分的排水系统;以及

(h) 针对防止接触有害水平的船上噪声和振动以及其他环境因素和化学物质的风险,起居舱室和娱乐及膳食服务设施须满足规则4.3中以及守则相关规定中对于健康和安全保护及事故预防的要求,并为海员提供一个可接受的职业环境和船上生活环境。

[1] 该规则已被于2008年5月13日生效的《2008年特殊用途船舶安全规则》取代。——校译者注

the requirements in Regulation 4.3, and the related provisions in the Code, on health and safety protection and accident prevention, with respect to preventing the risk of exposure to hazardous levels of noise and vibration and other ambient factors and chemicals on board ships, and to provide an acceptable occupational and onboard living environment for seafarers.

7. With respect to requirements for ventilation and heating:

(a) sleeping rooms and mess rooms shall be adequately ventilated;

(b) ships, except those regularly engaged in trade where temperate climatic conditions do not require this, shall be equipped with air conditioning for seafarer accommodation, for any separate radio room and for any centralized machinery control room;

(c) all sanitary spaces shall have ventilation to the open air, independently of any other part of the accommodation; and

(d) adequate heat through an appropriate heating system shall be provided, except in ships exclusively on voyages in tropical climates.

8. With respect to requirements for lighting, subject to such special arrangements as may be permitted in passenger ships, sleeping rooms and mess rooms shall be lit by natural light and provided with adequate artificial light.

9. When sleeping accommodation on board ships is required, the following requirements for sleeping rooms apply:

(a) in ships other than passenger ships, an individual sleeping room shall be provided for each seafarer; in the case of ships of less than 3,000 gross tonnage or special purpose ships, exemptions from this requirement may be granted by the competent author-

7. 关于通风和供暖的要求：

(a) 卧室和餐厅须通风良好；

(b) 除常年在温和的气候条件下航行不需要空调的船舶以外，须为船舶上的海员起居舱室、任何独立的报务室和任何机器集控室配备空调设备；

(c) 所有卫生处所须有直接通向露天的通风，并与起居舱室的任何其他部分相独立；以及

(d) 除专门在热带气候中航行的船舶外，须通过适当的供暖系统提供充分的取暖。

8. 就照明的要求而言，卧室和餐厅须有自然采光并配备足够的人工灯光，但受限于客船上可能允许的特殊布置。

9. 当要求船上有就寝的起居舱室时，适用以下对卧室的要求：

(a) 在除客船以外的船舶上，须为每一海员提供单独的卧室；对于低于3 000总吨的船舶或特殊用途船舶，主管当局在与有关船东组织和海员组织协商后可准予免除此要求；

ity after consultation with the shipowners' and seafarers' organizations concerned;

(b) separate sleeping rooms shall be provided for men and for women;

(c) sleeping rooms shall be of adequate size and properly equipped so as to ensure reasonable comfort and to facilitate tidiness;

(d) a separate berth for each seafarer shall in all circumstances be provided;

(e) the minimum inside dimensions of a berth shall be at least 198 centimetres by 80 centimetres;

(f) in single berth seafarers' sleeping rooms the floor area shall not be less than:

(i) 4.5 square metres in ships of less than 3,000 gross tonnage;

(ii) 5.5 square metres in ships of 3,000 gross tonnage or over but less than 10,000 gross tonnage;

(iii) 7 square metres in ships of 10,000 gross tonnage or over;

(g) however, in order to provide single berth sleeping rooms on ships of less than 3,000 gross tonnage, passenger ships and special purpose ships, the competent authority may allow a reduced floor area;

(h) in ships of less than 3,000 gross tonnage other than passenger ships and special purpose ships, sleeping rooms may be occupied by a maximum of two seafarers; the floor area of such sleeping rooms shall not be less than 7 square metres;

(i) on passenger ships and special purpose ships the floor area of sleeping rooms for seafarers not performing the duties of ships' officers shall not be less than:

(b) 须为男性和女性提供分开的卧室；

(c) 卧室须有足够的尺寸并配备适当的陈设，以保证合理的舒适及便于保持整洁；

(d) 在所有情况下都须为每名海员提供单独的床位；

(e) 每个床位的最小内部尺度须至少为198厘米长、80厘米宽；

(f) 在单床位的海员卧室内，地板面积不得小于：

(i) 在3 000总吨以下的船舶上，4.5平方米；

(ii) 在3 000总吨或以上但低于10 000总吨的船舶上，5.5平方米；

(iii) 在10 000总吨或以上的船舶上，7平方米；

(g) 但是，为了在3 000总吨以下的船舶上、客船上和特殊用途船舶上提供单床位的卧室，主管当局可允许减少地板面积；

(h) 对于客船和特殊用途船舶以外的3 000总吨以下的船舶，卧室最多可由两名海员居住；此类卧室的地板面积不得少于7平方米；

(i) 在客船和特殊用途船舶上，不履行船舶高级船员职责的海员的卧室地板面积不得少于：

(i) 7.5 square metres in rooms accommodating two persons;

(ii) 11.5 square metres in rooms accommodating three persons;

(iii) 14.5 square metres in rooms accommodating four persons;

(j) on special purpose ships sleeping rooms may accommodate more than four persons; the floor area of such sleeping rooms shall not be less than 3.6 square metres per person;

(k) on ships other than passenger ships and special purpose ships, sleeping rooms for seafarers who perform the duties of ships' officers, where no private sitting room or day room is provided, the floor area per person shall not be less than:

(i) 7.5 square metres in ships of less than 3,000 gross tonnage;

(ii) 8.5 square metres in ships of 3,000 gross tonnage or over but less than 10,000 gross tonnage;

(iii) 10 square metres in ships of 10,000 gross tonnage or over;

(l) on passenger ships and special purpose ships the floor area for seafarers performing the duties of ships' officers where no private sitting room or day room is provided, the floor area per person for junior officers shall not be less than 7.5 square metres and for senior officers not less than 8.5 square metres; junior officers are understood to be at the operational level, and senior officers at the management level;

(m) the master, the chief engineer and the chief navigating officer shall have, in addition to their sleeping rooms, an adjoining sitting room, day room or equivalent additional space; ships of less than 3,000 gross tonnage may be exempted by the competent authority from this requirement after consultation with the shipowners' and seafarers' organizations concerned;

(i) 双人间,7.5 平方米;

(ii) 三人间,11.5 平方米;

(iii) 四人间,14.5 平方米;

(j) 在特殊用途船舶上,卧室可容纳四人以上;此类卧室的地板面积不得小于每人 3.6 平方米;

(k) 在客船和特殊用途船舶以外的船舶上,对于履行船舶高级船员职责的海员的卧室,如果不提供专用起居室或休息室,地板面积每人不得少于:

(i) 在 3 000 总吨以下的船舶上,7.5 平方米;

(ii) 在 3 000 总吨或以上但低于 10 000 总吨的船舶上,8.5 平方米;

(iii) 在 10 000 总吨或以上的船舶上,10 平方米;

(l) 在客船和特殊用途船舶上,对于履行船舶高级船员职责的海员的卧室,如果不提供专用起居室或休息室,每人所占的地板面积对于低级别的高级船员不得少于 7.5 平方米,对于高级别的高级船员不得少于 8.5 平方米;低级别的高级船员被理解为处于操作级,高级别的高级船员处于管理级;

(m) 除卧室外,船长、轮机长和大副还须有相连的起居室、休息室或等效的额外空间;主管当局经与有关船东组织和海员组织协商后,可对 3 000总吨以下的船舶免除此要求;

(n) for each occupant, the furniture shall include a clothes locker of ample space (minimum 475 litres) and a drawer or equivalent space of not less than 56 litres; if the drawer is incorporated in the clothes locker then the combined minimum volume of the clothes locker shall be 500 litres; it shall be fitted with a shelf and be able to be locked by the occupant so as to ensure privacy;

(o) each sleeping room shall be provided with a table or desk, which may be of the fixed, drop-leaf or slide-out type, and with comfortable seating accommodation as necessary.

10. With respect to requirements for mess rooms:

(a) mess rooms shall be located apart from the sleeping rooms and as close as practicable to the galley; ships of less than 3,000 gross tonnage may be exempted by the competent authority from this requirement after consultation with the shipowners' and seafarers' organizations concerned; and

(b) mess rooms shall be of adequate size and comfort and properly furnished and equipped (including ongoing facilities for refreshment), taking account of the number of seafarers likely to use them at any one time; provision shall be made for separate or common mess room facilities as appropriate.

11. With respect to requirements for sanitary facilities:

(a) all seafarers shall have convenient access on the ship to sanitary facilities meeting minimum standards of health and hygiene and reasonable standards of comfort, with separate sanitary facilities being provided for men and for women;

(b) there shall be sanitary facilities within easy access of the navigating bridge and the machinery space or near the engine room control centre; ships of less than 3,000 gross tonnage may be ex-

(n) 对于每个居住者，家具须包括一个宽敞的衣柜（至少475升）和不小于56升的抽屉或等效空间；如果抽屉与衣柜为一体，则衣柜的合并容积须至少为500升；衣柜须设搁板，并能够由居住者上锁以确保隐私；

(o) 每间卧室须备有一张桌子或书桌，可以为固定式、铰链垂边式或滑出式，并按需要配备舒适的座位。

10. 关于餐厅的要求：

(a) 餐厅的位置须远离卧室，并尽实际可行地靠近厨房；主管当局在与有关船东组织和海员组织协商后可对低于3 000总吨的船舶免除此要求；以及

(b) 考虑到任一时间可能用餐的海员人数，餐厅须足够宽敞和舒适，并配备适当的家具和设备（包括提供茶点的常开设施）；须视情况配备分开的或共用的餐厅设施。

11. 关于卫生设施的要求：

(a) 所有海员须能够方便地在船上使用满足最低健康和卫生标准以及合理的舒适标准的卫生设施，为男性和女性提供分开的卫生设施；

(b) 在驾驶台和机器处所容易到达之处或靠近机舱控制中心处须设有卫生设施；主管当局在与有关船东组织和海员组织协商后可对低于3 000总吨的船舶免除此要求；

empted by the competent authority from this requirement after consultation with the shipowners' and seafarers' organizations concerned;

(c) in all ships a minimum of one toilet, one wash basin and one tub or shower or both for every six persons or less who do not have personal facilities shall be provided at a convenient location;

(d) with the exception of passenger ships, each sleeping room shall be provided with a washbasin having hot and cold running fresh water, except where such a washbasin is situated in the private bathroom provided;

(e) in passenger ships normally engaged on voyages of not more than four hours' duration, consideration may be given by the competent authority to special arrangements or to a reduction in the number of facilities required; and

(f) hot and cold running fresh water shall be available in all wash places.

12. With respect to requirements for hospital accommodation, ships carrying 15 or more seafarers and engaged in a voyage of more than three days' duration shall provide separate hospital accommodation to be used exclusively for medical purposes; the competent authority may relax this requirement for ships engaged in coastal trade; in approving on-board hospital accommodation, the competent authority shall ensure that the accommodation will, in all weathers, be easy of access, provide comfortable housing for the occupants and be conducive to their receiving prompt and proper attention.

13. Appropriately situated and furnished laundry facilities shall be available.

(c) 在所有船舶上，须在方便的位置为没有个人设施的每六人或以下提供至少一个厕所、一个洗脸池和一个浴缸和(或)淋浴；

(d) 除了客船以外，每个卧室均须配备带有冷热自来淡水的洗脸池，除非这样的洗脸池位于所提供的私人浴室中；

(e) 对于航行时间通常不超过四小时的客船，主管当局可考虑做出特殊安排或减少所要求的设施数目；以及

(f) 所有盥洗场所均须有冷热自来淡水。

12. 就医务室的要求而言，载有15名或以上海员且所从事的航程时间超过三天的船舶须设有独立的医务室，专供医疗使用；对从事沿岸航行的船舶，主管当局可放宽此项要求；在批准船上医务室时，主管当局须确保该舱室在各种天气中都容易进出，为使用者提供舒服的居住条件并有助于其获得迅速和适当的照料。

13. 须提供位置合适并有适当家具的洗衣设施。

14. All ships shall have a space or spaces on open deck to which the seafarers can have access when off duty, which are of adequate area having regard to the size of the ship and the number of seafarers on board.

15. All ships shall be provided with separate offices or a common ship's office for use by deck and engine departments; ships of less than 3,000 gross tonnage may be exempted by the competent authority from this requirement after consultation with the shipowners' and seafarers' organizations concerned.

16. Ships regularly trading to mosquito-infested ports shall be fitted with appropriate devices as required by the competent authority.

17. Appropriate seafarers' recreational facilities, amenities and services, as adapted to meet the special needs of seafarers who must live and work on ships, shall be provided on board for the benefit of all seafarers, taking into account Regulation 4. 3 and the associated Code provisions on health and safety protection and accident prevention.

18. The competent authority shall require frequent inspections to be carried out on board ships, by or under the authority of the master, to ensure that seafarer accommodation is clean, decently habitable and maintained in a good state of repair. The results of each such inspection shall be recorded and be available for review.

19. In the case of ships where there is need to take account, without discrimination, of the interests of seafarers having differing and distinctive religious and social practices, the competent authority may, after consultation with the shipowners' and seafarers' organ-

14. 所有船舶，顾及到其尺度和船上海员的人数，须在露天甲板上安排一块或数块具有充足面积的场所，供不当班的海员使用。

15. 所有船舶须配备多个分开的办公室或一个共用的船舶办公室，供甲板部和轮机部使用；主管当局在与有关船东组织和海员组织协商后可对低于3 000总吨的船舶免除此要求。

16. 经常驶往蚊虫猖獗的港口的船舶须按主管当局的要求安装适当的装置。

17. 为了所有海员的利益，在船上须提供适合于满足必须在船上生活和工作的海员的特殊需求的适当海员娱乐设施、康乐设施和服务，同时考虑到规则4.3和相关守则中关于健康和安全保护及事故预防的规定。

18. 主管当局须要求由船长或在船长的授权下，在船上开展经常性的检查，以确保海员起居舱室干净、体面地适宜居住并且被维护到良好的状态。每次此种检查的结果均须记录并能在审核时提供。

19. 对于需要对有不同和特别宗教与社会习惯的海员的利益给予一视同仁考虑的船舶，主管当局经与有关船东组织和海员组织协商后，可以允许对本标准进行适当的变动适用，条件是这种变动不会导致总体设施劣于实施本标准所带来的结果。

izations concerned, permit fairly applied variations in respect of this Standard on condition that such variations do not result in overall facilities less favourable than those which would result from the application of this Standard.

20. Each Member may, after consultation with the shipowners' and seafarers' organizations concerned, exempt ships of less than 200 gross tonnage where it is reasonable to do so, taking account of the size of the ship and the number of persons on board in relation to the requirements of the following provisions of this Standard:

(a) paragraphs 7(b), 11(d) and 13; and

(b) paragraph 9(f) and (h) to (l) inclusive, with respect to floor area only.

21. Any exemptions with respect to the requirements of this Standard may be made only where they are expressly permitted in this Standard and only for particular circumstances in which such exemptions can be clearly justified on strong grounds and subject to protecting the seafarers' health and safety.

Guideline B3. 1—Accommodation and recreational facilities

Guideline B3. 1. 1—Design and construction

1. External bulkheads of sleeping rooms and mess rooms should be adequately insulated. All machinery casings and all boundary bulkheads of galleys and other spaces in which heat is produced should be adequately insulated where there is a possibility of resulting heat effects in adjoining accommodation or passageways. Measures should also be taken to provide protection from heat effects of steam or hot-water service pipes or both.

20. 各成员国，考虑到船舶的尺度和船上人员的数量与本标准下述条款的要求的关系，经与有关船东组织和海员组织协商后，如这样做合理，可以对 200 总吨以下的船舶予以免除：

(a) 第 7(b)、11(d)和 13 款；以及

(b) 第 9(f)和(h)至(l)款，仅涉及地板面积。

21. 针对本标准要求的任何免除，只有在本标准明确准许且只有在特定的情形下，此种免除基于充分理由明显合理时才可做出，并受限于对海员健康和安全的保护。

导则 B3.1—起居舱室和娱乐设施

导则 B3.1.1—设计和建造

1. 卧室和餐厅的外部舱壁应充分地隔离。如果有可能在毗邻起居舱室或过道处产生发热影响，所有机器外罩以及厨房和其他发热处所的所有界限舱壁应予充分隔热。还应采取措施，提供免受蒸汽和(或)热水管道发热影响的保护。

2. Sleeping rooms, mess rooms, recreation rooms and alleyways in the accommodation space should be adequately insulated to prevent condensation or overheating.

3. The bulkhead surfaces and deckheads should be of material with a surface easily kept clean. No form of construction likely to harbour vermin should be used.

4. The bulkhead surfaces and deckheads in sleeping rooms and mess rooms should be capable of being easily kept clean and light in colour with a durable, nontoxic finish.

5. The decks in all seafarer accommodation should be of approved material and construction and should provide a non-slip surface impervious to damp and easily kept clean.

6. Where the floorings are made of composite materials, the joints with the sides should be profiled to avoid crevices.

Guideline B3.1.2—Ventilation

1. The system of ventilation for sleeping rooms and mess rooms should be controlled so as to maintain the air in a satisfactory condition and to ensure a sufficiency of air movement in all conditions of weather and climate.

2. Air-conditioning systems, whether of a centralized or individual unit type, should be designed to:

(a) maintain the air at a satisfactory temperature and relative humidity as compared to outside air conditions, ensure a sufficiency of air changes in all air-conditioned spaces, take account of the particular characteristics of operations at sea and not produce excessive noises or vibrations; and

2. 卧室、餐厅、娱乐室和起居舱室内的通道应充分隔热，以防止蒸汽凝结或温度过高。

3. 舱壁表面和天花板应为表面易于保持清洁的材料。不应使用容易隐藏害虫的构造方式。

4. 卧室和餐厅的舱壁表面和天花板应能够易于保持清洁并应使用耐久、无毒的浅色表层涂料。

5. 所有海员起居舱室的甲板应为认可的材料和构造，其表面应能防滑、防潮并易于保持清洁。

6. 如果地板用复合材料制成，其与侧壁的搭接应严丝合缝，避免留下缝隙。

导则 B3.1.2—通风

1. 卧室和餐厅的通风系统应受到控制，以使空气的状况令人满意，并确保在所有的天气和气候状况下都有充分的空气流通。

2. 空调系统，无论其为中央空调还是分体空调，均应设计成：

(a) 相比于室外空气状况，使室内空气保持满意的温度和相对湿度，保证在有空调的全部处所均有充分的空气交换，考虑到海上作业的独有特点，并避免产生过度的噪声或振动；以及

(b) facilitate easy cleaning and disinfection to prevent or control the spread of disease.

3. Power for the operation of the air conditioning and other aids to ventilation required by the preceding paragraphs of this Guideline should be available at all times when seafarers are living or working on board and conditions so require. However, this power need not be provided from an emergency source.

Guideline B3.1.3—Heating

1. The system of heating the seafarer accommodation should be in operation at all times when seafarers are living or working on board and conditions require its use.

2. In all ships in which a heating system is required, the heating should be by means of hot water, warm air, electricity, steam or equivalent. However, within the accommodation area, steam should not be used as a medium for heat transmission. The heating system should be capable of maintaining the temperature in seafarer accommodation at a satisfactory level under normal conditions of weather and climate likely to be met within the trade in which the ship is engaged. The competent authority should prescribe the standard to be provided.

3. Radiators and other heating apparatus should be placed and, where necessary, shielded so as to avoid risk of fire or danger or discomfort to the occupants.

Guideline B3.1.4—Lighting

1. In all ships, electric light should be provided in the seafarer accommodation. If there are not two independent sources of electricity for lighting, additional lighting should be provided by properly

(b) 便于轻易清洁和灭菌，以防止或控制疾病的传播。

3. 如果海员在船上生活或工作且情况需要，本导则以上条款要求的空调和其他通风设备工作所需的运转动力应随时可用。但是，此动力不必由应急电源提供。

导则 B3.1.3—供暖

1. 如果海员在船上生活或工作且情况需要，海员起居舱室的供暖系统应一直开放使用。

2. 在所有需要供暖系统的船上，应通过热水、热气、电力、蒸汽或等效方式供暖。但是，在起居舱室区域，不应使用蒸汽作为传热媒介。供暖系统应能在船舶所从事的营运范围内可能遇到的正常天气和气候状况下，使海员起居舱室的温度保持在满意的水平。主管当局应对要达到的标准做出规定。

3. 应设置散热器和其他供暖装置，在必要时，应装保护罩以避免火灾风险或对居住者构成危险或带来不便。

导则 B3.1.4—照明

1. 在所有船舶上，应为海员起居舱室配备电灯。如果没有两个独立的照明电源，应通过适当建造的灯具或照明装置提供应急使用的附加照明。

constructed lamps or lighting apparatus for emergency use.

2. In sleeping rooms an electric reading lamp should be installed at the head of each berth.

3. Suitable standards of natural and artificial lighting should be fixed by the competent authority.

Guideline B3. 1. 5—Sleeping rooms

1. There should be adequate berth arrangements on board, making it as comfortable as possible for the seafarer and any partner who may accompany the seafarer.

2. Where the size of the ship, the activity in which it is to be engaged and its layout make it reasonable and practicable, sleeping rooms should be planned and equipped with a private bathroom, including a toilet, so as to provide reasonable comfort for the occupants and to facilitate tidiness.

3. As far as practicable, sleeping rooms of seafarers should be so arranged that watches are separated and that no seafarers working during the day share a room with watchkeepers.

4. In the case of seafarers performing the duty of petty officers there should be no more than two persons per sleeping room.

5. Consideration should be given to extending the facility referred to in Standard A3. 1, paragraph 9 (m), to the second engineer officer when practicable.

6. Space occupied by berths and lockers, chests of drawers and seats should be included in the measurement of the floor area. Small or irregularly shaped spaces which do not add effectively to the space available for free movement and cannot be used for installing furni-

2. 在卧室内，应在每个床位的床头安装一盏台灯。

3. 自然采光和人工照明的适当标准应由主管当局确定。

导则 B3.1.5—卧室

1. 船上应有充分的床位安排，使海员及可能陪伴其的任何伴侣尽可能舒适。

2. 在船舶的尺度、其所从事的活动及其布置使这样做合理可行时，卧室应规划和配备一个包括厕所的私人浴室，从而为居住者提供合理的舒适性并便于整洁。

3. 海员卧室的安排应尽实际可行地将值班班次隔开，且不使日间工作的海员与值班人员同住一间。

4. 对于履行准高级船员[1]职责的海员，每间卧室居住的人数不应超过两人。

5. 可行时，应考虑将标准 A3.1 第 9(m)款中所述的设施扩展到大管轮。

6. 在丈量地板面积时，应包括床位和储物柜、抽屉柜和座位所占空间。不应包括那些不能有效增加可供自由走动空间的并且不能用来放置家具的小的和形状不规则的空间。

---

[1] 其英文为 petty officer，原义为“海军士官”。《1949 年船员起居舱室公约(修订)》(第 92 号)第二条第(f)款对 petty officer 进行了定义并在中文中译成“准高级船员”，现沿用这一译法。该公约对 petty officer 的定义是：“以监督的职位或特殊责任的职位工作的、由国内法律或条例定为准高级船员的普通船员，或者，在无任何有关法律或条例时，由集体协议或惯例定为准高级船员的普通船员。”实践中，petty officer 主要是指水手长、机工长、木匠等职位。——校译者注

ture should be excluded.

7. Berths should not be arranged in tiers of more than two; in the case of berths placed along the ship's side, there should be only a single tier where a sidelight is situated above a berth.

8. The lower berth in a double tier should be not less than 30 centimetres above the floor; the upper berth should be placed approximately midway between the bottom of the lower berth and the lower side of the deckhead beams.

9. The framework and the lee-board, if any, of a berth should be of approved material, hard, smooth, and not likely to corrode or to harbour vermin.

10. If tubular frames are used for the construction of berths, they should be completely sealed and without perforations which would give access to vermin.

11. Each berth should be fitted with a comfortable mattress with cushioning bottom or a combined cushioning mattress, including a spring bottom or a spring mattress. The mattress and cushioning material used should be made of approved material. Stuffing of material likely to harbour vermin should not be used.

12. When one berth is placed over another, a dust-proof bottom should be fitted beneath the bottom mattress or spring bottom of the upper berth.

13. The furniture should be of smooth, hard material not liable to warp or corrode.

14. Sleeping rooms should be fitted with curtains or equivalent for the sidelights.

7. 不应将床位布置成超过两层；如果床位靠船舷摆放，若床位上方有舷窗，应只设置单层床位。

8. 双层床中的下床位在地板上的高度不应小于30厘米；上床位应大约位于下床位底部与天花板横梁底侧之间的中间。

9. 床位的框架和挡板，如有，应使用经认可的材料，质地坚硬而光滑，不易腐蚀或隐藏害虫。

10. 如使用管状框架建造床位，则应将框架完全封闭，不留孔穴，以免害虫进入。

11. 每张床位应配备带有缓冲底板的舒服床垫或包括弹簧底板或弹簧垫在内的复合缓冲床垫。使用的床垫和缓冲材料应以经认可的材料制造。不应使用易于隐藏害虫的填充材料。

12. 如一个床位置于另一个之上，上床位的底垫或弹簧垫的下面应垫上一层防灰尘的底板。

13. 家具应以光滑、坚硬、不易变形或腐蚀的材料制作。

14. 卧室内的舷窗应装有窗帘或等效物。

15. Sleeping rooms should be fitted with a mirror, small cabinets for toilet requisites, a book rack and a sufficient number of coat hooks.

Guideline B3.1.6—Mess rooms

1. Mess room facilities may be either common or separate. The decision in this respect should be taken after consultation with seafarers' and shipowners' representatives and subject to the approval of the competent authority. Account should be taken of factors such as the size of the ship and the distinctive cultural, religious and social needs of the seafarers.

2. Where separate mess room facilities are to be provided to seafarers, then separate mess rooms should be provided for:

(a) master and officers; and

(b) petty officers and other seafarers.

3. On ships other than passenger ships, the floor area of mess rooms for seafarers should be not less than 1.5 square metres per person of the planned seating capacity.

4. In all ships, mess rooms should be equipped with tables and appropriate seats, fixed or movable, sufficient to accommodate the greatest number of seafarers likely to use them at any one time.

5. There should be available at all times when seafarers are on board:

(a) a refrigerator, which should be conveniently situated and of sufficient capacity for the number of persons using the mess room or mess rooms;

(b) facilities for hot beverages; and

15. 每间卧室应装有一面镜子、存放必要盥洗用具的多个小柜、一个书架和足够数量的衣服挂钩。

导则 B3.1.6—餐厅

1. 餐厅设施既可以共用也可以分开。关于此方面的决定应在与海员的和船东的代表协商后做出并有待于主管当局的批准。应考虑到诸如船舶的尺度和海员不同的文化、宗教和社会需要等方面的因素。

2. 如果向海员提供分开的餐厅设施，则分开的餐厅应提供给：

(a) 船长和高级船员；以及

(b) 准高级船员和其他海员。

3. 在客船以外的船舶上，海员餐厅的地板面积应不少于按计划容纳人数每人 1.5 平方米。

4. 所有船舶的餐厅应配备餐桌和相应的座位，无论是固定式还是可移动式，足以容纳在任何同一时间可能使用它们的最大海员人数。

5. 当海员在船上时，应随时提供：

(a) 一台冰箱，其设置应方便且对使用餐厅的人数而言，有足够的容量；

(b) 制作热饮料的设备；以及

(c) cool water facilities.

6. Where available pantries are not accessible to mess rooms, adequate lockers for mess utensils and proper facilities for washing utensils should be provided.

7. The tops of tables and seats should be of damp-resistant material.

Guideline B3.1.7—Sanitary accommodation

1. Washbasins and tub baths should be of adequate size and constructed of approved material with a smooth surface not liable to crack, flake or corrode.

2. All toilets should be of an approved pattern and provided with an ample flush of water or with some other suitable flushing means, such as air, which are available at all times and independently controllable.

3. Sanitary accommodation intended for the use of more than one person should comply with the following:

(a) floors should be of approved durable material, impervious to damp, and should be properly drained;

(b) bulkheads should be of steel or other approved material and should be watertight up to at least 23 centimetres above the level of the deck;

(c) the accommodation should be sufficiently lit, heated and ventilated;

(d) toilets should be situated convenient to, but separate from, sleeping rooms and wash rooms, without direct access from the sleeping rooms or from a passage between sleeping rooms and

(c) 冷水设备。

6. 如果可用的餐具室不与餐厅相通，应提供充足的餐具柜和洗涤餐具的适当设备。

7. 桌面和椅面应为防潮材料。

导则 B3.1.7—卫生设施

1. 洗脸池和浴缸[1]应具备适当的尺寸，用表面光滑，不易开裂、剥落或腐蚀的认可材料制成。

2. 所有厕所均应为认可的样式，有足够的冲水力或其他一些适合的冲洗方式，例如空气，随时可用且能够独立控制。

3. 计划不止一人使用的卫生设施应符合以下各项：

(a) 地面应为认可的耐久材料，防潮，并应适当排干；

(b) 舱壁应为钢材或其他认可的材料，并应水密至甲板面以上至少 23 厘米；

(c) 设施内应有充分的照明、供暖和通风；

(d) 厕所应位于卧室和盥洗室方便到达之处，但又要与之隔开，不能从卧室直接进入，也不能从卧室和厕所之间无其他入口的通道直接进入；该要求不适用于厕所位于总居住人数不超过四名海员的两间卧室之间的舱室内的情况；以及

---

[1] 其英文为 tub baths，其规范的含义是指“缸浴”，即在浴缸(tub)中的洗浴。但从该词所在条款的含义以及该词的并列词 washbasins(洗脸池)的含义来看，tub baths 应为 bath tubs(浴缸)。中文译文即按 bath tubs 来翻译。本公约中使用 tub 表示“浴缸”，共出现了三次，而 tub baths 仅出现在本款中。其原因是本款照搬了《1949 年船员起居舱室公约(修订)》(第 92 号)第十三条第 7 款，但未与本公约其他条款的措辞相协调。——校译者注

toilets to which there is no other access; this requirement does not apply where a toilet is located in a compartment between two sleeping rooms having a total of not more than four seafarers; and

(e) where there is more than one toilet in a compartment, they should be sufficiently screened to ensure privacy.

4. The laundry facilities provided for seafarers' use should include:

(a) washing machines;

(b) drying machines or adequately heated and ventilated drying rooms; and

(c) irons and ironing boards or their equivalent.

Guideline B3.1.8—Hospital accommodation

1. The hospital accommodation should be designed so as to facilitate consultation and the giving of medical first aid and to help prevent the spread of infectious diseases.

2. The arrangement of the entrance, berths, lighting, ventilation, heating and water supply should be designed to ensure the comfort and facilitate the treatment of the occupants.

3. The number of hospital berths required should be prescribed by the competent authority.

4. Sanitary accommodation should be provided for the exclusive use of the occupants of the hospital accommodation, either as part of the accommodation or in close proximity thereto. Such sanitary accommodation should comprise a minimum of one toilet, one washbasin and one tub or shower.

(e) 如同一舱室有不止一个厕位，应将其充分遮挡，确保隐私。

4. 供海员使用的洗衣设施应包括：

(a) 洗衣机；

(b) 烘干机或具有足够加热和通风的烘干室；以及

(c) 熨斗和熨衣板或其等效物。

导则 B3.1.8—医务室

1. 医务室的设计应便于会诊和进行医疗急救，并有助于防止传染性疾病的传播。

2. 入口、床位、照明、通风、取暖及供水的布置设计，应保证舒适和便于使用者的治疗。

3. 所需病床的数量应由主管当局规定。

4. 应为医务室的使用者提供专用的卫生设施，既可作为医务室的一部分也可与其紧邻。此类卫生设施应包括至少一个厕所、一个洗脸池和一个浴缸或淋浴。

Guideline B3.1.9—Other facilities

1. Where separate facilities for engine department personnel to change their clothes are provided, they should be:

(a) located outside the machinery space but with easy access to it; and

(b) fitted with individual clothes lockers as well as with tubs or showers or both and washbasins having hot and cold running fresh water.

Guideline B3.1.10—Bedding, mess utensils and miscellaneous provisions

1. Each Member should consider applying the following principles:

(a) clean bedding and mess utensils should be supplied by the shipowner to all seafarers for use on board during service on the ship, and such seafarers should be responsible for their return at times specified by the master and on completion of service in the ship;

(b) bedding should be of good quality, and plates, cups and other mess utensils should be of approved material which can be easily cleaned; and

(c) towels, soap and toilet paper for all seafarers should be provided by the shipowner.

Guideline B3.1.11—Recreational facilities, mail and ship visit arrangements

1. Recreational facilities and services should be reviewed frequently to ensure that they are appropriate in the light of changes in the needs of seafarers resulting from technical, operational and other

导则 B3.1.9—其他设施

1. 如果为轮机部人员提供更换衣服的独立设施，这些设施应：

(a) 设在机器处所之外但易于进入机器处所的位置；以及

(b) 配备个人衣柜以及通有冷热自来淡水的浴缸和(或)淋浴及洗脸池。

导则 B3.1.10—卧具、餐具和杂项规定

1. 各成员国应考虑适用以下原则：

(a) 船东应向全体海员提供洁净的卧具和餐具供其在船上服务期间在船上使用，海员应有责任按船长具体规定的时间以及在完成该船上的服务时归还这些用品；

(b) 卧具应质量良好，盘子、杯子和其他餐具应为认可的材料制成，便于清洗；以及

(c) 全体海员的毛巾、肥皂和卫生纸应由船东提供。

导则 B3.1.11—娱乐设施、邮件和上船探访安排

1. 对娱乐设施和服务应予经常审查，以保证其适应因航运业技术、操作和其他方面的发展所带来的海员需求的改变。

developments in the shipping industry.

2. Furnishings for recreational facilities should as a minimum include a bookcase and facilities for reading, writing and, where practicable, games.

3. In connection with the planning of recreation facilities, the competent authority should give consideration to the provision of a canteen.

4. Consideration should also be given to including the following facilities at no cost to the seafarer, where practicable:

(a) a smoking room;

(b) television viewing and the reception of radio broadcasts;

(c) showing of films, the stock of which should be adequate for the duration of the voyage and, where necessary, changed at reasonable intervals;

(d) sports equipment including exercise equipment, table games and deck games;

(e) where possible, facilities for swimming;

(f) a library containing vocational and other books, the stock of which should be adequate for the duration of the voyage and changed at reasonable intervals;

(g) facilities for recreational handicrafts;

(h) electronic equipment such as a radio, television, video recorders, DVD/CD player, personal computer and software and cassette recorder/player;

(i) where appropriate, the provision of bars on board for seafarers unless these are contrary to national, religious or social customs; and

2. 娱乐设施的配备应至少包括一个书柜及阅读和书写设施，以及在实际可行时，游戏设施。

3. 涉及娱乐设施的规划时，主管当局应考虑设立一个小卖部。

4. 在可行时，还应考虑包括以下不向海员收费的设施：

(a) 一个吸烟室；

(b) 观看电视和收听无线电广播；

(c) 放映电影，存片应足够航程期间使用，并在必要时，每隔适当时间予以更换；

(d) 运动器械，包括锻炼器械、桌面游戏器械和甲板游戏器械；

(e) 如可能，游泳设施；

(f) 藏有业务书籍和其他书籍的图书室，其藏书量应够航程期间使用，并且每隔适当时间予以更换；

(g) 娱乐性手工设施；

(h) 电子设备，例如收音机、电视机、录像机、DVD/CD播放机、个人电脑和软件以及盒式录放机；

(i) 如适宜，在船上为海员提供酒吧，除非有悖于国家、宗教或社会习俗；以及

(j) reasonable access to ship-to-shore telephone communications, and email and Internet facilities, where available, with any charges for the use of these services being reasonable in amount.

5. Every effort should be given to ensuring that the forwarding of seafarers' mail is as reliable and expeditious as possible. Efforts should also be considered for avoiding seafarers being required to pay additional postage when mail has to be readdressed owing to circumstances beyond their control.

6. Measures should be considered to ensure, subject to any applicable national or international laws or regulations, that whenever possible and reasonable seafarers are expeditiously granted permission to have their partners, relatives and friends as visitors on board their ship when in port. Such measures should meet any concerns for security clearances.

7. Consideration should be given to the possibility of allowing seafarers to be accompanied by their partners on occasional voyages where this is practicable and reasonable. Such partners should carry adequate insurance cover against accident and illness; the shipowners should give every assistance to the seafarer to effect such insurance.

Guideline B3. 1. 12—Prevention of noise and vibration

1. Accommodation and recreational and catering facilities should be located as far as practicable from the engines, steering gear rooms, deck winches, ventilation, heating and air-conditioning equipment and other noisy machinery and apparatus.

2. Acoustic insulation or other appropriate sound-absorbing materials should be used in the construction and finishing of bulkheads, deckheads and decks within the sound-producing spaces as well as

(j) 提供合理的船—岸电话通信及电子邮件和互连网设施(如有),使用这些服务的任何收费在数额上合理。

5. 应尽力保证尽可能稳妥迅速地转递海员的邮件。还应考虑努力避免使海员在超出其控制的情形下转寄邮件时加付邮资。

6. 在任何适用的国内或国际法律或条例的限制下,只要可能和合理,应考虑采取措施保证船舶在港口停留期间,从速批准海员的伴侣、亲属和朋友登船探视。此种措施应满足任何关于保安审查的考虑。

7. 应考虑在可行和合理的情况下允许海员的伴侣偶尔陪伴其几个航程的可能性。此类伴侣应带有充分的意外和疾病保险;船东应为海员投保这种保险给予一切帮助。

导则 B3.1.12—防止噪声和振动

1. 起居舱室和娱乐及膳食服务设施的位置应尽实际可行地远离机器、舵机室、甲板绞车、通风、取暖和空调设备以及其他有噪声的机械和装置。

2. 发出声音处所内的舱壁、天花板和甲板应使用隔音材料或其他适当的吸音材料建造和做表面修饰,并为机器处所安装隔音的自动关闭门。

self-closing noise-isolating doors for machinery spaces.

3. Engine rooms and other machinery spaces should be provided, wherever practicable, with soundproof centralized control rooms for engine-room personnel. Working spaces, such as the machine shop, should be insulated, as far as practicable, from the general engine-room noise and measures should be taken to reduce noise in the operation of machinery.

4. The limits for noise levels for working and living spaces should be in conformity with the ILO international guidelines on exposure levels, including those in the ILO code of practice entitled *Ambient factors in the workplace*, 2001, and, where applicable, the specific protection recommended by the International Maritime Organization, and with any subsequent amending and supplementary instruments for acceptable noise levels on board ships. A copy of the applicable instruments in English or the working language of the ship should be carried on board and should be accessible to seafarers.

5. No accommodation or recreational or catering facilities should be exposed to excessive vibration.

Regulation 3.2—Food and catering

Purpose: To ensure that seafarers have access to good quality food and drinking water provided under regulated hygienic conditions

1. Each Member shall ensure that ships that fly its flag carry on board and serve food and drinking water of appropriate quality, nutritional value and quantity that adequately covers the requirements of the ship and takes into account the differing cultural and religious backgrounds.

3. 凡可行，应在机舱和其他机器处所为机舱人员设立隔音的集控室。工作场所，例如机修间，应尽实际可行地隔离机舱的一般噪声，并应采取措施减少机器运转时的噪声。

4. 工作和生活处所的噪声水平限制，应符合ILO关于接触水平的国际性导则，包括标题为《2001年工作场所环境因素》的ILO实务守则中的导则和，在适用时，国际海事组织建议的具体保护，以及符合任何关于船上可接受噪声水平的后续修正和补充文件。适用文件的英文或船上工作语言的文本应随船携带并使海员能够使用。

5. 起居舱室或娱乐或膳食服务设施不应接触过度的振动。

规则 3.2—食品和膳食服务

目的：确保海员获得根据规范的卫生条件提供的优质食品和饮用水

1. 各成员国须确保悬挂其旗帜的船舶随船携带并供应充分满足船舶需求的质量、营养价值和数量均合适的食品和饮用水，同时考虑不同的文化和宗教背景。

2. Seafarers on board a ship shall be provided with food free of charge during the period of engagement.

3. Seafarers employed as ships' cooks with responsibility for food preparation must be trained and qualified for their position on board ship.

Standard A3.2—Food and catering

1. Each Member shall adopt laws and regulations or other measures to provide minimum standards for the quantity and quality of food and drinking water and for the catering standards that apply to meals provided to seafarers on ships that fly its flag, and shall undertake educational activities to promote awareness and implementation of the standards referred to in this paragraph.

2. Each Member shall ensure that ships that fly its flag meet the following minimum standards:

(a) food and drinking water supplies, having regard to the number of seafarers on board, their religious requirements and cultural practices as they pertain to food, and the duration and nature of the voyage, shall be suitable in respect of quantity, nutritional value, quality and variety;

(b) the organization and equipment of the catering department shall be such as to permit the provision to the seafarers of adequate, varied and nutritious meals prepared and served in hygienic conditions; and

(c) catering staff shall be properly trained or instructed for their positions.

3. Shipowners shall ensure that seafarers who are engaged as ships' cooks are trained, qualified and found competent for the pos-

2. 须为受聘期间的船上海员免费提供食品。

3. 作为负责烹制食品的船上厨师而受雇的海员必须就其在船上的职位经过培训并取得资格。

标准 A3.2—食品和膳食服务

1. 各成员国须通过法律和条例或其他措施，为悬挂其旗帜船舶上的食品和饮用水的数量和质量及适用于供应给海员各餐的膳食服务标准规定最低标准，并须开展教育活动促进对本款所述标准的认识和实施。

2. 各成员国须确保悬挂其旗帜的船舶满足以下最低标准：

(a) 考虑到船上海员人数、其与食品相关的宗教要求和文化习惯以及航程的时间和性质，供应在数量、营养价值、质量和品种方面均为适当的食品和饮用水；

(b) 膳食服务部的组织和设备须容许为海员提供在卫生的条件下烹制和供应充足、多品种和有营养的餐食；以及

(c) 膳食服务人员须就其职位接受过适当培训或指导。

3. 船东须确保作为船上厨师受聘的海员按有关成员国的法律和条例所规定的要求接受过培训、合格并认定为胜任其职位。

ition in accordance with requirements set out in the laws and regulations of the Member concerned.

4. The requirements under paragraph 3 of this Standard shall include a completion of a training course approved or recognized by the competent authority, which covers practical cookery, food and personal hygiene, food storage, stock control, and environmental protection and catering health and safety.

5. On ships operating with a prescribed manning of less than ten which, by virtue of the size of the crew or the trading pattern, may not be required by the competent authority to carry a fully qualified cook, anyone processing food in the galley shall be trained or instructed in areas including food and personal hygiene as well as handling and storage of food on board ship.

6. In circumstances of exceptional necessity, the competent authority may issue a dispensation permitting a non-fully qualified cook to serve in a specified ship for a specified limited period, until the next convenient port of call or for a period not exceeding one month, provided that the person to whom the dispensation is issued is trained or instructed in areas including food and personal hygiene as well as handling and storage of food on board ship.

7. In accordance with the ongoing compliance procedures under Title 5, the competent authority shall require that frequent docu-mented inspections be carried out on board ships, by or under the authority of the master, with respect to:

(a) supplies of food and drinking water;

4. 本标准第 3 款下的要求须包括完成主管当局批准或认可的培训课程，涉及实用厨艺、食品和个人卫生、食品储存、备料管理以及环境保护和膳食服务的卫生和安全。

5. 在以少于十人的规定配员进行营运的船舶上，由于船员数目或航行形式，主管当局可能不要求配备完全具有资格的厨师，在厨房加工食品的任何人员均须在包括食品和个人卫生以及船上处理和储存食品方面受到过培训或指导。

6. 在极其必要的情况下，主管当局可签发特免证明，允许不完全具备资格的厨师在具体规定的有限时间内为某特定船舶服务，直到下一个方便的停靠港或不超过一个月的时间，条件是获发特免证明的人员在包括食品和个人卫生以及船上处理和储存食品方面受到过培训或指导。

7. 根据标题五下的持续符合程序，主管当局须要求由船长或经船长授权，在船舶上对以下方面开展经常性的有记录的检查：

(a) 食品和饮用水供应；

(b) all spaces and equipment used for the storage and handling of food and drinking water; and

(c) galley and other equipment for the preparation and service of meals.

8. No seafarer under the age of 18 shall be employed or engaged or work as a ship's cook.

Guideline B3.2—Food and catering

Guideline B3.2.1—Inspection, education, research and publication

1. The competent authority should, in cooperation with other relevant agencies and organizations, collect up-to-date information on nutrition and on methods of purchasing, storing, preserving, cooking and serving food, with special reference to the requirements of catering on board a ship. This information should be made available, free of charge or at reasonable cost, to manufacturers of and traders in ships' food supplies and equipment, masters, stewards and cooks, and to shipowners' and seafarers' organizations concerned. Appropriate forms of publicity, such as manuals, brochures, posters, charts or advertisements in trade journals, should be used for this purpose.

2. The competent authority should issue recommendations to avoid wastage of food, facilitate the maintenance of a proper standard of hygiene, and ensure the maximum practicable convenience in working arrangements.

3. The competent authority should work with relevant agencies and organizations to develop educational materials and on-board information concerning methods of ensuring proper food supply and

(b) 用于储存和处理食品和饮用水的所有场所和设备;以及

(c) 用于烹制和供应餐食的厨房和其他设备。

8. 不满 18 岁的海员不得作为船上的厨师受雇或受聘或工作。

导则 B3.2—食品和膳食服务

导则 B3.2.1—检查、教育、研究和出版

1. 主管当局应与其他相关机构和组织合作,收集有关营养和有关购买、储存、保存、烹调和供应食品的方法的最新信息,并特别注意船上膳食服务的要求。此类信息应免费或以合理的价格提供给供应船用食品和设备的生产厂和经销商、船长、服务员和厨师以及有关船东组织和海员组织。为此目的,应利用诸如手册、小册子、招贴画、图表或在行业期刊上的广告等适当的宣传形式。

2. 主管当局应发布建议,以避免食品浪费,促进保持适当的卫生标准,并确保工作安排中最大实际可行的方便。

3. 主管当局应与有关机构和组织合作,制定关于保证适当的食品供应和膳食服务方法的教育性材料和船上信息。

catering services.

4. The competent authority should work in close cooperation with the shipowners' and seafarers' organizations concerned and with national or local authorities dealing with questions of food and health, and may where necessary utilize the services of such authorities.

Guideline B3.2.2—Ships' cooks

1. Seafarers should only be qualified as ships' cooks if they have:

(a) served at sea for a minimum period to be prescribed by the competent authority, which could be varied to take into account existing relevant qualifications or experience;

(b) passed an examination prescribed by the competent authority or passed an equivalent examination at an approved training course for cooks.

2. The prescribed examination may be conducted and certificates granted either directly by the competent authority or, subject to its control, by an approved school for the training of cooks.

3. The competent authority should provide for the recognition, where appropriate, of certificates of qualification as ships' cooks issued by other Members, which have ratified this Convention or the Certification of Ships' Cooks Convention, 1946 (No. 69), or other approved body.

4．主管当局应与有关船东组织和海员组织以及处理食品和健康问题的国家或地方当局密切合作，并在必要时，可利用该类当局的服务。

导则 B3.2.2—船上厨师

1．海员应满足以下条件才有资格成为船上厨师：

(a) 在海上已服务了主管当局确定的最低期限，考虑到现有的相关资格或经验，此期限可有所变化；

(b) 通过了主管当局规定的考试或通过了经认可的厨师培训课程的等效考试。

2．可直接由主管当局或在其监督下由经认可的烹饪培训学校开展规定的考试并颁发证书。

3．主管当局应规定，在适宜时，承认由批准了本公约或《1946 年船上厨师发证公约》(第 69 号)的其他成员国签发的或其他认可机构签发的船上厨师资格证书。

TITLE 4. HEALTH PROTECTION, MEDICAL CARE, WELFARE AND SOCIAL SECURITY PROTECTION

Regulation 4.1—Medical care on board ship and ashore

Purpose: To protect the health of seafarers and ensure their prompt access to medical care on board ship and ashore

1. Each Member shall ensure that all seafarers on ships that fly its flag are covered by adequate measures for the protection of their health and that they have access to prompt and adequate medical care whilst working on board.

2. The protection and care under paragraph 1 of this Regulation shall, in principle, be provided at no cost to the seafarers.

3. Each Member shall ensure that seafarers on board ships in its territory who are in need of immediate medical care are given access to the Member's medical facilities on shore.

4. The requirements for on-board health protection and medical care set out in the Code include standards for measures aimed at providing seafarers with health protection and medical care as comparable as possible to that which is generally available to workers ashore.

Standard A4.1—Medical care on board ship and ashore

1. Each Member shall ensure that measures providing for health protection and medical care, including essential dental care, for seafarers working on board a ship that flies its flag are adopted which:

(a) ensure the application to seafarers of any general provisions on

标题四　健康保护、医护、福利和社会保障保护

规则 4.1—船上和岸上医护

目的：保护海员健康并确保其迅速得到船上和岸上医护

1. 各成员国须确保在悬挂其旗帜船舶上的所有海员均被保护其健康的充分措施所覆盖，并且他们在船上工作期间能够得到迅速和适当的医护。

2. 按本规则第 1 款提供的保护和护理须原则上不由海员支付费用。

3. 各成员国须确保在其领土内的船舶上需要紧急医护的海员能够使用其岸上医疗设施。

4. 守则中规定的船上健康保护和医护要求包括旨在向海员提供尽可能相当于岸上工人一般能够得到的健康保护和医护的措施标准。

标准 A4.1—船上和岸上医护

1. 各成员国须确保采取措施向在悬挂其旗帜的船舶上工作的海员提供健康保护和医护，包括必需的牙科护理，这些措施：

(a) 保证将任何与海员职责相关的关于职业健康保护和医护的任何一般规定以及针对船上工作的特殊规定适用于海员；

occupational health protection and medical care relevant to their duties, as well as of special provisions specific to work on board ship;

(b) ensure that seafarers are given health protection and medical care as comparable as possible to that which is generally available to workers ashore, including prompt access to the necessary medicines, medical equipment and facilities for diagnosis and treatment and to medical information and expertise;

(c) give seafarers the right to visit a qualified medical doctor or dentist without delay in ports of call, where practicable;

(d) ensure that, to the extent consistent with the Member's national law and practice, medical care and health protection services while a seafarer is on board ship or landed in a foreign port are provided free of charge to seafarers; and

(e) are not limited to treatment of sick or injured seafarers but include measures of a preventive character such as health promotion and health education programmes.

2. The competent authority shall adopt a standard medical report form for use by the ships' masters and relevant onshore and on-board medical personnel. The form, when completed, and its contents shall be kept confidential and shall only be used to facilitate the treatment of seafarers.

3. Each Member shall adopt laws and regulations establishing requirements for on-board hospital and medical care facilities and equipment and training on ships that fly its flag.

4. National laws and regulations shall as a minimum provide for the following requirements:

(b) 保证向海员提供尽可能相当于岸上工人一般能够得到的健康保护和医护，包括迅速得到诊断和治疗所必需的药品、医疗设备和设施以及医疗信息和专业技能；

(c) 如可行，在停靠港不延误地给予海员去看合格医生或牙医的权利；

(d) 在与成员国国内法律和惯例一致的限度内，保证免费向船上海员或在外国港口下地的海员提供医护和健康保护服务；以及

(e) 不局限于对患病或受伤海员的治疗，但包括预防性措施，如健康宣传和健康教育计划。

2. 主管当局须选定一个标准的医疗报告表格，供船长和相关的岸上和船上医疗人员使用。填好后的该表格及其内容须予保密，且须只用于方便对海员的治疗。

3. 各成员国须通过法律和条例，对悬挂其旗帜船舶上的船上医务室及医护设施和设备以及培训做出要求。

4. 国内法律和条例最低限度须规定以下要求：

(a) all ships shall carry a medicine chest, medical equipment and a medical guide, the specifics of which shall be prescribed and subject to regular inspection by the competent authority; the national requirements shall take into account the type of ship, the number of persons on board and the nature, destination and duration of voyages and relevant national and international recommended medical standards;

(b) ships carrying 100 or more persons and ordinarily engaged on international voyages of more than three days' duration shall carry a qualified medical doctor who is responsible for providing medical care; national laws or regulations shall also specify which other ships shall be required to carry a medical doctor, taking into account, inter alia, such factors as the duration, nature and conditions of the voyage and the number of seafarers on board;

(c) ships which do not carry a medical doctor shall be required to have either at least one seafarer on board who is in charge of medical care and administering medicine as part of their regular duties or at least one seafarer on board competent to provide medical first aid; persons in charge of medical care on board who are not medical doctors shall have satisfactorily completed training in medical care that meets the requirements of the International Convention on Standards of Training, Certification and Watchkeeping for Seafarers, 1978, as amended ("STCW"); seafarers designated to provide medical first aid shall have satisfactorily completed training in medical first aid that meets the requirements of STCW; national laws or regulations shall specify the level of approved training required taking into account, inter alia, such factors as the duration, nature and conditions of the voyage and the number of seafarers on board; and

(a) 所有船舶均须携带医药箱、医疗设备和医疗指南，具体内容须由主管当局规定并受其定期检查；国内要求须考虑船舶类型、船上人员的数量及航程性质、目的地和航程时间以及相关的国内和国际的建议医疗标准；

(b) 载有100人或以上，通常从事三天以上国际航行的船舶须载有一名合格的医生负责提供医护；国内法律或条例还须具体规定哪些其他船舶须被要求载有一名医生，尤其考虑到诸如航程的时间、性质和条件以及船上海员人数等因素；

(c) 须要求不载有医生的船舶，要么在船上至少有一名海员，其一部分正式职责是负责医护和分发药品，要么船上至少有一名海员胜任提供医疗急救；不是医生但负责船上医护的人员须满意地完成了符合经修正的《1978年海员培训、发证和值班标准国际公约》（“《STCW公约》”）要求的医护培训；被指定提供医疗急救的海员须满意地完成了符合《STCW公约》要求的医疗急救培训；国内法律或条例须具体规定所要求的认可培训水平，尤其考虑到诸如航程时间、性质和条件以及船上海员的数量等因素；以及

(d) the competent authority shall ensure by a prearranged system that medical advice by radio or satellite communication to ships at sea, including specialist advice, is available 24 hours a day; medical advice, including the onward transmission of medical messages by radio or satellite communication between a ship and those ashore giving the advice, shall be available free of charge to all ships irrespective of the flag that they fly.

Guideline B4.1—Medical care on board ship and ashore

Guideline B4.1.1—Provision of medical care

1. When determining the level of medical training to be provided on board ships that are not required to carry a medical doctor, the competent authority should require that:

(a) ships which ordinarily are capable of reaching qualified medical care and medical facilities within eight hours should have at least one designated seafarer with the approved medical first-aid training required by STCW which will enable such persons to take immediate, effective action in case of accidents or illnesses likely to occur on board a ship and to make use of medical advice by radio or satellite communication; and

(b) all other ships should have at least one designated seafarer with approved training in medical care required by STCW, including practical training and training in life-saving techniques such as intravenous therapy, which will enable the persons concerned to participate effectively in coordinated schemes for medical assistance to ships at sea, and to provide the sick or injured with a satisfactory standard of medical care during the period they are likely to remain on board.

(d) 主管当局须通过一个预先安排的机制，保证船舶在海上能够每天24小时均可得到通过无线电或卫星通信提供的医疗指导，包括专家指导；医疗指导，包括船舶与岸上提供医疗咨询的各方之间通过无线电或卫星通信转发的医疗讯息，均须向所有船舶免费提供，无论其悬挂哪一国旗帜。

导则B4.1—船上和岸上医护

导则B4.1.1—医护的提供

1. 在确定为不要求载有医生的船舶提供的医疗培训水平时，主管当局应要求：

(a) 通常能够在八小时内获得合格的医护和医疗设施的船舶应至少有一名指定海员接受过《STCW公约》所要求的经认可的医疗急救培训，使这类人员在发生了船上可能出现的事故或疾病时能够立即采取有效行动并通过无线电或卫星通信使用医疗建议；以及

(b) 所有其他船舶应至少有一名指定的海员接受过《STCW公约》所要求的经认可的医护培训，包括实训以及诸如静脉治疗这类救生技能的培训，使有关人员能有效参与对海上船舶的医疗援助协调方案，并能在病员或伤员可能继续留在船上期间，向他们提供满意标准的医护。

2. The training referred to in paragraph 1 of this Guideline should be based on the contents of the most recent editions of the *International Medical Guide for Ships*, the *Medical First Aid Guide for Use in Accidents Involving Dangerous Goods*, the *Document for Guidance—An International Maritime Training Guide*, and the medical section of the *International Code of Signals* as well as similar national guides.

3. Persons referred to in paragraph 1 of this Guideline and such other seafarers as may be required by the competent authority should undergo, at approximately five year intervals, refresher courses to enable them to maintain and increase their knowledge and skills and to keep up-to-date with new developments.

4. The medicine chest and its contents, as well as the medical equipment and medical guide carried on board, should be properly maintained and inspected at regular intervals, not exceeding 12 months, by responsible persons designated by the competent authority, who should ensure that the labelling, expiry dates and conditions of storage of all medicines and directions for their use are checked and all equipment functioning as required. In adopting or reviewing the ship's medical guide used nationally, and in determining the contents of the medicine chest and medical equipment, the competent authority should take into account international recommendations in this field, including the latest edition of the *International Medical Guide for Ships*, and other guides mentioned in paragraph 2 of this Guideline.

5. Where a cargo which is classified dangerous has not been included in the most recent edition of the *Medical First Aid Guide for Use in Accidents Involving Dangerous Goods*, the necessary informa-

2. 本导则第1款所述的培训应基于以下文件最新版本的内容:《国际船舶医疗指南》、《用于涉及危险品事故的医疗急救指南》、《指导文件——国际海事培训指南》,以及《国际信号规则》的医疗部分及类似的本国指南。

3. 本导则第1款所述的人员和主管当局可能要求的其他海员,每隔大约五年应参加更新课程,以便能够保持和增加其知识与技能并跟上新的发展。

4. 船上携带的医药箱及其内容以及医疗设备和医疗指南应予以妥善维护并由主管当局指定的负责人员以不超过12个月的间隔进行定期检查,这些人员应确保全部药品的标签、失效日期和存放条件及其使用说明均已核对,所有设备功能合乎要求。在通过或审定国内使用的船舶医疗指南以及在确定医药箱的内容和医疗设备时,主管当局应考虑此领域的国际建议,包括最新版本的《国际船舶医疗指南》和本导则第2款提及的其他指南。

5. 如果归类为危险的货物尚未列入最新版本的《用于涉及危险品事故的医疗急救指南》,应向海员提供关于该物质的性质、涉及的风险、必要的个人保护装置、相关的医疗程序和专用解毒剂方面的必要信息。凡载运危险品时,船上应备有此类专用解毒剂和个人保护装置。此信息应纳入到规则4.3和相关守则规定中所述的关于职业安全和健康的船舶方针和计划中。

tion on the nature of the substances, the risks involved, the necessary personal protective devices, the relevant medical procedures and specific antidotes should be made available to the seafarers. Such specific antidotes and personal protective devices should be on board whenever dangerous goods are carried. This information should be integrated with the ship's policies and programmes on occupational safety and health described in Regulation 4. 3 and related Code provisions.

6. All ships should carry a complete and up-to-date list of radio stations through which medical advice can be obtained; and, if equipped with a system of satellite communication, carry an up-to-date and complete list of coast earth stations through which medical advice can be obtained. Seafarers with responsibility for medical care or medical first aid on board should be instructed in the use of the ship's medical guide and the medical section of the most recent edition of the *International Code of Signals* so as to enable them to understand the type of information needed by the advising doctor as well as the advice received.

Guideline B4. 1. 2—Medical report form

1. The standard medical report form for seafarers required under Part A of this Code should be designed to facilitate the exchange of medical and related information concerning individual seafarers between ship and shore in cases of illness or injury.

Guideline B4. 1. 3—Medical care ashore

1. Shore-based medical facilities for treating seafarers should be adequate for the purposes. The doctors, dentists and other medical personnel should be properly qualified.

6. 所有船舶均应携带一份无线电台的完整和最新清单，通过这些电台能够获得医疗指导；并且，如果装备了卫星通信系统，则还应携带一份海岸地球站的最新和完整清单，通过这些地球站能够获得医疗指导。应指导负责船上医护或医疗急救的海员使用船舶医疗指南以及最新版《国际信号规则》的医疗部分，以使他们能够理解提供指导的医生所需的信息类型以及所收到的指导。

导则 B4.1.2—医疗报告表格

1. 本守则 A 部分所要求的海员标准医疗报告表格应设计成便于在海员生病或受伤时，在船舶与岸上之间交换有关其个人的医疗信息及相关信息。

导则 B4.1.3—岸上医护

1. 用于治疗海员的岸上医疗设施应充分符合其目的。医生、牙医和其他医务人员应具备适当的资格。

2. Measures should be taken to ensure that seafarers have access when in port to:

(a) outpatient treatment for sickness and injury;

(b) hospitalization when necessary; and

(c) facilities for dental treatment, especially in cases of emergency.

3. Suitable measures should be taken to facilitate the treatment of seafarers suffering from disease. In particular, seafarers should be promptly admitted to clinics and hospitals ashore, without difficulty and irrespective of nationality or religious belief, and, whenever possible, arrangements should be made to ensure, when necessary, continuation of treatment to supplement the medical facilities available to them.

Guideline B4.1.4—Medical assistance to other ships and international cooperation

1. Each Member should give due consideration to participating in international cooperation in the area of assistance, programmes and research in health protection and medical care. Such cooperation might cover:

(a) developing and coordinating search and rescue efforts and arranging prompt medical help and evacuation at sea for the seriously ill or injured on board a ship through such means as periodic ship position reporting systems, rescue coordination centres and emergency helicopter services, in conformity with the International Convention on Maritime Search and Rescue, 1979, as amended, and the *International Aeronautical and Maritime Search and Rescue (IAMSAR) Manual*;

(b) making optimum use of all ships carrying a doctor and stationing

2. 应采取措施确保海员在港口时能够：

(a) 在患病和受伤时得到门诊治疗；

(b) 在必要时住院；以及

(c) 得到牙科治疗的便利，特别是在紧急情况下。

3. 应采取适当措施便利患病海员的治疗。特别是，应没有困难地立即接收海员进入岸上的诊室和医院，不论其国籍或宗教信仰并且，凡可能时，应做出安排确保必要时的连续治疗，以补充海员可用的医疗设施。

导则 B4.1.4—对其他船舶的医疗援助和国际合作

1. 各成员国应充分考虑参与健康保护和医护的援助、计划和研究领域的国际合作。此种合作可包括：

(a) 按照经修正的《1979 年国际海上搜寻救助公约》和《国际航空和海上搜寻与救助(IAMSAR)手册》，制定和协调搜寻和救助行动，并通过定期船位报告制度、救助协调中心和应急直升机服务等手段，迅速安排船上重病员或重伤员的海上治疗帮助和转移；

(b) 最充分地利用载有医生的所有船舶并向海上派驻能够提供医院和救助设施的船舶；

ships at sea which can provide hospital and rescue facilities;

(c) compiling and maintaining an international list of doctors and medical care facilities available worldwide to provide emergency medical care to seafarers;

(d) landing seafarers ashore for emergency treatment;

(e) repatriating seafarers hospitalized abroad as soon as practicable, in accordance with the medical advice of the doctors responsible for the case, which takes into account the seafarer's wishes and needs;

(f) arranging personal assistance for seafarers during repatriation, in accordance with the medical advice of the doctors responsible for the case, which takes into account the seafarer's wishes and needs;

(g) endeavouring to set up health centres for seafarers to:

(i) conduct research on the health status, medical treatment and preventive health care of seafarers; and

(ii) train medical and health service staff in maritime medicine;

(h) collecting and evaluating statistics concerning occupational accidents, diseases and fatalities of seafarers and integrating and harmonizing the statistics with any existing national system of statistics on occupational accidents and diseases covering other categories of workers;

(i) organizing international exchanges of technical information, training material and personnel, as well as international training courses, seminars and working groups;

(j) providing all seafarers with special curative and preventive health and medical services in port, or making available to them general

(c) 汇编和保持一份世界范围内能向海员提供应急医护的医生和医护设施的国际名录；

(d) 接海员上岸进行紧急治疗；

(e) 根据负责医生考虑了海员本人愿望和需要的医疗建议，尽实际可行地及早将在国外住院的海员遣返回国；

(f) 根据负责医生考虑了海员本人愿望和需要的医疗建议，在遣返期间为海员安排专人协助；

(g) 努力建立海员健康中心，以便：

(i) 对海员的健康状况、医疗和预防性保健开展研究；和

(ii) 培训航海医学方面的医疗和健康服务人员；

(h) 搜集和评价有关海员职业事故、疾病和伤亡的统计资料，把这些统计资料纳入国内任何现行的包括其他类别工人的职业事故和疾病的统计资料系统中并与之协调；

(i) 组织技术情报、培训材料和人员的国际交流，以及国际培训课程、研讨会和工作组；

(j) 在港口向所有海员提供专门的治疗和预防性健康和医疗服务，或使他们能得到一般性的保健、医疗和康复服务；以及

health, medical and rehabilitation services; and

(k) arranging for the repatriation of the bodies or ashes of deceased seafarers, in accordance with the wishes of the next of kin and as soon as practicable.

2. International cooperation in the field of health protection and medical care for seafarers should be based on bilateral or multilateral agreements or consultations among Members.

Guideline B4.1.5—Dependants of seafarers

1. Each Member should adopt measures to secure proper and sufficient medical care for the dependants of seafarers domiciled in its territory pending the development of a medical care service which would include within its scope workers generally and their dependants where such services do not exist and should inform the International Labour Office concerning the measures taken for this purpose.

Regulation 4.2—Shipowners' liability

Purpose: To ensure that seafarers are protected from the financial consequences of sickness, injury or death occurring in connection with their employment

1. Each Member shall ensure that measures, in accordance with the Code, are in place on ships that fly its flag to provide seafarers employed on the ships with a right to material assistance and support from the shipowner with respect to the financial consequences of sickness, injury or death occurring while they are serving under a seafarers' employment agreement or arising from their employment under such agreement.

(k) 根据已故海员最近亲属[1]的意愿，尽实际可行地及早安排将其遗体或骨灰运回。

2. 海员健康保护和医护领域的国际合作应以成员国间的双边或多边协议或协商为基础。

导则 B4.1.5—海员的受扶养人

1. 在其领土内若不存在范围通常包括工人及其受扶养人的医护服务，则各成员国在发展此种服务之前，应采取措施保障海员在其领土内居住的受扶养人得到妥善和充分的医护，并应将其为此目的而采取的措施通报国际劳工局。

规则 4.2—船东的责任

目的：确保海员得到保护，免受相关于其就业而发生的疾病、受伤或死亡的经济后果

1. 针对海员根据其就业协议在服务期间发生的或在此种协议下就业所引起的疾病、受伤或死亡的经济后果，各成员国须确保，根据守则，在悬挂其旗帜的船舶上存在措施，以便向在船上就业的海员提供从船东那里获得物质援助和支持的权利。

[1] 对应的英文为 next of kin，指最亲近的血亲和姻亲，即父母、子女和配偶，其范围相当于我国《继承法》中的第一顺序继承人。我国法律中的“近亲属”，除父母、子女和配偶外，还包括兄弟姐妹等，因此与本公约中的“最近亲属”不同。——校译者注

2. This Regulation does not affect any other legal remedies that a seafarer may seek.

Standard A4.2—Shipowners' liability

1. Each Member shall adopt laws and regulations requiring that shipowners of ships that fly its flag are responsible for health protection and medical care of all seafarers working on board the ships in accordance with the following minimum standards:

(a) shipowners shall be liable to bear the costs for seafarers working on their ships in respect of sickness and injury of the seafarers occurring between the date of commencing duty and the date upon which they are deemed duly repatriated, or arising from their employment between those dates;

(b) shipowners shall provide financial security to assure compensation in the event of the death or long-term disability of seafarers due to an occupational injury, illness or hazard, as set out in national law, the seafarers' employment agreement or collective agreement;

(c) shipowners shall be liable to defray the expense of medical care, including medical treatment and the supply of the necessary medicines and therapeutic appliances, and board and lodging away from home until the sick or injured seafarer has recovered, or until the sickness or incapacity has been declared of a permanent character; and

(d) shipowners shall be liable to pay the cost of burial expenses in the case of death occurring on board or ashore during the period of engagement.

2. National laws or regulations may limit the liability of the

2. 本规则不影响海员可能寻求的任何其他法律救济。

标准 A4.2—船东的责任

1. 各成员国须通过法律和条例,要求悬挂其旗帜的船舶的船东根据以下最低标准,对在船上工作的所有海员的健康保护和医护负责:

(a) 对于在其船上工作的海员从开始履行职责之日起到其被视为妥善遣返之日期间所发生的或源自这些日期之间就业的疾病和受伤,船东须有责任承担费用;

(b) 船东须提供财务担保,以保证在海员因职业伤害、疾病或危害而死亡或长期残疾的情况下获得按国内法律、海员就业协议或集体协议所规定的赔偿;

(c) 船东须有责任支付医护费用,包括医疗及提供必要的药品和治疗器械,以及离家在外的膳宿,直到该患病或受伤海员康复,或直到该疾病或机能丧失被宣布为永久性;以及

(d) 在受雇期间如果在船上或岸上发生死亡,船东须有责任支付丧葬费用。

2. 国内法律或条例可以把船东支付医护和膳宿费用的责任限制在从受伤或开始患病之日起不得少于16周的期限内。

shipowner to defray the expense of medical care and board and lodging to a period which shall not be less than 16 weeks from the day of the injury or the commencement of the sickness.

3. Where the sickness or injury results in incapacity for work the shipowner shall be liable:

(a) to pay full wages as long as the sick or injured seafarers remain on board or until the seafarers have been repatriated in accordance with this Convention; and

(b) to pay wages in whole or in part as prescribed by national laws or regulations or as provided for in collective agreements from the time when the seafarers are repatriated or landed until their recovery or, if earlier, until they are entitled to cash benefits under the legislation of the Member concerned.

4. National laws or regulations may limit the liability of the shipowner to pay wages in whole or in part in respect of a seafarer no longer on board to a period which shall not be less than 16 weeks from the day of the injury or the commencement of the sickness.

5. National laws or regulations may exclude the shipowner from liability in respect of:

(a) injury incurred otherwise than in the service of the ship;

(b) injury or sickness due to the wilful misconduct of the sick, injured or deceased seafarer; and

(c) sickness or infirmity intentionally concealed when the engagement is entered into.

6. National laws or regulations may exempt the shipowner from liability to defray the expense of medical care and board and lodging and burial expenses in so far as such liability is assumed by the public

3. 如果疾病或受伤造成工作能力丧失，船东须有责任：

(a) 支付全额工资，只要患病或受伤海员还留在船上或者直到海员根据本公约得到遣返；以及

(b) 从海员被遣返或上岸之时起，按照国内法律或条例的规定或集体协议中的规定支付全额或部分工资，直到其康复或者，如更早，直到其有权根据有关成员国的立法获得现金津贴。

4. 国内法律或条例可将船东向一名离船海员支付全额或部分工资的责任限制在从受伤或开始患病之日起不得少于16周的期限内。

5. 国内法律或条例可就以下情况免除船东的责任：

(a) 在船舶服务之外发生的受伤；

(b) 受伤或患病是因患病、受伤或死亡海员的故意不当行为所致；以及

(c) 在达成聘用时故意隐瞒的疾病或病症。

6. 只要支付医护和膳宿费用及丧葬费用的责任由公共当局承担，国内法律或条例可免除船东的此种责任。

authorities.

7. Shipowners or their representatives shall take measures for safeguarding property left on board by sick, injured or deceased seafarers and for returning it to them or to their next of kin.

Guideline B4.2—Shipowners' liability

1. The payment of full wages required by Standard A4.2, paragraph 3(a), may be exclusive of bonuses.

2. National laws or regulations may provide that a shipowner shall cease to be liable to bear the costs of a sick or injured seafarer from the time at which that seafarer can claim medical benefits under a scheme of compulsory sickness insurance, compulsory accident insurance or workers' compensation for accidents.

3. National laws or regulations may provide that burial expenses paid by the shipowner shall be reimbursed by an insurance institution in cases in which funeral benefit is payable in respect of the deceased seafarer under laws or regulations relating to social insurance or workers' compensation.

Regulation 4.3—Health and safety protection and accident prevention

Purpose: To ensure that seafarers' work environment on board ships promotes occupational safety and health

1. Each Member shall ensure that seafarers on ships that fly its flag are provided with occupational health protection and live, work and train on board ship in a safe and hygienic environment.

2. Each Member shall develop and promulgate national guide-

7. 船东或其代表须采取措施保护患病、受伤或死亡海员留在船上的财物并将其归还给海员或其最近亲属。

导则 B4.2—船东的责任

1. 标准 A4.2 第 3(a)款所要求的支付全额工资可不包括奖金。

2. 国内法律或条例可以规定,从患病或受伤海员能够根据疾病强制保险计划、事故强制保险计划或工人事故赔偿计划索取医疗津贴之时起,船东停止负责承担该海员的费用。

3. 如果根据有关社会保险或工人赔偿的法律或条例可对死亡海员支付殡葬补助,国内法律或条例可规定保险机构须偿付船东已支付的丧葬费用。

规则 4.3—健康和安全保护及事故预防

目的:确保海员的船上工作环境促进职业安全和健康

1. 各成员国须确保悬挂其旗帜的船舶上的海员得到职业健康保护,并且在一个安全和卫生的环境下在船上生活、工作和培训。

2. 各成员国须在与有代表性的船东组织和海员组织协商后,并考虑到国际组织、国内管理机关和海运业组织所建议的适用守则、导则和标准,为悬挂其旗帜船舶上的职业安全和健康管理制定和颁布本国导则。

lines for the management of occupational safety and health on board ships that fly its flag, after consultation with representative shipowners' and seafarers' organizations and taking into account applicable codes, guidelines and standards recommended by international organizations, national administrations and maritime industry organizations.

3. Each Member shall adopt laws and regulations and other measures addressing the matters specified in the Code, taking into account relevant international instruments, and set standards for occupational safety and health protection and accident prevention on ships that fly its flag.

Standard A4. 3—Health and safety protection and accident prevention

1. The laws and regulations and other measures to be adopted in accordance with Regulation 4. 3, paragraph 3, shall include the following subjects:

(a) the adoption and effective implementation and promotion of occupational safety and health policies and programmes on ships that fly the Member's flag, including risk evaluation as well as training and instruction of seafarers;

(b) reasonable precautions to prevent occupational accidents, injuries and diseases on board ship, including measures to reduce and prevent the risk of exposure to harmful levels of ambient factors and chemicals as well as the risk of injury or disease that may arise from the use of equipment and machinery on board ships;

(c) on-board programmes for the prevention of occupational accidents, injuries and diseases and for continuous improvement in

3. 各成员国须通过法律和条例及其他措施处理守则中具体规定的事项，同时考虑到相关的国际文件，并为悬挂其旗帜的船舶上的职业安全和健康保护及事故预防制定标准。

标准 A4.3—健康和安全保护及事故预防

1. 根据规则 4.3 第 3 款通过的法律和条例及其他措施须包括以下主题：

(a) 在悬挂成员国旗帜的船舶上通过和有效实施并促进职业安全和健康方针和计划，包括风险评价及对海员的培训和指导；

(b) 防止船上职业事故、伤害和疾病的合理预防措施，包括减少和防止接触有害水平的环境因素和化学品的风险以及可能源自使用船上设备和机械的伤害或疾病的风险的措施；

(c) 防止职业事故、伤害和疾病及不断改善职业安全和健康保护的船上计划，让海员代表和所有其他有关人员参与其实施，同时考虑到预防性的措施，包括工程和设计控制、对集体和个人的任务采取替代工序和程序以及使用个人保护设备；以及

occupational safety and health protection, involving seafarers' representatives and all other persons concerned in their implementation, taking account of preventive measures, including engineering and design control, substitution of processes and procedures for collective and individual tasks, and the use of personal protective equipment; and

(d) requirements for inspecting, reporting and correcting unsafe conditions and for investigating and reporting on-board occupational accidents.

2. The provisions referred to in paragraph 1 of this Standard shall:

(a) take account of relevant international instruments dealing with occupational safety and health protection in general and with specific risks, and address all matters relevant to the prevention of occupational accidents, injuries and diseases that may be applicable to the work of seafarers and particularly those which are specific to maritime employment;

(b) clearly specify the obligation of shipowners, seafarers and others concerned to comply with the applicable standards and with the ship's occupational safety and health policy and programme with special attention being paid to the safety and health of seafarers under the age of 18;

(c) specify the duties of the master or a person designated by the master, or both, to take specific responsibility for the implementation of and compliance with the ship's occupational safety and health policy and programme; and

(d) specify the authority of the ship's seafarers appointed or elected as safety representatives to participate in meetings of the ship's

(d) 检查、报告和纠正不安全状况的要求以及调查和报告船上职业事故的要求。

2. 本标准第1款所述的规定须：

(a) 对于应对一般性的和具有特定风险的职业安全和健康保护的相关国际文件予以考虑，并对相关于预防那些可能适用于海员工作的，特别是那些海上就业所特有的，职业事故、伤害和疾病的所有事项进行处理；

(b) 明确地具体规定船东、海员和其他有关人员遵守适用的标准及船上职业安全和健康方针和计划的义务，并特别注意18岁以下海员的安全和健康；

(c) 具体规定船长和(或)船长指定的人员的职责，以承担实施和遵守船舶职业安全和健康方针和计划的具体责任；以及

(d) 具体规定船上被任命或选举为安全代表参与船舶安全委员会会议的海员的权利。在有五名或更多海员的船上须成立此委员会。

safety committee. Such a committee shall be established on board a ship on which there are five or more seafarers.

3. The laws and regulations and other measures referred to in Regulation 4.3, paragraph 3, shall be regularly reviewed in consultation with the representatives of the shipowners' and seafarers' organizations and, if necessary, revised to take account of changes in technology and research in order to facilitate continuous improvement in occupational safety and health policies and programmes and to provide a safe occupational environment for seafarers on ships that fly the Member's flag.

4. Compliance with the requirements of applicable international instruments on the acceptable levels of exposure to workplace hazards on board ships and on the development and implementation of ships' occupational safety and health policies and programmes shall be considered as meeting the requirements of this Convention.

5. The competent authority shall ensure that:

(a) occupational accidents, injuries and diseases are adequately reported, taking into account the guidance provided by the International Labour Organization with respect to the reporting and recording of occupational accidents and diseases;

(b) comprehensive statistics of such accidents and diseases are kept, analysed and published and, where appropriate, followed up by research into general trends and into the hazards identified; and

(c) occupational accidents are investigated.

6. Reporting and investigation of occupational safety and health matters shall be designed to ensure the protection of seafarers' personal data, and shall take account of the guidance provided by the In-

3. 规则4.3第3款中所述的法律和条例及其他措施，须与船东组织和海员组织的代表协商予以定期审查，并在必要时加以修订，以便考虑到技术和研究的变化，从而促进对职业安全和健康方针和计划的不断改善，并为悬挂该成员国旗帜船舶上的海员提供一个安全的职业环境。

4. 符合适用的国际文件关于接触船上工作场所危害的可接受水平的要求以及关于制定和实施船上职业安全和健康方针和计划的要求，须被认为满足了本公约的要求。

5. 主管当局须确保：

(a) 考虑到国际劳工组织提供的关于报告和记录职业事故和疾病的指导，使职业事故、伤害和疾病得到充分报告；

(b) 此类事故和疾病的全面统计资料得以保持、分析和公布，并且在适宜时，通过对总体趋势和所识别的危害进行研究而得以跟踪；以及

(c) 对职业事故开展调查。

6. 职业安全和健康事项的报告和调查的安排须确保海员的个人资料得到保护，并须考虑国际劳工组织关于此事项提供的指导。

ternational Labour Organization on this matter.

7. The competent authority shall cooperate with shipowners' and seafarers' organizations to take measures to bring to the attention of all seafarers information concerning particular hazards on board ships, for instance, by posting official notices containing relevant instructions.

8. The competent authority shall require that shipowners conducting risk evaluation in relation to management of occupational safety and health refer to appropriate statistical information from their ships and from general statistics provided by the competent authority.

Guideline B4.3—Health and safety protection and accident prevention

Guideline B4.3.1—Provisions on occupational accidents, injuries and diseases

1. The provisions required under Standard A4.3 should take into account the ILO code of practice entitled *Accident prevention on board ship at sea and in port*, 1996, and subsequent versions and other related ILO and other international standards and guidelines and codes of practice regarding occupational safety and health protection, including any exposure levels that they may identify.

2. The competent authority should ensure that the national guidelines for the management of occupational safety and health address the following matters, in particular:

(a) general and basic provisions;

(b) structural features of the ship, including means of access and asbestos-related risks;

7. 主管当局须与船东组织和海员组织合作，采取措施使所有海员注意有关船上特殊危害的信息，例如通过张贴包含相关指导的正式通告。

8. 主管当局须要求对有关职业安全和健康的管理开展风险评价的船东，参考来自其船舶的和来自主管当局所提供一般性统计资料的适当统计信息。

导则 B4.3—健康和安全保护及事故预防

导则 B4.3.1—关于职业事故、伤害和疾病的规定

1. 标准 A4.3 所要求的规定应考虑到标题为《1996 年海上和港口防止船上事故》的 ILO 实务守则及其以后的版本，以及关于职业安全和健康保护的其他相关的 ILO 和其他国际标准和导则及实务守则，包括其可能确认的任何接触水平。

2. 主管当局应确保管理职业安全和健康的本国导则特别处理以下事项：

(a) 一般和基本规定；

(b) 船舶结构特征，包括出入通道和与石棉有关的风险；

(c) machinery;

(d) the effects of the extremely low or high temperature of any surfaces with which seafarers may be in contact;

(e) the effects of noise in the workplace and in shipboard accommodation;

(f) the effects of vibration in the workplace and in shipboard accommodation;

(g) the effects of ambient factors, other than those referred to in subparagraphs (e) and (f), in the workplace and in shipboard accommodation, including tobacco smoke;

(h) special safety measures on and below deck;

(i) loading and unloading equipment;

(j) fire prevention and fire-fighting;

(k) anchors, chains and lines;

(l) dangerous cargo and ballast;

(m) personal protective equipment for seafarers;

(n) work in enclosed spaces;

(o) physical and mental effects of fatigue;

(p) the effects of drug and alcohol dependency;

(q) HIV/AIDS protection and prevention; and

(r) emergency and accident response.

3. The assessment of risks and reduction of exposure on the matters referred to in paragraph 2 of this Guideline should take account of the physical occupational health effects, including manual handling of loads, noise and vibration, the chemical and biological occupational health effects, the mental occupational health effects,

(c) 机器；
(d) 海员可能接触到的任何极端低温或高温表面的影响；
(e) 工作场所和船上起居舱室中的噪声影响；
(f) 工作场所和船上起居舱室中的振动影响；
(g) 工作场所和船上起居舱室中除第(e)和(f)项中所述以外的环境因素的影响，包括吸烟的影响；
(h) 甲板上面和下面的特别安全措施；
(i) 装卸设备；
(j) 防火和灭火；
(k) 锚、链索和绳索；
(l) 危险货物和压载；
(m) 海员个人保护设备；
(n) 在封闭处所工作；
(o) 疲劳对身心的影响；
(p) 药物和酒精依赖的影响；
(q) 艾滋病毒/艾滋病的保护和预防；以及
(r) 应急和事故反应。

3. 对本导则第2款所述事项的风险评估和接触的减少应考虑到：身体方面的职业健康影响，包括手动操作重荷，噪声和振动，化学和生物学方面的职业健康影响，精神方面的职业健康影响，疲劳的身心健康影响以及职业事故。必要的措施应充分考虑到预防性原则，根据这一原则，除其他外，从源头降低风险，使工作适合于个人，特别是关于工作场所的设计，用无危险或危险性小的来取代危险的，均优先于海员的个人保护设备。

the physical and mental health effects of fatigue, and occupational accidents. The necessary measures should take due account of the preventive principle according to which, among other things, combating risk at the source, adapting work to the individual, especially as regards the design of workplaces, and replacing the dangerous by the nondangerous or the less dangerous, have precedence over personal protective equipment for seafarers.

4. In addition, the competent authority should ensure that the implications for health and safety are taken into account, particularly in the following areas:

(a) emergency and accident response;

(b) the effects of drug and alcohol dependency; and

(c) HIV/AIDS protection and prevention.

Guideline B4.3.2—Exposure to noise

1. The competent authority, in conjunction with the competent international bodies and with representatives of shipowners' and seafarers' organizations concerned, should review on an ongoing basis the problem of noise on board ships with the objective of improving the protection of seafarers, in so far as practicable, from the adverse effects of exposure to noise.

2. The review referred to in paragraph 1 of this Guideline should take account of the adverse effects of exposure to excessive noise on the hearing, health and comfort of seafarers and the measures to be prescribed or recommended to reduce shipboard noise to protect seafarers. The measures to be considered should include the following:

(a) instruction of seafarers in the dangers to hearing and health of prolonged exposure to high noise levels and in the proper use of

4. 此外，主管当局应确保考虑健康和安全所受的影响，特别是在以下方面：

(a) 应急和事故反应；

(b) 药物和酒精依赖的影响；以及

(c) 艾滋病毒/艾滋病的保护和预防。

导则 B4.3.2—接触噪声

1. 主管当局应与主管的国际机构和有关船东组织和海员组织的代表一起，以尽实际可行地改进保护海员免受接触噪声的不利影响为目标，不断审议船上的噪声问题。

2. 本导则第1款中所述的审议应考虑到接触过量噪声对海员的听觉、健康和舒适产生的不利影响，以及为减少船上噪声、保护海员所要规定或建议的措施。要考虑的措施应包括：

(a) 向海员讲解长时间接触高分贝噪声水平对听觉和健康的危害，以及噪声防护装置和器材的妥善使用；

noise protection devices and equipment;

(b) provision of approved hearing protection equipment to seafarers where necessary; and

(c) assessment of risk and reduction of exposure levels to noise in all accommodation and recreational and catering facilities, as well as engine rooms and other machinery spaces.

Guideline B4.3.3—Exposure to vibration

1. The competent authority, in conjunction with the competent international bodies and with representatives of shipowners' and seafarers' organizations concerned, and taking into account, as appropriate, relevant international standards, should review on an ongoing basis the problem of vibration on board ships with the objective of improving the protection of seafarers, in so far as practicable, from the adverse effects of vibration.

2. The review referred to in paragraph 1 of this Guideline should cover the effect of exposure to excessive vibration on the health and comfort of seafarers and the measures to be prescribed or recommended to reduce shipboard vibration to protect seafarers. The measures to be considered should include the following:

(a) instruction of seafarers in the dangers to their health of prolonged exposure to vibration;

(b) provision of approved personal protective equipment to seafarers where necessary; and

(c) assessment of risks and reduction of exposure to vibration in all accommodation and recreational and catering facilities by adopting measures in accordance with the guidance provided by the ILO code of practice entitled *Ambient factors in the workplace*,

(b) 必要时向海员提供经认可的听觉保护设备;以及

(c) 进行风险评估并减少所有起居舱室及娱乐和膳食服务设施以及机舱和其他机器处所中噪声的接触水平。

导则 B4.3.3—接触振动

1. 主管当局应与主管的国际机构和有关船东组织和海员组织的代表一起,并视情况考虑到相关的国际标准,以尽实际可行地改进保护海员免受振动的不利影响为目标,不断审议船上的振动问题。

2. 本导则第 1 款所述的审议应包括接触过度的振动对海员健康和舒适的影响,以及为减少船上振动、保护海员所要规定或建议的措施。要考虑的措施应包括:

(a) 向海员讲解长时间接触振动对其健康的危害;

(b) 必要时向海员提供认可的个人保护设备;以及

(c) 进行风险评估并根据标题为《2001 年工作场所的环境因素》的 ILO 实务守则及其任何后续修订本提供的指导采取措施,减少所有起居舱室及娱乐和膳食服务设施内接触的振动,并考虑到接触这些场所内的振动和接触工作场所内的振动之间的区别。

2001, and any subsequent revisions, taking account of the difference between exposure in those areas and in the workplace.

Guideline B4.3.4—Obligations of shipowners

1. Any obligation on the shipowner to provide protective equipment or other accident prevention safeguards should, in general, be accompanied by provisions requiring their use by seafarers and by a requirement for seafarers to comply with the relevant accident prevention and health protection measures.

2. Account should also be taken of Articles 7 and 11 of the Guarding of Machinery Convention, 1963 (No. 119), and the corresponding provisions of the Guarding of Machinery Recommendation, 1963 (No. 118), under which the obligation to ensure compliance with the requirement that machinery in use is properly guarded, and its use without appropriate guards prevented, rests on the employer, while there is an obligation on the worker not to use machinery without the guards being in position nor to make inoperative the guards provided.

Guideline B4.3.5—Reporting and collection of statistics

1. All occupational accidents and occupational injuries and diseases should be reported so that they can be investigated and comprehensive statistics can be kept, analysed and published, taking account of protection of the personal data of the seafarers concerned. Reports should not be limited to fatalities or to accidents involving the ship.

2. The statistics referred to in paragraph 1 of this Guideline should record the numbers, nature, causes and effects of occupational accidents and occupational injuries and diseases, with a clear indi-

导则 B4.3.4—船东的义务

1. 一般而言，任何关于船东提供防护性设备或其他事故预防的保障措施的义务，都应附带要求海员对其予以使用的规定以及海员遵守有关事故预防和健康保护措施的要求。

2. 还应考虑《1963 年机器防护公约》(第 119 号)第七和十一条以及《1963 年机器防护建议书》(第 118 号)的相应规定，根据这些规定，雇主有义务确保符合对使用的机器进行适当的防护、防止使用无适当保护装置机器的要求，而工人则有义务不使用未安装保护装置的机器，亦不停用提供的这些保护装置。

导则 B4.3.5—报告和收集统计资料

1. 一切职业事故以及职业伤害和疾病均应报告，从而能够对其开展调查以及保持、分析和公布全面的统计资料，并考虑到保护有关海员的个人数据。报告不应局限于伤亡事故或涉及船舶的事故。

2. 本导则第 1 款中所述的统计资料应记录职业事故及职业伤害和疾病的次数、性质、原因和后果，如适用，还明确指出在船上的部门、事故的类型以及在海上还是在港口。

cation, as applicable, of the department on board a ship, the type of accident and whether at sea or in port.

3. Each Member should have due regard to any international system or model for recording accidents to seafarers which may have been established by the International Labour Organization.

Guideline B4.3.6—Investigations

1. The competent authority should undertake investigations into the causes and circumstances of all occupational accidents and occupational injuries and diseases resulting in loss of life or serious personal injury, and such other cases as may be specified in national laws or regulations.

2. Consideration should be given to including the following as subjects of investigation:

(a) working environment, such as working surfaces, layout of machinery, means of access, lighting and methods of work;

(b) incidence in different age groups of occupational accidents and occupational injuries and diseases;

(c) special physiological or psychological problems created by the shipboard environment;

(d) problems arising from physical stress on board a ship, in particular as a consequence of increased workload;

(e) problems arising from and effects of technical developments and their influence on the composition of crews; and

(f) problems arising from any human failures.

3. 各成员国应充分注意到国际劳工组织可能业已确立的记录海员事故的任何国际制度或模式。

导则 B4.3.6—调查

1. 主管当局应对所有造成死亡或重伤的职业事故及职业伤害和疾病以及国内法律或条例可能具体规定的其他事件的原因和情况进行调查。

2. 应考虑将以下内容列入调查主题：

(a) 工作环境，如作业面、机器布置、出入通道、照明和工作方法；

(b) 不同年龄组中职业事故及职业伤害和疾病的发生率；

(c) 船上环境造成的特殊的生理或心理问题；

(d) 在船上的身体压力，特别是工作量增加引起的身体压力所产生的问题；

(e) 技术进步带来的问题和后果及其对船员构成的影响；以及

(f) 任何人为失误产生的问题。

Guideline B4.3.7—National protection and prevention programmes

1. In order to provide a sound basis for measures to promote occupational safety and health protection and prevention of accidents, injuries and diseases which are due to particular hazards of maritime employment, research should be undertaken into general trends and into such hazards as are revealed by statistics.

2. The implementation of protection and prevention programmes for the promotion of occupational safety and health should be so organized that the competent authority, shipowners and seafarers or their representatives and other appropriate bodies may play an active role, including through such means as information sessions, on-board guidelines on maximum exposure levels to potentially harmful ambient workplace factors and other hazards or outcomes of a systematic risk evaluation process. In particular, national or local joint occupational safety and health protection and accident prevention committees or ad hoc working parties and on-board committees, on which shipowners' and seafarers' organizations concerned are represented, should be established.

3. Where such activity takes place at company level, the representation of seafarers on any safety committee on board that shipowner's ships should be considered.

Guideline B4.3.8—Content of protection and prevention programmes

1. Consideration should be given to including the following in the functions of the committees and other bodies referred to in Guideline B4.3.7, paragraph 2:

导则 B4.3.7—国内保护和预防计划

1. 为了给促进职业安全和健康保护及防止源于海上就业特有危害的事故、伤害和疾病的措施打下完备的基础，应对总的趋势以及统计资料所揭示的危害进行研究。

2. 应组织实施促进职业安全和健康的保护和预防计划，使主管当局、船东和海员或其代表及其他相应机构可以发挥积极作用，包括采用诸如信息通报会、关于有潜在危害的工作场所环境因素和其他危害的最高接触水平的船上导则，或系统性风险评价过程的结果等方式。特别是应成立由有关船东组织和海员组织的代表参加的全国性或地方性职业安全和健康保护及事故预防联合委员会或特设工作组和船上委员会。

3. 如果在公司的层面上开展此类活动，应考虑在该船东的船舶上的任何安全委员会中都有海员的代表参加。

导则 B4.3.8—保护和预防计划的内容

1. 应考虑在导则 B4.3.7 第 2 款所述委员会和其他机构的职能中包括以下内容：

(a) the preparation of national guidelines and policies for occupational safety and health management systems and for accident prevention provisions, rules and manuals;

(b) the organization of occupational safety and health protection and accident prevention training and programmes;

(c) the organization of publicity on occupational safety and health protection and accident prevention, including films, posters, notices and brochures; and

(d) the distribution of literature and information on occupational safety and health protection and accident prevention so that it reaches seafarers on board ships.

2. Relevant provisions or recommendations adopted by the appropriate national authorities or organizations or international organizations should be taken into account by those preparing texts of occupational safety and health protection and accident prevention measures or recommended practices.

3. In formulating occupational safety and health protection and accident prevention programmes, each Member should have due regard to any code of practice concerning the safety and health of seafarers which may have been published by the International Labour Organization.

Guideline B4. 3. 9—Instruction in occupational safety and health protection and the prevention of occupational accidents

1. The curriculum for the training referred to in Standard A4. 3, paragraph 1(a), should be reviewed periodically and brought up to date in the light of development in types and sizes of ships and in

(a) 制订职业安全和健康管理系统和事故预防的规定、规章和手册的本国导则和政策；

(b) 组织职业安全和健康保护及事故预防的培训和计划；

(c) 组织对职业安全和健康保护及事故预防的宣传，包括电影、宣传画、告示和小册子；以及

(d) 散发有关职业安全和健康保护及事故预防的材料和信息，以便让在船上的海员得到。

2. 起草职业安全和健康保护及事故预防措施或建议做法的人员，应考虑到相应的国内当局或组织或国际组织所通过的有关规定或建议。

3. 在制订职业安全和健康保护及事故预防的计划时，各成员国应充分注意到国际劳工组织可能业已出版的关于海员安全和健康的任何实务守则。

导则 B4.3.9—职业安全和健康保护及职业事故预防的指导

1. 应定期审议标准 A4.3 第 1(a)款中所述的全套培训课程，并根据船舶类型和尺度及其设备的发展以及船上配员实践、国籍、语言和工作组织方面的变化对其加以更新。

their equipment, as well as changes in manning practices, nationality, language and the organization of work on board ships.

2. There should be continuous occupational safety and health protection and accident prevention publicity. Such publicity might take the following forms:

(a) educational audiovisual material, such as films, for use in vocational training centres for seafarers and where possible shown on board ships;

(b) display of posters on board ships;

(c) inclusion in periodicals read by seafarers of articles on the hazards of maritime employment and on occupational safety and health protection and accident prevention measures; and

(d) special campaigns using various publicity media to instruct seafarers, including campaigns on safe working practices.

3. The publicity referred to in paragraph 2 of this Guideline should take account of the different nationalities, languages and cultures of seafarers on board ships.

Guideline B4.3.10—Safety and health education of young seafarers

1. Safety and health regulations should refer to any general provisions on medical examinations before and during employment and on the prevention of accidents and the protection of health in employment, which may be applicable to the work of seafarers. Such regulations should specify measures which will minimize occupational dangers to young seafarers in the course of their duties.

2. Except where a young seafarer is recognized as fully qualified in a pertinent skill by the competent authority, the regulations

2. 对职业安全和健康保护及事故预防的宣传应持续不断。宣传可采取如下形式：

(a) 在海员职业培训中心内使用的以及，可能时，在船上播放的诸如电影等教育性视听材料；

(b) 在船上张贴宣传画；

(c) 在海员阅读的期刊上登载关于海上就业中的危害以及关于职业安全和健康保护及事故预防措施的文章；以及

(d) 利用各种宣传媒体来指导海员的专题活动，包括有关安全工作实践的活动。

3. 本导则第2款所述的宣传应考虑到船上海员的不同国籍、语言和文化。

导则 B4.3.10—未成年海员的安全和健康教育

1. 安全和健康的条例应参照对就业之前和期间体检的以及对就业中事故预防和健康保护的，可能适用于海员工作的任何一般性规定。这些条例应具体规定尽量减少未成年海员在履行职责过程中的职业危害的措施。

2. 除非未成年海员经主管当局认可完全具备相关技能的资格，否则，条例应做出具体规定，限制未成年海员在没有适当监督和指导的情况下从事存在特殊事故风险或对其健康或体格发育有不利影响风险的，或要求具有一定程度的成熟度、经验或技能的某些类型的工作。在确定该条例要限制的工作类型时，主管当局可特别考虑到涉及以下方面的工作：

should specify restrictions on young seafarers undertaking, without appropriate supervision and instruction, certain types of work presenting special risk of accident or of detrimental effect on their health or physical development, or requiring a particular degree of maturity, experience or skill. In determining the types of work to be restricted by the regulations, the competent authority might consider in particular work involving:

(a) the lifting, moving or carrying of heavy loads or objects;

(b) entry into boilers, tanks and cofferdams;

(c) exposure to harmful noise and vibration levels;

(d) operating hoisting and other power machinery and tools, or acting as signallers to operators of such equipment;

(e) handling mooring or tow lines or anchoring equipment;

(f) rigging;

(g) work aloft or on deck in heavy weather;

(h) nightwatch duties;

(i) servicing of electrical equipment;

(j) exposure to potentially harmful materials, or harmful physical agents such as dangerous or toxic substances and ionizing radiations;

(k) the cleaning of catering machinery; and

(l) the handling or taking charge of ships' boats.

3. Practical measures should be taken by the competent authority or through the appropriate machinery to bring to the attention of young seafarers information concerning the prevention of accidents and the protection of their health on board ships. Such measures could include adequate instruction in courses, official accident pre-

(a) 搬起、挪动或运送重荷或重物；

(b) 进入锅炉、液舱和隔离舱；

(c) 接触有害水平的噪声和振动；

(d) 操作起重或其他动力机械和工具，或充任此类设备操作人员的信号员；

(e) 操作系泊缆或拖缆或锚泊设备；

(f) 索具作业；

(g) 高空作业或恶劣天气中甲板作业；

(h) 夜间值班职责；

(i) 电气设备维修；

(j) 接触有潜在危害的物质，或诸如危险或有毒物质及电离辐射等有害的物理因素[1]；

(k) 清洗餐饮机械；以及

(l) 操作或掌管船上小艇。

3. 应由主管当局或通过适当机制采取切实措施，使未成年海员注意到关于船上防止事故和保护其健康的信息。这些措施可包括适当的课程讲授、针对未成年人的官方事故预防宣传以及对未成年海员的专业指导和监督。

---

[1] 其英文为 physical agents，指噪声、高温、振动、微波、紫外辐射等对身体健康有害的物理现象。我国制定有《物理因素作业人员健康监护》，针对这些有害现象规定了保护措施。——校译者注

vention publicity intended for young persons and professional instruction and supervision of young seafarers.

4. Education and training of young seafarers both ashore and on board ships should include guidance on the detrimental effects on their health and well-being of the abuse of alcohol and drugs and other potentially harmful substances, and the risk and concerns relating to HIV/AIDS and of other health risk related activities.

Guideline B4.3.11—International cooperation

1. Members, with the assistance as appropriate of intergovernmental and other international organizations, should endeavour, in cooperation with each other, to achieve the greatest possible uniformity of action for the promotion of occupational safety and health protection and prevention of accidents.

2. In developing programmes for promoting occupational safety and health protection and prevention of accidents under Standard A4.3, each Member should have due regard to relevant codes of practice published by the International Labour Organization and the appropriate standards of international organizations.

3. Members should have regard to the need for international cooperation in the continuous promotion of activity related to occupational safety and health protection and prevention of occupational accidents. Such cooperation might take the form of:

(a) bilateral or multilateral arrangements for uniformity in occupational safety and health protection and accident prevention standards and safeguards;

(b) exchange of information on particular hazards affecting seafarers and on means of promoting occupational safety and health pro-

4. 在岸上和船上对未成年海员的教育和培训应包括，滥用酒精和药物及其他潜在有害的物质、相关于艾滋病毒/艾滋病的风险和担忧以及其他与健康风险有关的活动，对其健康和幸福的危害作用的指导。

导则 B4.3.11—国际合作

1. 视情况在政府间和其他国际组织的帮助下，成员国应相互合作，为促进职业安全和健康保护及事故预防，努力采取尽最大可能的统一行动。

2. 在根据标准 A4.3 制订促进职业安全和健康保护及事故预防的计划时，各成员国应充分注意到国际劳工组织出版的相关实务守则和国际组织的相应标准。

3. 成员国应注意到在不断促进与职业安全和健康保护及职业事故预防有关的活动方面进行国际合作的必要性。此类合作可采取以下形式：

(a) 统一在职业安全和健康保护及事故预防的标准和保障方面的双边或多边安排；

(b) 交流关于影响海员的特殊风险和关于促进职业安全和健康保护及事故预防的方法的信息；

tection and preventing accidents;

(c) assistance in testing of equipment and inspection according to the national regulations of the flag State;

(d) collaboration in the preparation and dissemination of occupational safety and health protection and accident prevention provisions, rules or manuals;

(e) collaboration in the production and use of training aids; and

(f) joint facilities for, or mutual assistance in, the training of seafarers in occupational safety and health protection, accident prevention and safe working practices.

Regulation 4.4—Access to shore-based welfare facilities

Purpose: To ensure that seafarers working on board a ship have access to shore-based facilities and services to secure their health and well-being

1. Each Member shall ensure that shore-based welfare facilities, where they exist, are easily accessible. The Member shall also promote the development of welfare facilities, such as those listed in the Code, in designated ports to provide seafarers on ships that are in its ports with access to adequate welfare facilities and services.

2. The responsibilities of each Member with respect to shore-based facilities, such as welfare, cultural, recreational and information facilities and services, are set out in the Code.

(c) 根据船旗国的国内条例，在设备测试以及检查方面提供帮助；

(d) 在编制和传播职业安全和健康保护及事故预防的规定、规章或手册方面开展合作；

(e) 在培训教具的制作和使用方面开展合作；以及

(f) 在对海员进行职业安全和健康保护、事故预防和安全工作实践的培训方面，共享设施或相互帮助。

规则 4.4—获得使用岸上福利设施

目的：确保在船上工作的海员能使用岸上设施和服务，以保障其健康和幸福

1. 各成员国须确保易于获得使用岸上福利设施，如其存在。成员国还须促进在指定的港口发展如守则中所列的福利设施，为在其港口的船舶上的海员提供充分的福利设施与服务。

2. 各成员国关于诸如福利、文化、娱乐及信息设施和服务等岸上设施的责任，在守则中规定。

Standard A4.4—Access to shore-based welfare facilities

1. Each Member shall require, where welfare facilities exist on its territory, that they are available for the use of all seafarers, irrespective of nationality, race, colour, sex, religion, political opinion or social origin and irrespective of the flag State of the ship on which they are employed or engaged or work.

2. Each Member shall promote the development of welfare facilities in appropriate ports of the country and determine, after consultation with the shipowners' and seafarers' organizations concerned, which ports are to be regarded as appropriate.

3. Each Member shall encourage the establishment of welfare boards which shall regularly review welfare facilities and services to ensure that they are appropriate in the light of changes in the needs of seafarers resulting from technical, operational and other developments in the shipping industry.

Guideline B4.4—Access to shore-based welfare facilities

Guideline B4.4.1—Responsibilities of Members

1. Each Member should:

(a) take measures to ensure that adequate welfare facilities and services are provided for seafarers in designated ports of call and that adequate protection is provided to seafarers in the exercise of their profession; and

(b) take into account, in the implementation of these measures, the special needs of seafarers, especially when in foreign countries

标准 A4.4—获得使用岸上福利设施

1. 各成员国须要求，如果在其领土内存在福利设施，将这些设施提供给所有海员使用，无论其国籍、种族、肤色、性别、宗教、政治见解或社会出身，也无论他们受雇或受聘或工作的船舶的船旗国。

2. 各成员国须促进在该国适当的港口发展福利设施，并在与有关船东组织和海员组织协商后，确定哪些港口要被视为适当。

3. 各成员国须鼓励设立福利委员会，该委员会须定期审查福利设施与服务，以确保其顺应因航运业技术、运营和其他方面的发展所带来的海员需求的改变。

导则 B4.4—获得使用岸上福利设施

导则 B4.4.1—成员国的责任

1. 各成员国应：

(a) 采取措施确保在指定的停靠港口向海员提供充分的福利设施与服务，并对从事其职业的海员提供充分的保护；以及

(b) 在实施这些措施时，考虑海员在其安全、健康和业余活动方面的特殊需要，特别是在外国和进入战区时。

and when entering war zones, in respect of their safety, health and spare-time activities.

2. Arrangements for the supervision of welfare facilities and services should include participation by representative shipowners' and seafarers' organizations concerned.

3. Each Member should take measures designed to expedite the free circulation among ships, central supply agencies and welfare establishments of welfare materials such as films, books, newspapers and sports equipment for use by seafarers on board their ships and in welfare centres ashore.

4. Members should cooperate with one another in promoting the welfare of seafarers at sea and in port. Such cooperation should include the following:

(a) consultations among competent authorities aimed at the provision and improvement of seafarers' welfare facilities and services, both in port and on board ships;

(b) agreements on the pooling of resources and the joint provision of welfare facilities in major ports so as to avoid unnecessary duplication;

(c) organization of international sports competitions and encouragement of the participation of seafarers in sports activities; and

(d) organization of international seminars on the subject of welfare of seafarers at sea and in port.

Guideline B4.4.2—Welfare facilities and services in ports

1. Each Member should provide or ensure the provision of such welfare facilities and services as may be required, in appropriate ports of the country.

2. 对福利设施与服务的监督安排应包括有代表性的有关船东组织和海员组织的参与。

3. 各成员国应采取措施，意在加速福利材料在船舶、中央供应机构和福利机构之间的自由周转，例如影片、图书、报纸和体育器材，供海员在其船舶上和岸上福利中心使用。

4. 成员国应相互合作，促进海员在海上和港口的福利。这种合作应包括以下内容：

(a) 为提供和改进海员在港口和船上的福利设施与服务，在主管当局之间进行协商；

(b) 就集中资源及在主要港口联合提供福利设施达成协议，以避免不必要的重复；

(c) 组织国际体育竞赛，并鼓励海员参加体育活动；以及

(d) 组织以海员在海上和港口的福利为主题的国际研讨会。

导则 B4.4.2—港口的福利设施与服务

1. 各成员国应在其国内的适当港口提供或确保提供可能要求的福利设施与服务。

2. Welfare facilities and services should be provided, in accordance with national conditions and practice, by one or more of the following:

(a) public authorities;

(b) shipowners' and seafarers' organizations concerned under collective agreements or other agreed arrangements; and

(c) voluntary organizations.

3. Necessary welfare and recreational facilities should be established or developed in ports. These should include:

(a) meeting and recreation rooms as required;

(b) facilities for sports and outdoor facilities, including competitions;

(c) educational facilities; and

(d) where appropriate, facilities for religious observances and for personal counselling.

4. These facilities may be provided by making available to seafarers in accordance with their needs facilities designed for more general use.

5. Where large numbers of seafarers of different nationalities require facilities such as hotels, clubs and sports facilities in a particular port, the competent authorities or bodies of the countries of origin of the seafarers and of the flag States, as well as the international associations concerned, should consult and cooperate with the competent authorities and bodies of the country in which the port is situated and with one another, with a view to the pooling of resources and to avoiding unnecessary duplication.

2. 应根据国内条件和惯例，由下列一方或几方提供福利设施与服务：

(a) 公共当局；

(b) 遵守集体协议或其他约定安排的有关船东组织和海员组织；以及

(c) 志愿组织。

3. 应在港口建立或发展必要的福利和娱乐设施。这些设施应包括：

(a) 要求的会议室和娱乐室；

(b) 体育设施和户外设施，包括比赛设施；

(c) 教育设施；以及

(d) 适当时，举行宗教仪式和个人咨询的设施。

4. 提供这些设施的方式，可以是按海员的需要向其提供设计成更针对一般性用途的设施。

5. 如果在某特定港口有人数众多的不同国籍海员需要诸如旅馆、俱乐部和体育设施等设施，海员来源国和船旗国的主管当局或机构以及有关国际性协会应与该港口所在国的主管当局和机构协商与合作，并进行相互间的协商与合作，旨在集中资源并避免不必要的重复。

6. Hotels or hostels suitable for seafarers should be available where there is need for them. They should provide facilities equal to those found in a good-class hotel, and should wherever possible be located in good surroundings away from the immediate vicinity of the docks. Such hotels or hostels should be properly supervised, the prices charged should be reasonable in amount and, where necessary and possible, provision should be made for accommodating seafarers' families.

7. These accommodation facilities should be open to all seafarers, irrespective of nationality, race, colour, sex, religion, political opinion or social origin and irrespective of the flag State of the ship on which they are employed or engaged or work. Without in any way infringing this principle, it may be necessary in certain ports to provide several types of facilities, comparable in standard but adapted to the customs and needs of different groups of seafarers.

8. Measures should be taken to ensure that, as necessary, technically competent persons are employed full time in the operation of seafarers' welfare facilities and services, in addition to any voluntary workers.

Guideline B4.4.3—Welfare boards

1. Welfare boards should be established, at the port, regional and national levels, as appropriate. Their functions should include:

(a) keeping under review the adequacy of existing welfare facilities and monitoring the need for the provision of additional facilities or the withdrawal of underutilized facilities; and

(b) assisting and advising those responsible for providing welfare facilities and ensuring coordination between them.

6. 在海员需要的地方，应有适合于他们的旅馆或招待所。这些旅馆或招待所应提供相当于上档次的饭店中具有的设施并，凡可能时，应位于周边环境良好、远离紧靠码头的区域。这些旅馆或招待所应受到适当的监督，收费价格应合理，并在需要和可能时，应为海员的家人提供住宿。

7. 这些住宿设施应向所有海员开放，无论其国籍、种族、肤色、性别、宗教、政治观点或社会出身，也不论他们受雇或受聘或工作的船舶的船旗国。在绝不违背此原则的前提下，可能有必要在某些港口提供几种类型的设施，标准相当但适合于不同海员群体的习惯和需要。

8. 除任何志愿工作者外，还应采取措施保证按照需要雇用全职的合格技术人员经营海员的福利设施与服务。

导则 B4.4.3—福利委员会

1. 应视情况在港口、地区和国家层面上成立福利委员会。其职能应包括：

(a) 持续审查现有福利设施是否充足，并监控有无需要提供更多设施或撤销利用不足的设施；以及

(b) 帮助提供福利设施的主管人员，并向他们提出建议，保证他们之间的协调。

2. Welfare boards should include among their members representatives of shipowners' and seafarers' organizations, the competent authorities and, where appropriate, voluntary organizations and social bodies.

3. As appropriate, consuls of maritime States and local representatives of foreign welfare organizations should, in accordance with national laws and regulations, be associated with the work of port, regional and national welfare boards.

Guideline B4.4.4—Financing of welfare facilities

1. In accordance with national conditions and practice, financial support for port welfare facilities should be made available through one or more of the following:

(a) grants from public funds;

(b) levies or other special dues from shipping sources;

(c) voluntary contributions from shipowners, seafarers, or their organizations; and

(d) voluntary contributions from other sources.

2. Where welfare taxes, levies and special dues are imposed, they should be used only for the purposes for which they are raised.

Guideline B4.4.5—Dissemination of information and facilitation measures

1. Information should be disseminated among seafarers concerning facilities open to the general public in ports of call, particularly transport, welfare, entertainment and educational facilities and places of worship, as well as facilities provided specifically for seafarers.

2. 福利委员会的成员中应包括船东组织和海员组织的代表、主管当局的代表以及在适当时，志愿组织和社会团体的代表。

3. 在适当时，应根据国内法律和条例使海运国家的领事和外国福利组织的当地代表参与港口、地区和国家福利委员会的工作。

导则 B4.4.4—福利设施的资金筹集

1. 根据国内条件和惯例，应通过以下一种或几种途径为港口福利设施提供财政支持：

(a) 公共基金拨款；

(b) 对航运资源的征税或其他专项收费；

(c) 船东、海员或其组织的自愿捐款；以及

(d) 其他来源的自愿捐款。

2. 如果征收福利税、税费和专项费，它们应仅用于其筹款之初衷。

导则 B4.4.5—信息传播和便利措施

1. 应在海员中传播有关停靠港内向普通公众开放的设施的信息，特别是有关交通、福利、娱乐与教育设施和礼拜场所，以及专门为海员提供的设施的信息。

2. Adequate means of transport at moderate prices should be available at any reasonable time in order to enable seafarers to reach urban areas from convenient locations in the port.

3. All suitable measures should be taken by the competent authorities to make known to shipowners and to seafarers entering port any special laws and customs, the contravention of which may jeopardize their freedom.

4. Port areas and access roads should be provided by the competent authorities with adequate lighting and signposting and regular patrols for the protection of seafarers.

Guideline B4.4.6—Seafarers in a foreign port

1. For the protection of seafarers in foreign ports, measures should be taken to facilitate:

(a) access to consuls of their State of nationality or State of residence; and

(b) effective cooperation between consuls and the local or national authorities.

2. Seafarers who are detained in a foreign port should be dealt with promptly under due process of law and with appropriate consular protection.

3. Whenever a seafarer is detained for any reason in the territory of a Member, the competent authority should, if the seafarer so requests, immediately inform the flag State and the State of nationality of the seafarer. The competent authority should promptly inform the seafarer of the right to make such a request. The State of nationality of the seafarer should promptly notify the seafarer's next of kin.

2. 为使海员能从港口内方便地点到达市区，应在任何合理时间内提供价格适中的充足交通工具。

3. 主管当局应采取所有适当措施使船东和进入港口的海员知晓那些倘若违反就可能危及其自由的任何特殊法律和习俗。

4. 主管当局应为港口区域和进出通道提供充分的照明和路标并定时巡逻，以保护海员。

导则 B4.4.6—在外国港口的海员

1. 为保护在外国港口的海员，应采取措施以便利于：

(a) 接触其国籍国或居住国的领事；以及

(b) 领事与地方或国家当局之间的有效合作。

2. 应按照正当的法律程序迅速处理在外国港口被拘禁的海员并给予适当的领事保护。

3. 不论出于任何原因，如果海员在一成员国领土内被拘禁，若该海员提出要求，主管当局应立即通知船旗国和海员的国籍国。主管当局应立即告知海员有提出此种要求的权利。海员的国籍国应立即通知海员的最近亲属。只要海员被拘禁，主管当局应允许这些国家的领事官员立即会见该海员，并在此后定期探视该海员。

The competent authority should allow consular officers of these States immediate access to the seafarer and regular visits thereafter so long as the seafarer is detained.

4. Each Member should take measures, whenever necessary, to ensure the safety of seafarers from aggression and other unlawful acts while ships are in their territorial waters and especially in approaches to ports.

5. Every effort should be made by those responsible in port and on board a ship to facilitate shore leave for seafarers as soon as possible after a ship's arrival in port.

Regulation 4.5—Social security

Purpose: To ensure that measures are taken with a view to providing seafarers with access to social security protection

1. Each Member shall ensure that all seafarers and, to the extent provided for in its national law, their dependants have access to social security protection in accordance with the Code without prejudice however to any more favourable conditions referred to in paragraph 8 of article 19 of the Constitution.

2. Each Member undertakes to take steps, according to its national circumstances, individually and through international cooperation, to achieve progressively comprehensive social security protection for seafarers.

3. Each Member shall ensure that seafarers who are subject to its social security legislation, and, to the extent provided for in its national law, their dependants, are entitled to benefit from social security protection no less favourable than that enjoyed by shoreworkers.

4. 当船舶位于一成员国的领水，特别是进入港口的航道时，凡有必要，该成员国应采取措施保证海员的安全，免受侵袭和其他非法行为。

5. 港口和船上的负责人员应尽一切努力，在船舶抵达港口后，方便海员尽可能及早上岸休假。

规则 4.5—社会保障

目的：确保采取措施向海员提供社会保障的保护

1. 各成员国须确保所有海员以及在其国内法律规定的范围内，其受扶养人，能够依据守则获得社会保障的保护，但不得妨碍《章程》第十九条第 8 款中所述的任何更优厚条件。

2. 各成员国承诺根据其国内情况采取步骤，独自或通过国际合作，逐步为海员实现全面的社会保障的保护。

3. 各成员国须确保受到其社会保障立法管辖的海员，以及在其国内法律规定的范围内，其受扶养人，有权享受不低于岸上工人所享受的社会保障的保护。

Standard A4.5—Social security

1. The branches to be considered with a view to achieving progressively comprehensive social security protection under Regulation 4.5 are: medical care, sickness benefit, unemployment benefit, old-age benefit, employment injury benefit, family benefit, maternity benefit, invalidity benefit and survivors' benefit, complementing the protection provided for under Regulations 4.1, on medical care, and 4.2, on shipowners' liability, and under other titles of this Convention.

2. At the time of ratification, the protection to be provided by each Member in accordance with Regulation 4.5, paragraph 1, shall include at least three of the nine branches listed in paragraph 1 of this Standard.

3. Each Member shall take steps according to its national circumstances to provide the complementary social security protection referred to in paragraph 1 of this Standard to all seafarers ordinarily resident in its territory. This responsibility could be satisfied, for example, through appropriate bilateral or multilateral agreements or contribution-based systems. The resulting protection shall be no less favourable than that enjoyed by shoreworkers resident in their territory.

4. Notwithstanding the attribution of responsibilities in paragraph 3 of this Standard, Members may determine, through bilateral and multilateral agreements and through provisions adopted in the framework of regional economic integration organizations, other rules concerning the social security legislation to which seafarers are subject.

标准 A4.5—社会保障

1. 为逐步实现规则 4.5 下的全面社会保障保护而将要考虑的分项是:医护、疾病津贴、失业津贴、老年津贴、工伤津贴、家庭津贴、生育津贴、病残津贴和遗属津贴,补充规则 4.1 下对医护规定的、规则 4.2 下对船东责任规定的保护以及本公约其他标题下规定的保护。

2. 在批准本公约时,各成员国根据规则 4.5 第 1 款所要提供的保护须包括本标准第 1 款所列九个分项中的至少三个。

3. 各成员国须根据其国内情况采取步骤,向通常在其领土内居住的所有海员提供本标准第 1 款所述的补充社会保障的保护。例如,此责任可通过适当的双边或多边协定或基于缴费的制度来履行。因而获得的保护须不低于居住在其领土内的岸上工人所享受的保护。

4. 尽管有本标准第 3 款中的责任归属,成员国可以通过双边和多边协定以及通过区域经济一体化组织框架中通过的规定,来决定关于管辖海员社会保障立法的其他规章。

5. Each Member's responsibilities with respect to seafarers on ships that fly its flag shall include those provided for by Regulations 4.1 and 4.2 and the related provisions of the Code, as well as those that are inherent in its general obligations under international law.

6. Each Member shall give consideration to the various ways in which comparable benefits will, in accordance with national law and practice, be provided to seafarers in the absence of adequate coverage in the branches referred to in paragraph 1 of this Standard.

7. The protection under Regulation 4.5, paragraph 1, may, as appropriate, be contained in laws or regulations, in private schemes or in collective bargaining agreements or in a combination of these.

8. To the extent consistent with their national law and practice, Members shall cooperate, through bilateral or multilateral agreements or other arrangements, to ensure the maintenance of social security rights, provided through contributory or non-contributory schemes, which have been acquired, or are in the course of acquisition, by all seafarers regardless of residence.

9. Each Member shall establish fair and effective procedures for the settlement of disputes.

10. Each Member shall at the time of ratification specify the branches for which protection is provided in accordance with paragraph 2 of this Standard. It shall subsequently notify the Director-General of the International Labour Office when it provides social security protection in respect of one or more other branches stated in paragraph 1 of this Standard. The Director-General shall maintain a register of this information and shall make it available to all interested parties.

5. 各成员国对悬挂其旗帜船舶上的海员的责任须包括规则 4.1 和规则 4.2 及守则相关条款所规定的责任，及其在国际法之下的一般义务中固有的责任。

6. 各成员国须考虑，在缺少本标准第 1 款所述分项的充分覆盖时，将根据国内法律和惯例向海员提供类似福利的各种方法。

7. 规则 4.5 第 1 款下的保护可视情况包含在法律或条例、私立机制或集体谈判协议中或这些情况的组合中。

8. 在与国内法律和惯例一致的范围内，成员国须通过双边或多边协定或其他安排进行合作，保证维持所有海员已经获得或正在获得过程中的通过缴费或不缴费的机制所提供的社会保障权利，无论其居住在何地。

9. 各成员国须建立公平而有效的争议解决程序。

10. 各成员国在批准公约时须具体规定其根据本标准第 2 款所提供保护的分项。在其提供有关本标准第 1 款中所述的一种或几种其他分项的社会保障保护时须随即通知国际劳工局局长。局长须保持一份此信息的记录簿，并须备所有利益各方索取。

11. The reports to the International Labour Office pursuant to article 22 of the Constitution, shall also include information regarding steps taken in accordance with Regulation 4. 5, paragraph 2, to extend protection to other branches.

Guideline B4. 5—Social security

1. The protection to be provided at the time of ratification in accordance with Standard A4. 5, paragraph 2, should at least include the branches of medical care, sickness benefit and employment injury benefit.

2. In the circumstances referred to in Standard A4. 5, paragraph 6, comparable benefits may be provided through insurance, bilateral and multilateral agreements or other effective means, taking into consideration the provisions of relevant collective bargaining agreements. Where such measures are adopted, seafarers covered by such measures should be advised of the means by which the various branches of social security protection will be provided.

3. Where seafarers are subject to more than one national legislation covering social security, the Members concerned should cooperate in order to determine by mutual agreement which legislation is to apply, taking into account such factors as the type and level of protection under the respective legislations which is more favourable to the seafarer concerned as well as the seafarer's preference.

4. The procedures to be established under Standard A4. 5, paragraph 9, should be designed to cover all disputes relevant to the claims of the seafarers concerned, irrespective of the manner in which the coverage is provided.

11. 按照《章程》第二十二条向国际劳工局提交的报告还须包括关于根据规则 4.5 第 2 款采取步骤将保护扩展到其他分项的信息。

导则 B4.5—社会保障

1. 在批准公约时根据标准 A4.5 第 2 款所要提供的保护应至少包括医护、疾病津贴和工伤津贴分项。

2. 在标准 A4.5 第 6 款所述的情况下,考虑到有关集体谈判协议的规定,可以通过保险、双边和多边协议或其他有效方式来提供类似的津贴。如果采取了此种措施,应将各种社会保障保护分项的提供方式告知被此种措施所覆盖的海员。

3. 如果海员受到不止一个涉及社会保障的国内立法的管辖,有关成员国应开展合作以便通过相互间的协议确定适用哪一国立法,并考虑到在各自立法中对相关海员更加优惠的保护种类和水平等因素以及海员的选择。

4. 根据标准 A4.5 第 9 款将要建立的程序应设计成覆盖与有关海员的索赔请求相关的所有争议,无论这种覆盖以何种方式提供。

5. Each Member which has national seafarers, non-national seafarers or both serving on ships that fly its flag should provide the social security protection in the Convention as applicable, and should periodically review the branches of social security protection in Standard A4. 5, paragraph 1, with a view to identifying any additional branches appropriate for the seafarers concerned.

6. The seafarers' employment agreement should identify the means by which the various branches of social security protection will be provided to the seafarer by the shipowner as well as any other relevant information at the disposal of the shipowner, such as statutory deductions from the seafarers' wages and shipowners' contributions which may be made in accordance with the requirements of identified authorized bodies pursuant to relevant national social security schemes.

7. The Member whose flag the ship flies should, in effectively exercising its jurisdiction over social matters, satisfy itself that the shipowners' responsibilities concerning social security protection are met, including making the required contributions to social security schemes.

5. 有本国海员和(或)非本国海员在悬挂其旗帜的船舶上服务的各成员国,应提供公约中适用的社会保障保护,并应定期审查标准 A4.5 第 1 款中的社会保障保护分项,旨在确定适合于有关海员的任何附加分项。

6. 海员就业协议应确认将由船东向海员提供各种分项的社会保障保护的方式以及由船东支配的任何其他相关信息,例如根据有关的国内社会保障制度按公认的授权机构的要求而可能做出的对海员工资的法定扣减以及船东缴费的情况。

7. 船舶所悬旗帜之成员国在对社会事项有效行使其管辖时,应自行确认船东履行了其关于社会保障保护的责任,包括向社会保障制度支付了所要求的缴费。

TITLE 5. COMPLIANCE AND ENFORCEMENT

1. The Regulations in this Title specify each Member's responsibility to fully implement and enforce the principles and rights set out in the Articles of this Convention as well as the particular obligations provided for under its Titles 1, 2, 3 and 4.

2. Paragraphs 3 and 4 of Article VI, which permit the implementation of Part A of the Code through substantially equivalent provisions, do not apply to Part A of the Code in this Title.

3. In accordance with paragraph 2 of Article VI, each Member shall implement its responsibilities under the Regulations in the manner set out in the corresponding Standards of Part A of the Code, giving due consideration to the corresponding Guidelines in Part B of the Code.

4. The provisions of this Title shall be implemented bearing in mind that seafarers and shipowners, like all other persons, are equal before the law and are entitled to the equal protection of the law and shall not be subject to discrimination in their access to courts, tribunals or other dispute resolution mechanisms. The provisions of this Title do not determine legal jurisdiction or a legal venue.

Regulation 5.1—Flag State responsibilities

Purpose: To ensure that each Member implements its responsibilities under this Convention with respect to ships that fly its flag

标题五　符合与执行

1. 本标题中的规则具体规定了各成员国充分实施和执行本公约正文条款所规定之原则和权利以及标题一、二、三和四之下所规定的具体义务的责任。

2. 允许通过实质上等效的规定来实施守则A部分的第六条第3和4款，不适用于本标题中的守则A部分。

3. 根据第六条第2款，各成员国须以守则A部分的相应标准所规定的方式实施其在规则下的责任，并充分考虑到守则B部分的相应导则。

4. 实施本标题的规定时须切记，同所有其他人一样，海员和船东在法律面前平等，有权受到法律的同等保护，不得在诉诸法院、裁判庭或其他争议解决机制方面受到歧视。本标题的规定并不决定法律管辖权或管辖地。

规则5.1—船旗国责任

目的：确保各成员国就悬挂其旗帜的船舶履行其在本公约下的责任

Regulation 5. 1. 1—General principles

1. Each Member is responsible for ensuring implementation of its obligations under this Convention on ships that fly its flag.

2. Each Member shall establish an effective system for the inspection and certification of maritime labour conditions, in accordance with Regulations 5. 1. 3 and 5. 1. 4 ensuring that the working and living conditions for seafarers on ships that fly its flag meet, and continue to meet, the standards in this Convention.

3. In establishing an effective system for the inspection and certification of maritime labour conditions, a Member may, where appropriate, authorize public institutions or other organizations (including those of another Member, if the latter agrees) which it recognizes as competent and independent to carry out inspections or to issue certificates or to do both. In all cases, the Member shall remain fully responsible for the inspection and certification of the working and living conditions of the seafarers concerned on ships that fly its flag.

4. A maritime labour certificate, complemented by a declaration of maritime labour compliance, shall constitute prima facie evidence that the ship has been duly inspected by the Member whose flag it flies and that the requirements of this Convention relating to working and living conditions of the seafarers have been met to the extent so certified.

5. Information about the system referred to in paragraph 2 of this Regulation, including the method used for assessing its effectiveness, shall be included in the Member's reports to the International Labour Office pursuant to article 22 of the Constitution.

规则 5.1.1——一般原则

1．各成员国有责任确保在悬挂其旗帜的船舶上实施其在本公约下的义务。

2．各成员国须根据规则 5.1.3 和 5.1.4 建立一个有效的海事劳工条件检查和发证体系，确保悬挂其旗帜船舶上的海员工作和生活条件符合并持续符合本公约中的标准。

3．在建立有效的海事劳工条件检查和发证体系时，如适宜，成员国可以授权经其认可具备能力和独立性的公共机构或其他组织（包括另一成员国的机构或组织，如果其同意）开展检查和（或）发证。在所有情况下，成员国须仍对悬挂其旗帜船舶上的有关海员工作和生活条件的检查和发证负全部责任。

4．由海事劳工符合声明补充的海事劳工证书，须构成船舶已经过其所悬挂旗帜的成员国的正规检查，且本公约关于海员工作和生活条件的要求已在其所证明的范围内得到满足的初步证据。

5．关于本规则第 2 款所述体系的信息，包括用来评估其有效性的方法的信息，须包括在成员国根据《章程》第二十二条提交给国际劳工局的报告中。

Standard A5.1.1—General principles

1. Each Member shall establish clear objectives and standards covering the administration of its inspection and certification systems, as well as adequate overall procedures for its assessment of the extent to which those objectives and standards are being attained.

2. Each Member shall require all ships that fly its flag to have a copy of this Convention available on board.

Guideline B5.1.1—General principles

1. The competent authority should make appropriate arrangements to promote effective cooperation between public institutions and other organizations, referred to in Regulations 5.1.1 and 5.1.2, concerned with seafarers' shipboard working and living conditions.

2. In order to better ensure cooperation between inspectors and shipowners, seafarers and their respective organizations, and to maintain or improve seafarers' working and living conditions, the competent authority should consult the representatives of such organizations at regular intervals as to the best means of attaining these ends. The manner of such consultation should be determined by the competent authority after consulting with shipowners' and seafarers' organizations.

Regulation 5.1.2—Authorization of recognized organizations

1. The public institutions or other organizations referred to in paragraph 3 of Regulation 5.1.1 ("recognized organizations") shall have been recognized by the competent authority as meeting the requirements in the Code regarding competency and independence. The inspection or certification functions which the recognized organiza-

标准 A5.1.1——一般原则

1. 各成员国须建立覆盖其检查和发证体系管理的明确目标和标准，以及对正在达到这些目标和标准的程度进行评估的适当的全面程序。

2. 各成员国须要求悬挂其旗帜的所有船舶均在船上携带一册本公约。

导则 B5.1.1——一般原则

1. 主管当局应做出适当的安排以促进规则 5.1.1 和 5.1.2 中所述的关注海员船上工作和生活条件的公共机构和其他组织之间的有效合作。

2. 为了更好地确保检查员与船东、海员及其各自组织之间的合作，并且为了保持或改善海员的工作和生活条件，主管当局应定期与这些组织的代表就达到这些目标的最佳途径进行协商。此种协商的方式应由主管当局在与船东组织和海员组织协商后确定。

规则 5.1.2—对认可组织的授权

1. 规则 5.1.1 第 3 款所述的公共机构或其他组织（“认可组织”）须经主管当局认可满足守则关于能力和独立性的要求。认可组织可以被授权实施的检查或发证职能须在守则明确提及由主管当局或认可组织所实施活动的范围之内。

tions may be authorized to carry out shall come within the scope of the activities that are expressly mentioned in the Code as being carried out by the competent authority or a recognized organization.

2. The reports referred to in paragraph 5 of Regulation 5. 1. 1 shall contain information regarding any recognized organization, the extent of authorizations given and the arrangements made by the Member to ensure that the authorized activities are carried out completely and effectively.

Standard A5. 1. 2—Authorization of recognized organizations

1. For the purpose of recognition in accordance with paragraph 1 of Regulation 5. 1. 2, the competent authority shall review the competency and independence of the organization concerned and determine whether the organization has demonstrated, to the extent necessary for carrying out the activities covered by the authorization conferred on it, that the organization:

(a) has the necessary expertise in the relevant aspects of this Convention and an appropriate knowledge of ship operations, including the minimum requirements for seafarers to work on a ship, conditions of employment, accommodation, recreational facilities, food and catering, accident prevention, health protection, medical care, welfare and social security protection;

(b) has the ability to maintain and update the expertise of its personnel;

(c) has the necessary knowledge of the requirements of this Convention as well as of applicable national laws and regulations and relevant international instruments; and

(d) is of the appropriate size, structure, experience and capability

2. 规则 5.1.1 第 5 款所述之报告须包含关于任何认可组织、所授权范围和成员国为确保所授权的活动得以完整和有效的实施所做安排的信息。

标准 A5.1.2—对认可组织的授权

1. 为根据规则 5.1.2 第 1 款的认可之目的，主管当局须审查有关组织的能力和独立性并确定该组织在开展对其授权的活动所必要的范围内是否已表明其：

(a) 具备本公约相关方面的必要专门知识和船舶操作的适当知识，包括对海员上船工作的最低要求、就业条件、起居舱室、娱乐设施、食品和膳食服务、事故预防、健康保护、医护、福利和社会保障保护方面的适当知识；

(b) 有能力维持和更新其人员的专门知识；

(c) 具备关于本公约的要求以及适用的国内法律和条例及相关国际文件的必要知识；以及

(d) 具有与其所被授权的类型和程度相称的适当规模、结构、经验和能力。

commensurate with the type and degree of authorization.

2. Any authorizations granted with respect to inspections shall, as a minimum, empower the recognized organization to require the rectification of deficiencies that it identifies in seafarers' working and living conditions and to carry out inspections in this regard at the request of a port State.

3. Each Member shall establish:

(a) a system to ensure the adequacy of work performed by recognized organizations, which includes information on all applicable national laws and regulations and relevant international instruments; and

(b) procedures for communication with and oversight of such organizations.

4. Each Member shall provide the International Labour Office with a current list of any recognized organizations authorized to act on its behalf and it shall keep this list up to date. The list shall specify the functions that the recognized organizations have been authorized to carry out. The Office shall make the list publicly available.

Guideline B5.1.2—Authorization of recognized organizations

1. The organization seeking recognition should demonstrate the technical, administrative and managerial competence and capacity to ensure the provision of timely service of satisfactory quality.

2. In evaluating the capability of an organization, the competent authority should determine whether the organization:

(a) has adequate technical, managerial and support staff;

(b) has sufficient qualified professional staff to provide the required

2. 所准予的关于检查的任何授权，在最低限度上须授权该认可组织要求纠正其发现的海员工作和生活条件方面的缺陷以及在港口国的要求下开展这方面的检查。

3. 各成员国须建立：

(a) 一个确保认可组织所做工作之恰当性的机制，包括关于所有适用的国内法律和条例及相关国际文件的信息；以及

(b) 与此类组织进行交流和对其进行监督的程序。

4. 各成员国须向国际劳工局提供一份授权代表其行事的任何认可组织的当前清单，并须保持对清单的更新。该清单须具体规定已授权认可组织履行的职能。劳工局须将该清单对公众开放。

导则 B5.1.2—对认可组织的授权

1. 寻求认可的组织应表明在技术、行政和管理方面的胜任和能力，确保提供满意质量的及时服务。

2. 在评价某一组织的能力时，主管当局应确定该组织是否：

(a) 具备适当的技术、管理和支持性工作人员；

(b) 具备充足的合格专业人员提供所要求的服务，代表充分的地理覆盖范围；

service, representing an adequate geographical coverage;

(c) has proven ability to provide a timely service of satisfactory quality; and

(d) is independent and accountable in its operations.

3. The competent authority should conclude a written agreement with any organization that it recognizes for purposes of an authorization. The agreement should include the following elements:

(a) scope of application;

(b) purpose;

(c) general conditions;

(d) the execution of functions under authorization;

(e) legal basis of the functions under authorization;

(f) reporting to the competent authority;

(g) specification of the authorization from the competent authority to the recognized organization; and

(h) the competent authority's supervision of activities delegated to the recognized organization.

4. Each Member should require the recognized organizations to develop a system for qualification of staff employed by them as inspectors to ensure the timely updating of their knowledge and expertise.

5. Each Member should require the recognized organizations to maintain records of the services performed by them such that they are able to demonstrate achievement of the required standards in the items covered by the services.

6. In establishing the oversight procedures referred to in Stand-

(c) 已证实有能力提供满意质量的及时服务；以及

(d) 运作独立并对其运作负责。

3. 主管当局应与其为授权之目的所认可的任何组织达成一份书面协议。该协议应包括以下要素：

(a) 适用范围；

(b) 目的；

(c) 一般条件；

(d) 经授权职能的行使；

(e) 经授权职能的法律基础；

(f) 向主管当局报告；

(g) 主管当局向认可组织授权的具体内容；以及

(h) 主管当局对认可组织代为行事活动的监督。

4. 各成员国应要求认可组织为被该组织雇用为检查员的人员的资格制定一项机制，以确保及时更新其知识和专门技能。

5. 各成员国应要求认可组织保持其所做服务的记录，从而使他们能够表明在服务所涉及的项目中达到所要求的标准。

6. 在建立标准 A5.1.2 第 3(b)款所述的监督程序时，各成员国应考虑到在国际海事组织的框架内通过的《对代表主管机关行事的组织授权的导则》。

ard A5. 1. 2, paragraph 3(b), each Member should take into account the *Guidelines for the Authorization of Organizations Acting on Behalf of the Administration*, adopted in the framework of the International Maritime Organization.

Regulation 5. 1. 3—Maritime labour certificate and declaration of maritime labour compliance

1. This Regulation applies to ships of:

(a) 500 gross tonnage or over, engaged in international voyages; and

(b) 500 gross tonnage or over, flying the flag of a Member and operating from a port, or between ports, in another country.

For the purpose of this Regulation, "international voyage" means a voyage from a country to a port outside such a country.

2. This Regulation also applies to any ship that flies the flag of a Member and is not covered by paragraph 1 of this Regulation, at the request of the shipowner to the Member concerned.

3. Each Member shall require ships that fly its flag to carry and maintain a maritime labour certificate certifying that the working and living conditions of seafarers on the ship, including measures for ongoing compliance to be included in the declaration of maritime labour compliance referred to in paragraph 4 of this Regulation, have been inspected and meet the requirements of national laws or regulations or other measures implementing this Convention.

4. Each Member shall require ships that fly its flag to carry and maintain a declaration of maritime labour compliance stating the national requirements implementing this Convention for the working and living conditions for seafarers and setting out the measures

规则5.1.3—海事劳工证书和海事劳工符合声明

1. 本规则适用于：

(a) 从事国际航行的500总吨或以上船舶；以及

(b) 悬挂一成员国的旗帜并从另一国的港口或在其港口之间运营的500总吨或以上船舶。

就本规则而言，“国际航行”系指从一国到该国以外的一个港口的航行。

2. 本规则还适用于悬挂成员国的旗帜但未被本规则第1款所覆盖的任何船舶，如果船东向相关成员国提出了请求。

3. 各成员国须要求悬挂其旗帜的船舶携带和保有一份海事劳工证书，证明该船舶上的海员工作和生活条件，包括本规则第4款所述的海事劳工符合声明中所要包括的持续符合措施，已经过检查并满足国内法律或条例或其他实施本公约之措施的要求。

4. 各成员国须要求悬挂其旗帜的船舶携带和保有一份海事劳工符合声明，陈述在海员的工作和生活条件方面实施本公约的国内要求，并列明船东为确保符合有关船舶上的要求所采取的措施。

adopted by the shipowner to ensure compliance with the requirements on the ship or ships concerned.

5. The maritime labour certificate and the declaration of maritime labour compliance shall conform to the model prescribed by the Code.

6. Where the competent authority of the Member or a recognized organization duly authorized for this purpose has ascertained through inspection that a ship that flies the Member's flag meets or continues to meet the standards of this Convention, it shall issue or renew a maritime labour certificate to that effect and maintain a publicly available record of that certificate.

7. Detailed requirements for the maritime labour certificate and the declaration of maritime labour compliance, including a list of the matters that must be inspected and approved, are set out in Part A of the Code.

Standard A5.1.3—Maritime labour certificate and declaration of maritime labour compliance

1. The maritime labour certificate shall be issued to a ship by the competent authority, or by a recognized organization duly authorized for this purpose, for a period which shall not exceed five years. A list of matters that must be inspected and found to meet national laws and regulations or other measures implementing the requirements of this Convention regarding the working and living conditions of seafarers on ships before a maritime labour certificate can be issued is found in Appendix A5-I.

2. The validity of the maritime labour certificate shall be subject to an intermediate inspection by the competent authority, or by a

5. 海事劳工证书和海事劳工符合声明须与守则所规定的范本相符。

6. 如果成员国主管当局或为此目的正式授权的认可组织通过检查确定,悬挂该成员国旗帜的船舶符合并持续符合本公约的标准,其须就此签发或换新海事劳工证书并保持一份对该证书的公开记录。

7. 海事劳工证书和海事劳工符合声明的详细要求,包括必须检查和核准事项的清单,在守则的A部分中规定。

标准 A5.1.3—海事劳工证书和海事劳工符合声明

1. 海事劳工证书须由主管当局或为此目的而正式授权的认可组织签发给船舶,期限不得超过五年。在可以签发海事劳工证书之前,在船上海员工作和生活条件方面,必须予以检查并表明满足国内法律和条例或其他实施本公约要求之措施的项目清单见附录A5-I。

2. 海事劳工证书的有效性须取决于主管当局或为此目的而正式授权的认可组织所进行的一次中间检查,以确保持续符合实施本公约的国内要求。如果仅开展一次中间检查且证书的有效期为五年,该检查须在证书的第二和第三个周年日之间进行。周年日系指每年对应于海事劳工证书到期日的月份和日期。中间检查的范围和深度须与证书换证检查相同。在中间检查通过后须对证书进行签注。

recognized organization duly authorized for this purpose, to ensure continuing compliance with the national requirements implementing this Convention. If only one intermediate inspection is carried out and the period of validity of the certificate is five years, it shall take place between the second and third anniversary dates of the certificate. Anniversary date means the day and month of each year which will correspond to the date of expiry of the maritime labour certificate. The scope and depth of the intermediate inspection shall be equal to an inspection for renewal of the certificate. The certificate shall be endorsed following satisfactory intermediate inspection.

3. Notwithstanding paragraph 1 of this Standard, when the renewal inspection has been completed within three months before the expiry of the existing maritime labour certificate, the new maritime labour certificate shall be valid from the date of completion of the renewal inspection for a period not exceeding five years from the date of expiry of the existing certificate.

4. When the renewal inspection is completed more than three months before the expiry date of the existing maritime labour certificate, the new maritime labour certificate shall be valid for a period not exceeding five years starting from the date of completion of the renewal inspection.

5. A maritime labour certificate may be issued on an interim basis:

(a) to new ships on delivery;

(b) when a ship changes flag; or

(c) when a shipowner assumes responsibility for the operation of a ship which is new to that shipowner.

3. 尽管有本标准第1款的规定，如果在现有海事劳工证书到期之前三个月内完成了换证检查，新海事劳工证书须从完成换证检查之日起有效，有效期自现有海事劳工证书到期之日起不得超过五年。

4. 如果在现有海事劳工证书到期之前三个月前完成了换证检查，新海事劳工证书的有效期从完成换证检查之日起不得超过五年。

5. 如有以下情形，海事劳工证书可以在临时的基础上签发：

(a) 刚交付的新船；

(b) 当船舶变更船旗时；或

(c) 当船东承担了对其而言为一艘新船的经营责任时。

6. An interim maritime labour certificate may be issued for a period not exceeding six months by the competent authority or a recognized organization duly authorized for this purpose.

7. An interim maritime labour certificate may only be issued following verification that:

(a) the ship has been inspected, as far as reasonable and practicable, for the matters listed in Appendix A5-I, taking into account verification of items under subparagraphs (b), (c) and (d) of this paragraph;

(b) the shipowner has demonstrated to the competent authority or recognized organization that the ship has adequate procedures to comply with this Convention;

(c) the master is familiar with the requirements of this Convention and the responsibilities for implementation; and

(d) relevant information has been submitted to the competent authority or recognized organization to produce a declaration of maritime labour compliance.

8. A full inspection in accordance with paragraph 1 of this Standard shall be carried out prior to expiry of the interim certificate to enable issue of the full-term maritime labour certificate. No further interim certificate may be issued following the initial six months referred to in paragraph 6 of this Standard. A declaration of maritime labour compliance need not be issued for the period of validity of the interim certificate.

9. The maritime labour certificate, the interim maritime labour certificate and the declaration of maritime labour compliance shall be drawn up in the form corresponding to the models given in Appendix

6. 临时海事劳工证书可由主管当局或为此目的而正式授权的认可组织签发，有效期不超过六个月。

7. 只有在核实了以下情况后才可签发临时海事劳工证书：

(a) 考虑到对本款第(b)、(c)和(d)项中项目的核实，尽合理和可行地对船舶进行了附录A5-I所列事项的检查；

(b) 船东已向主管当局或认可组织表明，船舶具备适当程序来符合本公约；

(c) 船长熟悉本公约的要求和实施责任；以及

(d) 有关信息已提交给主管当局或认可组织来制作海事劳工符合声明。

8. 在临时证书到期前，须根据本标准第1款进行全面检查，以便能够签发正式的海事劳工证书。在本标准第6款所述的最初六个月后不得再续发临时证书。在临时证书有效期内不必签发海事劳工符合声明。

9. 海事劳工证书、临时海事劳工证书和海事劳工符合声明的格式须编制成与附录A5-II中所列的范本相符。

A5-II.

10. The declaration of maritime labour compliance shall be attached to the maritime labour certificate. It shall have two parts:

(a) Part I shall be drawn up by the competent authority which shall: (i) identify the list of matters to be inspected in accordance with paragraph 1 of this Standard; (ii) identify the national requirements embodying the relevant provisions of this Convention by providing a reference to the relevant national legal provisions as well as, to the extent necessary, concise information on the main content of the national requirements; (iii) refer to ship-type specific requirements under national legislation; (iv) record any substantially equivalent provisions adopted pursuant to paragraph 3 of Article VI; and (v) clearly indicate any exemption granted by the competent authority as provided in Title 3; and

(b) Part II shall be drawn up by the shipowner and shall identify the measures adopted to ensure ongoing compliance with the national requirements between inspections and the measures proposed to ensure that there is continuous improvement.

The competent authority or recognized organization duly authorized for this purpose shall certify Part II and shall issue the declaration of maritime labour compliance.

11. The results of all subsequent inspections or other verifications carried out with respect to the ship concerned and any significant deficiencies found during any such verification shall be recorded, together with the date when the deficiencies were found to have been remedied. This record, accompanied by an English-language translation where it is not in English, shall, in accordance with national laws or regulations, be inscribed upon or appended to the declaration

10. 海事劳工符合声明须附在海事劳工证书之后。声明须有两个部分：

(a) 第I部分须由主管当局编制，该部分须：(i)明确根据本标准第1款将检查的事项清单；(ii)通过援引有关的国内法律规定来明确那些体现了本公约有关规定的国内要求，以及在必要的范围内明确这些国内要求主要内容的简明信息；(iii)提及国内立法中针对具体船舶类型的要求；(iv)记录任何根据第六条第3款所采用的实质上等效的规定；并且(v)明确指出标题三中规定的由主管当局准许的任何免除；以及

(b) 第II部分须由船东编制并须明确所采取的确保在两次检查之间持续符合国内要求的措施和为确保不断改进而建议的措施。

主管当局或为此目的而正式授权的认可组织须对第II部分予以认证并须签发海事劳工符合声明。

11. 对有关船舶实施的所有后续检查或其他核实的结果以及在任何此种核实过程中发现的重大缺陷都须予以记录，并记录认定该缺陷得以纠正的日期。该记录，如果不是英文则连同英译文一起，须根据国内法律或条例写入或附于海事劳工符合声明，或用一些其他方式提供给海员、船旗国检查员、港口国的授权官员及船东的和海员的代表。

of maritime labour compliance or made available in some other way to seafarers, flag State inspectors, authorized officers in port States and shipowners' and seafarers' representatives.

12. A current valid maritime labour certificate and declaration of maritime labour compliance, accompanied by an English-language translation where it is not in English, shall be carried on the ship and a copy shall be posted in a conspicuous place on board where it is available to the seafarers. A copy shall be made available in accordance with national laws and regulations, upon request, to seafarers, flag State inspectors, authorized officers in port States, and shipowners' and seafarers' representatives.

13. The requirement for an English-language translation in paragraphs 11 and 12 of this Standard does not apply in the case of a ship not engaged in an international voyage.

14. A certificate issued under paragraph 1 or 5 of this Standard shall cease to be valid in any of the following cases:

(a) if the relevant inspections are not completed within the periods specified under paragraph 2 of this Standard;

(b) if the certificate is not endorsed in accordance with paragraph 2 of this Standard;

(c) when a ship changes flag;

(d) when a shipowner ceases to assume the responsibility for the operation of a ship; and

(e) when substantial changes have been made to the structure or equipment covered in Title 3.

15. In the case referred to in paragraph 14(c), (d) or (e) of this Standard, a new certificate shall only be issued when the competent

12. 一份当前有效的海事劳工证书和海事劳工符合声明，在非英语的情况辅以英译文，须随船携带，并须将一份副本张贴在船上海员能够到达的显著位置。如有要求，须根据国内法律和条例向海员、船旗国检查员、港口国授权官员以及船东的和海员的代表提供一份副本。

13. 本标准第 11 和 12 款对英译文的要求不适用于船舶不从事国际航行的情况。

14. 根据本标准第 1 或 5 款签发的证书须在以下任何情况下停止有效：

(a) 如果在本标准第 2 款具体规定的期限内没有完成相关检查；

(b) 如果证书没有根据本标准第 2 款予以签注；

(c) 船舶变更船旗；

(d) 如果船东不再承担船舶的经营责任；以及

(e) 如果对标题三所包括的结构或设备做出了实质性变动。

15. 在本标准第 14(c)、(d)或(e)款所述的情况下，只有在签发新证书的主管当局或认可组织对船舶符合本标准要求的情况完全满意时才须签发新证书。

authority or recognized organization issuing the new certificate is fully satisfied that the ship is in compliance with the requirements of this Standard.

16. A maritime labour certificate shall be withdrawn by the competent authority or the recognized organization duly authorized for this purpose by the flag State, if there is evidence that the ship concerned does not comply with the requirements of this Convention and any required corrective action has not been taken.

17. When considering whether a maritime labour certificate should be withdrawn in accordance with paragraph 16 of this Standard, the competent authority or the recognized organization shall take into account the seriousness or the frequency of the deficiencies.

Guideline B5.1.3—Maritime labour certificate and declaration of maritime labour compliance

1. The statement of national requirements in Part I of the declaration of maritime labour compliance should include or be accompanied by references to the legislative provisions relating to seafarers' working and living conditions in each of the matters listed in Appendix A5-I. Where national legislation precisely follows the requirements stated in this Convention, a reference may be all that is necessary. Where a provision of the Convention is implemented through substantial equivalence as provided under Article VI, paragraph 3, this provision should be identified and a concise explanation should be provided. Where an exemption is granted by the competent authority as provided in Title 3, the particular provision or provisions concerned should be clearly indicated.

16. 如果有证据表明有关船舶不符合本公约的要求且没有采取所要求的任何纠正行动，海事劳工证书须由主管当局或船旗国为此目的而正式授权的认可组织予以撤销。

17. 在考虑是否应根据本标准第16款撤销海事劳工证书时，主管当局或认可组织须考虑到缺陷的严重性或频发程度。

导则 B5.1.3—海事劳工证书和海事劳工符合声明

1. 海事劳工符合声明第Ⅰ部分中对国内要求的陈述应包括或后附对附录A5-Ⅰ中所列各事项中与海员工作和生活条件有关的立法规定的引用。如果国内立法严格遵循了本公约中规定的要求，只需做出必要的提及即可。如果公约的规定是通过第六条第3款规定的实质上等效来实施的，则应明确该规定，并应提供简明的解释。如果主管当局准许了标题三中所规定的免除，则应明确指出有关的具体规定。

2. The measures referred to in Part II of the declaration of maritime labour compliance, drawn up by the shipowner, should, in particular, indicate the occasions on which ongoing compliance with particular national requirements will be verified, the persons responsible for verification, the records to be taken, as well as the procedures to be followed where non-compliance is noted. Part II may take a number of forms. It could make reference to other more comprehensive documentation covering policies and procedures relating to other aspects of the maritime sector, for example documents required by the *International Safety Management (ISM) Code* or the information required by Regulation 5 of the SOLAS Convention, Chapter XI-1 relating to the ship's Continuous Synopsis Record.

3. The measures to ensure ongoing compliance should include general international requirements for the shipowner and master to keep themselves informed of the latest advances in technology and scientific findings concerning workplace design, taking into account the inherent dangers of seafarers' work, and to inform the seafarers' representatives accordingly, thereby guaranteeing a better level of protection of the seafarers' working and living conditions on board.

4. The declaration of maritime labour compliance should, above all, be drafted in clear terms designed to help all persons concerned, such as flag State inspectors, authorized officers in port States and seafarers, to check that the requirements are being properly implemented.

5. An example of the kind of information that might be contained in a declaration of maritime labour compliance is given in Appendix B5-I.

6. When a ship changes flag as referred to in Standard A5. 1. 3,

2. 船东所编制的海事劳工符合声明第Ⅱ部分中所述的措施，应特别指明对持续符合特定的国内要求将进行核实的场合、负责核实的人员、将做出的记录以及发现不符合情况时将遵循的程序。第Ⅱ部分可采用多种格式。它可以提及其他涵盖与海运行业其他方面有关的政策和程序的更全面性的文件，例如《国际安全管理(ISM)规则》所要求的文件或《SOLAS公约》第XI-1章第5条关于船舶“连续概要记录”所要求的信息。

3. 确保持续符合的措施应包括对船东和船长使自己不断了解关于工作场所设计的科技成果最新进展的一般性国际要求，并考虑到海员工作固有的危险，并相应地告知海员代表，从而保证船上海员工作和生活条件的更好保护水平。

4. 首要的是，海事劳工符合声明的编写应用词明确，意在帮助所有相关人员，如船旗国检查员、港口国的授权官员和海员，来核查各项要求正在得到妥善实施。

5. 附录B5-I给出了一份海事劳工符合声明中可能载明的信息种类的范例。

6. 如果船舶按标准A5.1.3第14(c)款所述变更了船旗，并且两个有关国家均批准了本公约，船舶原先有权悬挂其旗帜的成员国应尽快将变更船旗前该船舶所携带的海事劳工证书和海事劳工符合声明的副本以及，如适用，相关的检查报告的副本转给另一成员国主管当局，如果该主管当局在变更船旗发生后三个月内提出了此要求。

paragraph 14(c), and where both States concerned have ratified this Convention, the Member whose flag the ship was formerly entitled to fly should, as soon as possible, transmit to the competent authority of the other Member copies of the maritime labour certificate and the declaration of maritime labour compliance carried by the ship before the change of flag and, if applicable, copies of the relevant inspection reports if the competent authority so requests within three months after the change of flag has taken place.

Regulation 5.1.4—Inspection and enforcement

1. Each Member shall verify, through an effective and coordinated system of regular inspections, monitoring and other control measures, that ships that fly its flag comply with the requirements of this Convention as implemented in national laws and regulations.

2. Detailed requirements regarding the inspection and enforcement system referred to in paragraph 1 of this Regulation are set out in Part A of the Code.

Standard A5.1.4—Inspection and enforcement

1. Each Member shall maintain a system of inspection of the conditions for seafarers on ships that fly its flag which shall include verification that the measures relating to working and living conditions as set out in the declaration of maritime labour compliance, where applicable, are being followed, and that the requirements of this Convention are met.

2. The competent authority shall appoint a sufficient number of qualified inspectors to fulfil its responsibilities under paragraph 1 of this Standard. Where recognized organizations have been authorized to carry out inspections, the Member shall require that personnel

规则 5.1.4—检查和执行

1. 各成员国须通过一个定期检查、监控和其他控制措施的有效和协调的机制，核实悬挂其旗帜的船舶符合由其国内法律和条例所实施的本公约的要求。

2. 关于本规则第 1 款所述的检查和执行机制的详细要求在守则 A 部分中规定。

标准 A5.1.4—检查和执行

1. 各成员国须维持一个对悬挂其旗帜船舶上的海员所提供条件进行检查的机制，其中须包括核实在适用时海事劳工符合声明中所列的与工作和生活条件有关的措施正在得以遵守，且满足本公约的要求。

2. 主管当局须任命充足数量的合格检查员来履行其在本标准第 1 款下的责任。如果认可组织经授权实施检查，成员国须要求实施检查的人员有资格承担这些职责，并须赋予其行使职责所必要的法定权力。

carrying out the inspection are qualified to undertake these duties and shall provide them with the necessary legal authority to perform their duties.

3. Adequate provision shall be made to ensure that the inspectors have the training, competence, terms of reference, powers, status and independence necessary or desirable so as to enable them to carry out the verification and ensure the compliance referred to in paragraph 1 of this Standard.

4. Inspections shall take place at the intervals required by Standard A5. 1. 3, where applicable. The interval shall in no case exceed three years.

5. If a Member receives a complaint which it does not consider manifestly unfounded or obtains evidence that a ship that flies its flag does not conform to the requirements of this Convention or that there are serious deficiencies in the implementation of the measures set out in the declaration of maritime labour compliance, the Member shall take the steps necessary to investigate the matter and ensure that action is taken to remedy any deficiencies found.

6. Adequate rules shall be provided and effectively enforced by each Member in order to guarantee that inspectors have the status and conditions of service to ensure that they are independent of changes of government and of improper external influences.

7. Inspectors, issued with clear guidelines as to the tasks to be performed and provided with proper credentials, shall be empowered:

(a) to board a ship that flies the Member's flag;

(b) to carry out any examination, test or inquiry which they may

3. 须做出充分的准备确保检查员具备必要或期望的培训、胜任能力、职责范围、权力、身份和独立性，从而使其能够进行核实并确保本标准第1款所述的符合情况。

4. 如适用，检查须按标准 A5.1.3 所要求的间隔进行。在任何情况下该间隔不得超过三年。

5. 如果成员国收到了其认为不是明显无根据的投诉，或者获得了证据，表明一艘悬挂其旗帜的船不符合本公约的要求，或在实施海事劳工符合声明中所列的措施方面有严重缺陷，该成员国须采取必要的步骤对该事项开展调查，并确保采取行动纠正所发现的任何缺陷。

6. 各成员国须制定适当的规章并加以有效执行，以保证检查员具有服务的身份和条件，确保其独立于政府更迭和不当外部影响。

7. 已获得关于所要执行任务的明确导则并持有适当委任证书的检查员须被授权：

(a) 登上悬挂该成员国旗帜的船舶；

(b) 为确定标准正在得到严格遵守，开展其可能认为必要的任何检查、测试或询查；以及

consider necessary in order to satisfy themselves that the standards are being strictly observed; and

(c) to require that any deficiency is remedied and, where they have grounds to believe that deficiencies constitute a serious breach of the requirements of this Convention (including seafarers' rights), or represent a significant danger to seafarers' safety, health or security, to prohibit a ship from leaving port until necessary actions are taken.

8. Any action taken pursuant to paragraph 7(c) of this Standard shall be subject to any right of appeal to a judicial or administrative authority.

9. Inspectors shall have the discretion to give advice instead of instituting or recommending proceedings when there is no clear breach of the requirements of this Convention that endangers the safety, health or security of the seafarers concerned and where there is no prior history of similar breaches.

10. Inspectors shall treat as confidential the source of any grievance or complaint alleging a danger or deficiency in relation to seafarers' working and living conditions or a violation of laws and regulations and give no intimation to the shipowner, the shipowner's representative or the operator of the ship that an inspection was made as a consequence of such a grievance or complaint.

11. Inspectors shall not be entrusted with duties which might, because of their number or nature, interfere with effective inspection or prejudice in any way their authority or impartiality in their relations with shipowners, seafarers or other interested parties. In particular, inspectors shall:

(c) 要求对任何缺陷予以纠正，并且，如果他们有理由相信某些缺陷构成了对本公约要求(包括海员的权利)的严重违反，或对海员的安全、健康或保安构成重大危险，禁止船舶离港，直到采取了必要的行动。

8. 对于根据本标准第7(c)款所采取的任何行动，须有向司法或行政当局申诉的任何权利。

9. 如果没有危及有关海员的安全、健康或保安的明显违反本公约要求的情况，且先前没有类似违反的历史，检查员须有提出劝诫而不提起或不建议正式程序[1]的决定权。

10. 检查员须对指称与海员工作和生活条件有关的危险或缺陷或者指称法律和条例被违反的任何抱怨或投诉来源保密，不向船东、船东代表或船舶经营人暗示进行某检查缘起于此类抱怨或投诉。

11. 不得委托检查员行使因其数量或性质可能会干扰有效检查的职责或在其与船东、海员或其他利益方的关系方面可能会以任何方式损害其权威或公正的职责。检查员特别须：

[1] 其英文为 proceedings，主要指对存在缺陷的船舶所采取的行政(处罚)程序。——校译者注

(a) be prohibited from having any direct or indirect interest in any operation which they are called upon to inspect; and

(b) subject to appropriate sanctions or disciplinary measures, not reveal, even after leaving service, any commercial secrets or confidential working processes or information of a personal nature which may come to their knowledge in the course of their duties.

12. Inspectors shall submit a report of each inspection to the competent authority. One copy of the report in English or in the working language of the ship shall be furnished to the master of the ship and another copy shall be posted on the ship's notice board for the information of the seafarers and, upon request, sent to their representatives.

13. The competent authority of each Member shall maintain records of inspections of the conditions for[1] seafarers on ships that fly its flag. It shall publish an annual report on inspection activities within a reasonable time, not exceeding six months, after the end of the year.

14. In the case of an investigation pursuant to a major incident, the report shall be submitted to the competent authority as soon as practicable, but not later than one month following the conclusion of the investigation.

15. When an inspection is conducted or when measures are taken under this Standard, all reasonable efforts shall be made to avoid a ship being unreasonably detained or delayed.

---

[1] 在最初公布的公约正式英文文本中，此处为 of，现修订为 for，即把 conditions of seafarers 修改为 conditions for seafarers，与本标准第 1 款中的表述相统一。——校译者注

(a) 禁止在其被召请检查的任何活动中有任何直接或间接的利益；以及

(b) 受到适当的制裁或纪律措施的约束，不泄露在其行使职责中可能了解到的任何商业秘密或保密工作程序或具有个人性质的信息，即使在离开岗位以后。

12. 检查员须就每一次检查向主管当局提交一份报告。须将报告的一份英文或船上工作语言的文本提供给船舶的船长，同时将另一份张贴在船舶的布告栏内供海员知晓并在有请求时送给他们的代表。

13. 对在悬挂其旗帜船舶上的海员所提供的条件，各成员国的主管当局须保持对其进行检查的记录。其须在年终之后不超过六个月的合理时间内发布关于检查活动的年度报告。

14. 如系重大事件后的调查，须尽实际可行地及早向主管当局提交报告，但不得晚于调查结束之后一个月。

15. 当根据本标准进行检查或采取措施时，须做出一切合理努力，避免船舶被不合理滞留或延误。

16. Compensation shall be payable in accordance with national laws and regulations for any loss or damage suffered as a result of the wrongful exercise of the inspectors' powers. The burden of proof in each case shall be on the complainant.

17. Adequate penalties and other corrective measures for breaches of the requirements of this Convention (including seafarers' rights) and for obstructing inspectors in the performance of their duties shall be provided for and effectively enforced by each Member.

Guideline B5.1.4—Inspection and enforcement

1. The competent authority and any other service or authority wholly or partly concerned with the inspection of seafarers' working and living conditions should have the resources necessary to fulfil their functions. In particular:

(a) each Member should take the necessary measures so that duly qualified technical experts and specialists may be called upon, as needed, to assist in the work of inspectors; and

(b) inspectors should be provided with conveniently situated premises, equipment and means of transport adequate for the efficient performance of their duties.

2. The competent authority should develop a compliance and enforcement policy to ensure consistency and otherwise guide inspection and enforcement activities related to this Convention. Copies of this policy should be provided to all inspectors and relevant law-enforcement officials and should be made available to the public and shipowners and seafarers.

3. The competent authority should establish simple procedures to enable it to receive information in confidence concerning possible

16. 对于因检查员错误地行使权力而遭受的任何损失或损害，须根据国内法律和条例予以赔偿。在每种情况下均须由申诉者承担举证责任。

17. 各成员国，对于违反本公约要求（包括海员权利）及妨碍检查员履行其职责的情况，须规定并有效执行适当处罚和其他纠正措施。

导则 B5.1.4—检查和执行

1. 主管当局和与海员工作和生活条件的检查全部或部分有关的任何其他服务机构或当局应有履行其职能所必需的资源。特别是：

(a) 各成员国应采取必要措施，使正规合格的技术专家和专业人员可在需要时被召请协助检查员的工作；以及

(b) 应为检查员配备地点方便的场所、设备和交通手段，足以使其高效地行使职责。

2. 主管当局应制定一项符合与执行方针，以确保一贯性并在其他方面指导与本公约有关的检查和执行活动。该方针的文本应提供给所有检查员和相关执法官员，并应使公众及船东和海员能够得到。

3. 主管当局应设立简便的程序，使其能够秘密接收海员直接或由其代表提出的关于可能违反本公约要求（包括海员权利）的信息，并允许检查员迅速调查此类事项，包括：

breaches of the requirements of this Convention (including seafarers' rights) presented by seafarers directly or by representatives of the seafarers, and permit inspectors to investigate such matters promptly, including:

(a) enabling masters, seafarers or representatives of the seafarers to request an inspection when they consider it necessary; and

(b) supplying technical information and advice to shipowners and seafarers and organizations concerned as to the most effective means of complying with the requirements of this Convention and of bringing about a continual improvement in seafarers' on-board conditions.

4. Inspectors should be fully trained and sufficient in numbers to secure the efficient discharge of their duties with due regard to:

(a) the importance of the duties which the inspectors have to perform, in particular the number, nature and size of ships subject to inspection and the number and complexity of the legal provisions to be enforced;

(b) the resources placed at the disposal of the inspectors; and

(c) the practical conditions under which inspections must be carried out in order to be effective.

5. Subject to any conditions for recruitment to the public service which may be prescribed by national laws and regulations, inspectors should have qualifications and adequate training to perform their duties and where possible should have a maritime education or experience as a seafarer. They should have adequate knowledge of seafarers' working and living conditions and of the English language.

6. Measures should be taken to provide inspectors with appro-

(a) 使船长、海员或海员代表能在他们认为必要时要求进行检查；以及

(b) 就遵守本公约的要求和不断改善海员的船上条件的最有效的方法向船东和海员及有关组织提供技术信息和建议。

4. 检查员应得到全面培训且人数充足，以保障高效履行其职责，并充分注意到：

(a) 检查员必须履行的职责的重要性，特别是应受检查的船舶数目、性质和尺度以及将要执行的法律条款的数量和复杂性；

(b) 可供检查员支配的资源；以及

(c) 为求有效而必须开展检查的实际条件。

5. 以国内法律和条例可能规定的公共部门的任何招聘条件为前提，检查员应具备行使其职责的资格和适当培训，并且在可能时，应受过海事教育或具有海员的经历。他们应充分了解海员的工作和生活条件并掌握英语。

6. 应采取措施使检查员在就业期间受到适当的进一步培训。

priate further training during their employment.

7. All inspectors should have a clear understanding of the circumstances in which an inspection should be carried out, the scope of the inspection to be carried out in the various circumstances referred to and the general method of inspection.

8. Inspectors provided with proper credentials under the national law should at a minimum be empowered:

(a) to board ships freely and without previous notice; however, when commencing the ship inspection, inspectors should provide notification of their presence to the master or person in charge and, where appropriate, to the seafarers or their representatives;

(b) to question the master, seafarer or any other person, including the shipowner or the shipowner's representative, on any matter concerning the application of the requirements under laws and regulations, in the presence of any witness that the person may have requested;

(c) to require the production of any books, log books, registers, certificates or other documents or information directly related to matters subject to inspection, in order to verify compliance with the national laws and regulations implementing this Convention;

(d) to enforce the posting of notices required under the national laws and regulations implementing this Convention;

(e) to take or remove, for the purpose of analysis, samples of products, cargo, drinking water, provisions, materials and substances used or handled;

(f) following an inspection, to bring immediately to the attention of

7. 所有检查员应清楚理解应开展检查的情形、在所提到的各种情形中将开展检查的范围和检查的一般方法。

8. 根据国内法律持有适当委任证书的检查员应至少被授权：

(a) 自由地登船且不经事先通知；但是，在开始对船舶进行检查时，检查员应将他们的到来通知船长或负责人，并在适宜时通知海员或其代表；

(b) 在受询问者可能要求的任何证人在场的情况下，就涉及法律和条例要求的适用之任何事项询问船长、海员或任何其他人员，包括船东或船东的代表；

(c) 要求出示任何书册、日志、登记册、证书或其他与受检事项直接相关的文件或资料，以便核实对实施本公约的国内法律和条例的符合情况；

(d) 根据实施本公约的国内法律和条例的要求执行对通知的张贴；

(e) 以进行分析为目的，提取或取走曾使用过或处理过的产品、货物、饮用水、伙食、材料和物质的样品；

(f) 在检查后立即提请船东、船舶经营人或船长注意那些可能会影响到船上人员健康与安全的缺陷；

the shipowner, the operator of the ship or the master, deficiencies which may affect the health and safety of those on board ship;

(g) to alert the competent authority and, if applicable, the recognized organization to any deficiency or abuse not specifically covered by existing laws or regulations and submit proposals to them for the improvement of the laws or regulations; and

(h) to notify the competent authority of any occupational injuries or diseases affecting seafarers in such cases and in such manner as may be prescribed by laws and regulations.

9. When a sample referred to in paragraph 8(e) of this Guideline is being taken or removed, the shipowner or the shipowner's representative, and where appropriate a seafarer, should be notified or should be present at the time the sample is taken or removed. The quantity of such a sample should be properly recorded by the inspector.

10. The annual report published by the competent authority of each Member, in respect of ships that fly its flag, should contain:

(a) a list of laws and regulations in force relevant to seafarers' working and living conditions and any amendments which have come into effect during the year;

(b) details of the organization of the system of inspection;

(c) statistics of ships or other premises subject to inspection and of ships and other premises actually inspected;

(d) statistics on all seafarers subject to its national laws and regulations;

(e) statistics and information on violations of legislation, penalties

(g) 提醒主管当局并在适用时提醒认可组织注意现行法律或条例没有明确包括的任何缺陷或弊病，并向其提出改善法律或条例的建议；以及

(h)按照法律和条例可能规定的情况和方式，将影响海员的任何职业伤害或疾病通知主管当局。

9. 如果提取或取走本导则第8(e)款中所述的样品，应通知船东或船东代表，并在适宜时通知海员，或者当提取或取走样品时他们应在现场。检查员对此类样品的数量应予妥善记录。

10. 各成员国主管当局就悬挂其旗帜船舶而发布的年度报告应载明：

(a) 与海员的工作和生活条件有关的有效法律和条例以及在该年度中生效的任何修正的清单；

(b) 检查机制的组织细节；

(c) 应受检查和实受检查的船舶或其他场所的统计资料；

(d) 受其国内法律和条例管辖的所有海员的统计资料；

(e) 关于违反立法、所给予的处罚以及滞留船舶案例的统计资料和信息；以及

imposed and cases of detention of ships; and

(f) statistics on reported occupational injuries and diseases affecting seafarers.

Regulation 5.1.5—On-board complaint procedures

1. Each Member shall require that ships that fly its flag have on-board procedures for the fair, effective and expeditious handling of seafarer complaints alleging breaches of the requirements of this Convention (including seafarers' rights).

2. Each Member shall prohibit and penalize any kind of victimization of a seafarer for filing a complaint.

3. The provisions in this Regulation and related sections of the Code are without prejudice to a seafarer's right to seek redress through whatever legal means the seafarer considers appropriate.

Standard A5.1.5—On-board complaint procedures

1. Without prejudice to any wider scope that may be given in national laws or regulations or collective agreements, the on-board procedures may be used by seafarers to lodge complaints relating to any matter that is alleged to constitute a breach of the requirements of this Convention (including seafarers' rights).

2. Each Member shall ensure that, in its laws or regulations, appropriate on board complaint procedures are in place to meet the requirements of Regulation 5.1.5. Such procedures shall seek to resolve complaints at the lowest level possible. However, in all cases, seafarers shall have a right to complain directly to the master and, where they consider it necessary, to appropriate external authorities.

3. The on-board complaint procedures shall include the right of

(f) 关于所报告的影响海员的职业伤害和疾病的统计资料。

规则 5.1.5—船上投诉程序

1. 各成员国须要求悬挂其旗帜的船舶具备公平、有效和迅速处理海员指称违反本公约要求(包括海员权利)的投诉的船上程序。

2. 各成员国须禁止和处罚对提出投诉的海员进行任何形式的迫害。

3. 本规则和守则的相关部分的规定不得损害海员通过其认为适当的任何法律手段寻求纠正的权利。

标准 A5.1.5—船上投诉程序

1. 在不损害国内法律或条例或集体协议可能规定更宽范围的情况下,海员可以使用船上程序提出关于任何被指称为构成违反本公约要求(包括海员权利)之事项的投诉。

2. 各成员国须在其法律或条例中确保存在适当的船上投诉程序以满足规则 5.1.5 的要求。此类程序须寻求在尽可能最低的层次解决投诉。但是,在任何情况下,海员须有权直接向船长投诉并在其认为必要时,向适当的外部当局投诉。

3. 船上投诉程序须包括海员在投诉程序期间由人陪同或由人代表的权利,并防止海员因提出投诉而受迫害的可能性。"迫害"一词包括任何人因海员提出并非明显无理取闹或恶意的投诉而采取的任何敌意行为。

the seafarer to be accompanied or represented during the complaints procedure, as well as safeguards against the possibility of victimization of seafarers for filing complaints. The term "victimization" covers any adverse action taken by any person with respect to a seafarer for lodging a complaint which is not manifestly vexatious or maliciously made.

4. In addition to a copy of their seafarers' employment agreement, all seafarers shall be provided with a copy of the on-board complaint procedures applicable on the ship. This shall include contact information for the competent authority in the flag State and, where different, in the seafarers' country of residence, and the name of a person or persons on board the ship who can, on a confidential basis, provide seafarers with impartial advice on their complaint and otherwise assist them in following the complaint procedures available to them on board the ship.

Guideline B5.1.5—On-board complaint procedures

1. Subject to any relevant provisions of an applicable collective agreement, the competent authority should, in close consultation with shipowners' and seafarers' organizations, develop a model for fair, expeditious and well-documented on-board complaint-handling procedures for all ships that fly the Member's flag. In developing these procedures the following matters should be considered:

(a) many complaints may relate specifically to those individuals to whom the complaint is to be made or even to the master of the ship. In all cases seafarers should also be able to complain directly to the master and to make a complaint externally; and

(b) in order to help avoid problems of victimization of seafarers making complaints about matters under this Convention, the proce-

4. 除其一份海员就业协议外，还须向所有海员提供一份适用于该船的船上投诉程序。该投拆程序须包括船旗国主管当局和海员居住国（如果与船旗国不同）主管当局的联络信息，以及能够在保密的基础上就海员的投诉向其提供公正的建议并在其他方面帮助其遵循船上可用投诉程序的船上人员的姓名。

导则 B5.1.5—船上投诉程序

1. 在适用的集体协议的任何相关规定的限制下，主管当局应与船东组织和海员组织密切协商，为悬挂该成员国旗帜的所有船舶制定公平、迅速和妥善记录的船上投诉处理程序的范本。在制定这些程序时，应考虑以下事项：

(a) 许多投诉可能与将要接收投诉的个人或甚至与船长具体相关。在各种情况下，海员还应能够直接向船长投诉及向外部投诉；以及

(b) 为了帮助就本公约事项提出投诉的海员避免受到迫害的问题，程序应鼓励指定一名能够就海员可用的程序向海员提出建议的船上人员，并且，如果提出投诉的海员要求，该指定人员还能够参加针对该投诉主题的任何会议或听证。

dures should encourage the nomination of a person on board who can advise seafarers on the procedures available to them and, if requested by the complainant seafarer, also attend any meetings or hearings into the subject matter of the complaint.

2. At a minimum the procedures discussed during the consultative process referred to in paragraph 1 of this Guideline should include the following:

(a) complaints should be addressed to the head of the department of the seafarer lodging the complaint or to the seafarer's superior officer;

(b) the head of department or superior officer should then attempt to resolve the matter within prescribed time limits appropriate to the seriousness of the issues involved;

(c) if the head of department or superior officer cannot resolve the complaint to the satisfaction of the seafarer, the latter may refer it to the master, who should handle the matter personally;

(d) seafarers should at all times have the right to be accompanied and to be represented by another seafarer of their choice on board the ship concerned;

(e) all complaints and the decisions on them should be recorded and a copy provided to the seafarer concerned;

(f) if a complaint cannot be resolved on board, the matter should be referred ashore to the shipowner, who should be given an appropriate time limit for resolving the matter, where appropriate, in consultation with the seafarers concerned or any person they may appoint as their representative; and

(g) in all cases seafarers should have a right to file their complaints directly with the master and the shipowner and competent au-

2. 本导则第1款所述的协商过程中所讨论的程序至少应包括以下内容：

(a) 投诉应提交给提出投诉的海员的部门负责人或该海员的上级高级船员；

(b) 部门负责人或上级高级船员应努力在与所涉问题的严重性相适应的规定时限内解决该事项；

(c) 如果部门负责人或上级高级船员对投诉的解决不能令海员满意，该海员可以将投诉提交给船长，船长则应亲自处理该事项；

(d) 海员应始终有权由其在相关船上选择的另一名海员陪同或代表；

(e) 应记录所有的投诉和对投诉的决定，并将一份提供给有关海员；

(f) 如果投诉不能在船上得到解决，该事项应交给岸上的船东，并应给予该船东适当的时限，适宜时，与有关海员或可能被他们指定为代表的任何人协商，来解决该事项；以及

(g) 在所有情况下海员均应有权直接向船长和船东及主管当局提出投诉。

thorities.

Regulation 5.1.6—Marine casualties

1. Each Member shall hold an official inquiry into any serious marine casualty, leading to injury or loss of life, that involves a ship that flies its flag. The final report of an inquiry shall normally be made public.

2. Members shall cooperate with each other to facilitate the investigation of serious marine casualties referred to in paragraph 1 of this Regulation.

Standard A5.1.6—Marine casualties

(No provisions)

Guideline B5.1.6—Marine casualties

(No provisions)

Regulation 5.2—Port State responsibilities

Purpose: To enable each Member to implement its responsibilities under this Convention regarding international cooperation in the implementation and enforcement of the Convention standards on foreign ships

Regulation 5.2.1—Inspections in port

1. Every foreign ship calling, in the normal course of its business or for operational reasons, in the port of a Member may be the subject of inspection in accordance with paragraph 4 of Article V for the purpose of reviewing compliance with the requirements of this Convention (including seafarers' rights) relating to the working and

规则 5.1.6—海上事故

1. 各成员国须对涉及悬挂其旗帜船舶的导致人员伤亡的任何严重海上事故开展官方询查[1]。询查的最后报告通常须予公布。

2. 成员国须相互合作,以便利于调查本规则第 1 款所述的严重海上事故。

标准 A5.1.6—海上事故

(无规定)

导则 B5.1.6—海上事故

(无规定)

规则 5.2—港口国责任

目的:使各成员国能够履行其本公约关于在外国船舶上实施和执行公约标准方面进行国际合作的责任

规则 5.2.1—在港口的检查

1. 每一外国船舶在正常的业务过程中或出于操作性原因停靠一成员国的港口时,可能成为根据第五条第 4 款所进行检查的对象,目的在于对本公约有关船上海员工作和生活条件的要求(包括海员权利)的符合情况进行核查。

---

[1] 本款源自《1976 年商船(最低标准)公约》(第 147 号)第 2 条第(g)款,保留了其中的用词 inquiry(在此改译成“询查”)。而下一款则是本公约新增条款,其中使用 investigation(调查)一词。两英文词在文义上有所区别,但在此处其含义应是相同的,因为对于严重海上事故各方均应进行正式的“调查”。其措辞的区别应是源于其所在条款来源的不同。——校译者注

living conditions of seafarers on the ship.

2. Each Member shall accept the maritime labour certificate and the declaration of maritime labour compliance required under Regulation 5. 1. 3 as prima facie evidence of compliance with the requirements of this Convention (including seafarers' rights). Accordingly, the inspection in its ports shall, except in the circumstances specified in the Code, be limited to a review of the certificate and declaration.

3. Inspections in a port shall be carried out by authorized officers in accordance with the provisions of the Code and other applicable international arrangements governing port State control inspections in the Member. Any such inspection shall be limited to verifying that the matter inspected is in conformity with the relevant requirements set out in the Articles and Regulations of this Convention and in Part A only of the Code.

4. Inspections that may be carried out in accordance with this Regulation shall be based on an effective port State inspection and monitoring system to help ensure that the working and living conditions for seafarers on ships entering a port of the Member concerned meet the requirements of this Convention (including seafarers' rights).

5. Information about the system referred to in paragraph 4 of this Regulation, including the method used for assessing its effectiveness, shall be included in the Member's reports pursuant to article 22 of the Constitution.

Standard A5. 2. 1—Inspections in port

1. Where an authorized officer, having come on board to carry out an inspection and requested, where applicable, the maritime la-

2. 各成员国须接受规则 5.1.3 所要求的海事劳工证书和海事劳工符合声明为符合本公约要求(包括海员权利)的初步证据。因此,除守则中具体规定的情况外,其港口内的检查须仅限于核查证书和声明。

3. 在港口内的检查须由授权官员根据守则和其他管辖该成员国内港口国监督检查的适用国际协议的规定来进行。任何此种检查须仅限于核实所检查的事项符合本公约正文条款和规则及守则中仅 A 部分所规定的相关要求。

4. 根据本规则可能开展的检查须以有效的港口国检查和监控机制为基础,以帮助确保进入有关成员国港口的船舶上的海员工作和生活条件满足本公约的要求(包括海员权利)。

5. 关于本规则第 4 款所述机制的信息,包括用于评估其有效性的方法的信息,须包括在成员国根据《章程》第二十二条提交的报告中。

标准 A5.2.1—在港口的检查

1. 如果授权官员登船进行检查并,如适用,要求出示海事劳工证书和海事劳工符合声明时发现:

bour certificate and the declaration of maritime labour compliance, finds that:

(a) the required documents are not produced or maintained or are falsely maintained or that the documents produced do not contain the information required by this Convention or are otherwise invalid; or

(b) there are clear grounds for believing that the working and living conditions on the ship do not conform to the requirements of this Convention; or

(c) there are reasonable grounds to believe that the ship has changed flag for the purpose of avoiding compliance with this Convention; or

(d) there is a complaint alleging that specific working and living conditions on the ship do not conform to the requirements of this Convention;

a more detailed inspection may be carried out to ascertain the working and living conditions on board the ship. Such inspection shall in any case be carried out where the working and living conditions believed or alleged to be defective could constitute a clear hazard to the safety, health or security of seafarers or where the authorized officer has grounds to believe that any deficiencies constitute a serious breach of the requirements of this Convention (including seafarers' rights).

2. Where a more detailed inspection is carried out on a foreign ship in the port of a Member by authorized officers in the circumstances set out in subparagraph (a), (b) or (c) of paragraph 1 of this Standard, it shall in principle cover the matters listed in Appendix A5-III.

(a) 未出示或未记载或虚假记载所要求的文件，或所出示的文件未包含本公约所要求的信息或因其他原因无效；或

(b) 有明显理由相信，该船上的工作和生活条件不符合本公约的要求；或

(c) 有合理的理由相信该船出于逃避符合本公约之目的而变更船旗；或

(d) 有投诉指称，船上的具体工作和生活条件不符合本公约的要求；

则可以进行更详细的检查以确定船上的工作和生活条件。如果被认为或被指称为存在缺陷的工作和生活条件会对海员的安全、健康或保安构成明显危害，或者授权官员有理由相信任何缺陷构成了对本公约要求（包括海员权利）的严重违反，则无论如何都须进行此种检查。

2. 如果在成员国港口由授权官员在本标准第1款第(a)、(b)或(c)项规定的情形中对外国船舶进行更详细的检查，该检查原则上须涵盖附录A5-III中所列的事项。

3. In the case of a complaint under paragraph 1(d) of this Standard, the inspection shall generally be limited to matters within the scope of the complaint, although a complaint, or its investigation, may provide clear grounds for a detailed inspection in accordance with paragraph 1(b) of this Standard. For the purpose of paragraph 1(d) of this Standard, "complaint" means information submitted by a seafarer, a professional body, an association, a trade union or, generally, any person with an interest in the safety of the ship, including an interest in safety or health hazards to seafarers on board.

4. Where, following a more detailed inspection, the working and living conditions on the ship are found not to conform to the requirements of this Convention, the authorized officer shall forthwith bring the deficiencies to the attention of the master of the ship, with required deadlines for their rectification. In the event that such deficiencies are considered by the authorized officer to be significant, or if they relate to a complaint made in accordance with paragraph 3 of this Standard, the authorized officer shall bring the deficiencies to the attention of the appropriate seafarers' and shipowners' organizations in the Member in which the inspection is carried out, and may:

(a) notify a representative of the flag State;

(b) provide the competent authorities of the next port of call with the relevant information.

5. The Member in which the inspection is carried out shall have the right to transmit a copy of the officer's report, which must be accompanied by any reply received from the competent authorities of the flag State within the prescribed deadline, to the Director-General of the International Labour Office with a view to such action as may

3. 在本标准第1(d)款的投诉的情况下，检查一般须限于投诉范围内的事项，尽管一项投诉或其调查可能为根据本标准第1(b)款进行更详细的检查提供明显理由。就本标准第1(d)款而言，“投诉”系指对海员、专业机构、协会、工会或总体而言，由那些对船舶安全有利害关系，包括对船上海员的安全或健康危害有利害关系的任何人提交的信息。

4. 如果在更详细检查后发现船上的工作和生活条件不符合本公约的要求，授权官员须随即提请该船的船长注意这些缺陷并随附对其纠正所要求的截止日期。如果授权官员认为这些缺陷为重大缺陷，或者这些缺陷涉及根据本标准第3款提出的投诉，授权官员须提请开展检查所在成员国的适当海员组织和船东组织注意这些缺陷，并且可以：

(a) 通知船旗国的代表；

(b) 向下一停靠港口的主管当局提供有关信息。

5. 开展检查所在的成员国须有权将该官员的一份报告，其后必须附有所收到的船旗国的主管当局在规定的截止时间内做出的任何回应，转送国际劳工局局长，旨在采取可能认为适当和迅速的行动，以便确保此信息的记录得以保持，并确保提请可能对利用相关追索程序有利害关系的各方对其注意。

be considered appropriate and expedient in order to ensure that a record is kept of such information and that it is brought to the attention of parties which might be interested in availing themselves of relevant recourse procedures.

6. Where, following a more detailed inspection by an authorized officer, the ship is found not to conform to the requirements of this Convention and:

(a) the conditions on board are clearly hazardous to the safety, health or security of seafarers; or

(b) the non-conformity constitutes a serious or repeated breach of the requirements of this Convention (including seafarers' rights);

the authorized officer shall take steps to ensure that the ship shall not proceed to sea until any non-conformities that fall within the scope of subparagraph (a) or (b) of this paragraph have been rectified, or until the authorized officer has accepted a plan of action to rectify such non-conformities and is satisfied that the plan will be implemented in an expeditious manner. If the ship is prevented from sailing, the authorized officer shall forthwith notify the flag State accordingly and invite a representative of the flag State to be present, if possible, requesting the flag State to reply within a prescribed deadline. The authorized officer shall also inform forthwith the appropriate shipowners' and seafarers' organizations in the port State in which the inspection was carried out.

7. Each Member shall ensure that its authorized officers are given guidance, of the kind indicated in Part B of the Code, as to the kinds of circumstances justifying detention of a ship under paragraph 6 of this Standard.

6. 如果授权官员进行更详细的检查后发现船舶不符合本公约的要求，并且：

(a) 船上条件明显危害海员的安全、健康或保安；或

(b) 不符合的情况构成对本公约要求（包括海员权利）的严重或屡次违反；

授权官员须采取步骤确保该船不得开航出海，直到属于本款第(a)或(b)项范围内的任何不符合情况得到纠正，或者直到授权官员接受了纠正该不符合情况的行动计划并认为该计划将会得到迅速实施。如果船舶被禁止开航，授权官员须相应地随即通知船旗国并请船旗国的代表到场，若可能，要求船旗国在规定的截止期限内答复。授权官员还须随即通知开展检查所在港口国的适当船东组织和海员组织。

7. 各成员国须确保对其授权官员，就本标准第 6 款中构成滞留船舶理由的情况类型，按守则 B 部分所指出的形式给以指导。

8. When implementing their responsibilities under this Standard, each Member shall make all possible efforts to avoid a ship being unduly detained or delayed. If a ship is found to be unduly detained or delayed, compensation shall be paid for any loss or damage suffered. The burden of proof in each case shall be on the complainant.

Guideline B5.2.1—Inspections in port

1. The competent authority should develop an inspection policy for authorized officers carrying out inspections under Regulation 5.2.1. The objective of the policy should be to ensure consistency and to otherwise guide inspection and enforcement activities related to the requirements of this Convention (including seafarers' rights). Copies of this policy should be provided to all authorized officers and should be available to the public and shipowners and seafarers.

2. When developing a policy relating to the circumstances warranting a detention of the ship under Standard A5.2.1, paragraph 6, of [1] the competent authority should consider that, with respect to the breaches referred to in Standard A5.2.1, paragraph 6(b), the seriousness could be due to the nature of the deficiency concerned. This would be particularly relevant in the case of the violation of fundamental rights and principles or seafarers' employment and social rights under Articles III and IV. For example, the employment of a person who is under age should be considered as a serious breach even if there is only one such person on board. In other cases, the number of different defects found during a particular inspection should be taken into account: for example, several instances of de-

---

[1] 此 of 似多余，可删除。——校译者注

8. 各成员国在履行其在本标准下的责任时,须尽一切可能努力避免船舶被不当滞留或延误。如果发现船舶被不当滞留或延误,须对所遭受的任何损失或损害予以赔偿。在每种情况下均须由申诉者承担举证责任。

导则 B5.2.1—在港口的检查

1. 主管当局应为按规则 5.2.1 进行检查的授权官员制定检查方针。方针的目标应为确保一贯性并在其他方面指导与本公约要求(包括海员权利)有关的检查和执行活动。该方针的文本应提供给所有授权官员,并应使公众及船东和海员能够得到。

2. 在制定关于标准 A5.2.1 第 6 款中构成滞留船舶正当理由之情形的方针时,主管当局应考虑到,关于标准 A5.2.1 第 6(b)款中所述的违反,其严重性可以源于有关缺陷的性质。这一点,在违反了第三条和第四条中的基本权利和原则或海员的就业和社会权利的情况下,将会特别贴切。例如,雇用一个未成年人应被视为严重违反,即使船上只有一个这样的人。在其他情况下,应考虑到在一次特定的检查中所发现的不同缺陷的数量:例如,在应被认为构成严重违反之前,可能需要有几个并不威胁安全或健康的关于起居舱室或食品和膳食服务的缺陷情况。

fects relating to accommodation or food and catering which do not threaten safety or health might be needed before they should be considered as constituting a serious breach.

3. Members should cooperate with each other to the maximum extent possible in the adoption of internationally agreed guidelines on inspection policies, especially those relating to the circumstances warranting the detention of a ship.

Regulation 5.2.2—Onshore seafarer complaint-handling procedures

1. Each Member shall ensure that seafarers on ships calling at a port in the Member's territory who allege a breach of the requirements of this Convention (including seafarers' rights) have the right to report such a complaint in order to facilitate a prompt and practical means of redress.

Standard A5.2.2—Onshore seafarer complaint-handling procedures

1. A complaint by a seafarer alleging a breach of the requirements of this Convention (including seafarers' rights) may be reported to an authorized officer in the port at which the seafarer's ship has called. In such cases, the authorized officer shall undertake an initial investigation.

2. Where appropriate, given the nature of the complaint, the initial investigation shall include consideration of whether the on-board complaint procedures provided under Regulation 5.1.5 have been explored. The authorized officer may also conduct a more detailed inspection in accordance with Standard A5.2.1.

3. The authorized officer shall, where appropriate, seek to pro-

3. 成员国应最大可能限度地相互合作，在检查方针方面通过国际一致的导则，特别是那些关于构成滞留船舶正当理由的情形的导则。

规则 5.2.2—海员投诉的岸上处理程序

1. 各成员国须确保，在该成员国领土内的港口停靠的船舶上的指称违反本公约要求(包括海员权利)的海员，有权对此类投诉做出报告，以促进采取迅速而实际的解决方式。

标准 A5.2.2—海员投诉的岸上处理程序

1. 海员指称违反本公约要求(包括海员权利)的投诉可向海员所在船舶停靠的港口的授权官员报告。在这种情况下，授权官员须开展初步调查。

2. 基于投诉的性质，适宜时，初步调查须包括考虑是否已用尽了规则 5.1.5 所规定的船上投诉程序。授权官员还可以根据标准 A5.2.1 开展更详细的检查。

3. 适宜时，授权官员须寻求促成在船舶层面上解决投诉。

mote a resolution of the complaint at the ship-board level.

4. In the event that the investigation or the inspection provided under this Standard reveals a non-conformity that falls within the scope of paragraph 6 of Standard A5. 2. 1, the provisions of that paragraph shall be applied.

5. Where the provisions of paragraph 4 of this Standard do not apply, and the complaint has not been resolved at the ship-board level, the authorized officer shall forthwith notify the flag State, seeking, within a prescribed deadline, advice and a corrective plan of action.

6. Where the complaint has not been resolved following action taken in accordance with paragraph 5 of this Standard, the port State shall transmit a copy of the authorized officer's report to the Director-General. The report must be accompanied by any reply received within the prescribed deadline from the competent authority of the flag State. The appropriate shipowners' and seafarers' organizations in the port State shall be similarly informed. In addition, statistics and information regarding complaints that have been resolved shall be regularly submitted by the port State to the Director-General. Both such submissions are provided in order that, on the basis of such action as may be considered appropriate and expedient, a record is kept of such information and is brought to the attention of parties, including shipowners' and seafarers' organizations, which might be interested in availing themselves of relevant recourse procedures.

7. Appropriate steps shall be taken to safeguard the confidentiality of complaints made by seafarers.

4. 如果根据本标准所规定的调查或检查发现的不符合情况属于标准 A5.2.1 第 6 款的范畴,须适用该款的规定。

5. 如果本标准第 4 款的规定不适用,且该投诉未能在船舶层面上得到解决,授权官员须随即通知船旗国,在规定的截止期限内征询建议及纠正的行动计划。

6. 如果按本标准第 5 款采取行动后投诉未能得到解决,港口国须将一份授权官员的报告送交局长。该报告必须附有在规定的截止限期内从船旗国主管当局那里收到的任何答复。须以类似的方式通知港口国内适当的船东组织和海员组织。此外,港口国须定期将关于已解决投诉的统计资料和信息提交给局长。对上述两种提交报告所做的规定,是为了在可能认为这类行动恰当且迅速的基础上,保持一份这类信息的记录,并使包括船东组织和海员组织在内的可能会对利用有关追索程序有利害关系的各方注意到该记录。

7. 须采取适当步骤为海员提出的投诉保密。

Guideline B5. 2. 2—Onshore seafarer complaint-handling procedures

1. Where a complaint referred to in Standard A5. 2. 2 is dealt with by an authorized officer, the officer should first check whether the complaint is of a general nature which concerns all seafarers on the ship, or a category of them, or whether it relates only to the individual case of the seafarer concerned.

2. If the complaint is of a general nature, consideration should be given to undertaking a more detailed inspection in accordance with Standard A5. 2. 1.

3. If the complaint relates to an individual case, an examination of the results of any on-board complaint procedures for the resolution of the complaint concerned should be undertaken. If such procedures have not been explored, the authorized officer should suggest that the complainant take advantage of any such procedures available. There should be good reasons for considering a complaint before any on-board complaint procedures have been explored. These would include the inadequacy of, or undue delay in, the internal procedures or the complainant's fear of reprisal for lodging a complaint.

4. In any investigation of a complaint, the authorized officer should give the master, the shipowner and any other person involved in the complaint a proper opportunity to make known their views.

5. In the event that the flag State demonstrates, in response to the notification by the port State in accordance with paragraph 5 of Standard A5. 2. 2, that it will handle the matter, and that it has in place effective procedures for this purpose and has submitted an acceptable plan of action, the authorized officer may refrain from any

导则 B5.2.2—海员投诉的岸上处理程序

1. 如果标准 A5.2.2 中所述的投诉由授权官员来处理,该官员应首先核查该投诉是否具有涉及该船上的所有海员或某一类海员的普遍性,或者是否只与该当事海员的个案有关。

2. 如果该投诉具有普遍性,应考虑根据标准 A5.2.1 进行一次更详细的检查。

3. 如果投诉只与个案有关,应对解决有关投诉的任何船上投诉程序的结果予以考察。如果还没有用尽该程序,授权官员应建议投诉人利用现有的任何此类程序。若在用尽任何船上投诉程序之前就对投诉予以考虑,应当有充分的理由。这些理由将包括内部程序不足或过分拖沓,或者投诉人害怕因提出投诉而受到报复。

4. 在对投诉的任何调查中,授权官员应给船长、船东和投诉所涉及的任何其他人员适当的机会来表明其观点。

5. 如果船旗国在对港口国根据标准 A5.2.2 第 5 款所发通知的答复中已表明其将处理该事项,且其具备为此目的的有效程序并提交了一份可接受的行动方案,授权官员可避开进一步涉及此投诉。

further involvement with the complaint.

Regulation 5.3—Labour-supplying responsibilities

Purpose: To ensure that each Member implements its responsibilities under this Convention as pertaining to seafarer recruitment and placement and the social protection of its seafarers

1. Without prejudice to the principle of each Member's responsibility for the working and living conditions of seafarers on ships that fly its flag, the Member also has a responsibility to ensure the implementation of the requirements of this Convention regarding the recruitment and placement of seafarers as well as the social security protection of seafarers that are its nationals or are resident or are otherwise domiciled in its territory, to the extent that such responsibility is provided for in this Convention.

2. Detailed requirements for the implementation of paragraph 1 of this Regulation are found in the Code.

3. Each Member shall establish an effective inspection and monitoring system for enforcing its labour-supplying responsibilities under this Convention.

4. Information about the system referred to in paragraph 3 of this Regulation, including the method used for assessing its effectiveness, shall be included in the Member's reports pursuant to article 22 of the Constitution.

Standard A5.3—Labour-supplying responsibilities

1. Each Member shall enforce the requirements of this Convention applicable to the operation and practice of seafarer recruitment

规则 5.3—劳工提供责任

目的：确保各成员国履行其在本公约下关于海员招募和安置以及对其海员社会保护的责任

1. 在不损害各成员国对悬挂其旗帜船舶上海员工作和生活条件进行负责的原则下，成员国还有责任确保实施本公约关于海员招募和安置的要求，以及对作为其国民或在其领土内定居或以其他方式居住的海员的社会保障保护的要求，只要本公约规定了此种责任。

2. 实施本规则第 1 款的详细要求见守则。

3. 各成员国须建立一个有效的检查和监控机制来执行其在本公约下的劳工提供责任。

4. 关于本规则第 3 款所述机制的信息，包括用于评估其有效性的方法的信息，须包括在成员国根据《章程》第二十二条提交的报告中。

标准 A5.3—劳工提供责任

1. 各成员国须通过一个检查和监控机制并通过对违反标准 A1.4 规定的发放许可证和其他操作性要求的法律程序，执行本公约中适用于在其领土上设立的海员招募和安置服务机构的运作和实践的要求。

and placement services established on its territory through a system of inspection and monitoring and legal proceedings for breaches of licensing and other operational requirements provided for in Standard A1. 4.

Guideline B5. 3—Labour-supplying responsibilities

1. Private seafarer recruitment and placement services established in the Member's territory and securing the services of a seafarer for a shipowner, wherever located, should be required to assume obligations to ensure the proper fulfilment by shipowners of the terms of their employment agreements concluded with seafarers.

导则 B5.3—劳工提供责任

1. 应要求在成员国领土内设立并为船东落实海员服务的私营海员招募和安置服务机构承担责任,确保由船东妥善履行与海员订立的就业协议条款,无论船东位于何处。

APPENDIX A5-I

The working and living conditions of seafarers that must be inspected and approved by the flag State before certifying a ship in accordance with Standard A5. 1. 3, paragraph 1:

Minimum age

Medical certification

Qualifications of seafarers

Seafarers' employment agreements

Use of any licensed or certified or regulated private recruitment and placement service

Hours of work or rest

Manning levels for the ship

Accommodation

On-board recreational facilities

Food and catering

Health and safety and accident prevention

On-board medical care

On-board complaint procedures

Payment of wages

附录 A5-I

在根据标准 A5.1.3 第 1 款向船舶发证之前，必须经过船旗国检查并核准的海员工作和生活条件：

最低年龄

健康证书

海员的资格

海员就业协议

使用任何有许可证的或经发证或规范的私营招募和安置服务机构

工作或休息时间

船舶配员水平

起居舱室

船上娱乐设施

食品和膳食服务

健康和安全及事故预防

船上医护

船上投诉程序

工资支付

APPENDIX A5-II

Maritime Labour Certificate

(*Note: This Certificate shall have a Declaration of Maritime Labour Compliance attached*)

Issued under the provisions of Article V and Title 5 of the Maritime Labour Convention, 2006
(referred to below as "the Convention")
under the authority of the Government of:

....

(full designation of the State whose flag the ship is entitled to fly)

by ....

(full designation and address of the competent authority or recognized organization duly authorized under the provisions of the Convention)

Particulars of the ship

Name of ship ....

Distinctive number or letters ....

Port of registry ....

Date of registry ....

Gross tonnage[①] ....

IMO number ....

Type of ship ....

---

① For ships covered by the tonnage measurement interim scheme adopted by the IMO, the gross tonnage is that which is included in the REMARKS column of the International Tonnage Certificate (1969). See Article II (1)(c) of the Convention.

附录 A5-II

海事劳工证书

（注：本证书后须附有“海事劳工符合声明”）

根据《2006年海事劳工公约》（以下简称“《公约》”）

第五条和标题五的规定，

经……………………………………政府授权，

（船舶有权悬挂其旗帜国家的全称）

由……………………………………签发

（主管当局或根据《公约》规定正式授权的认可组织的全称和地址）

船舶细节

船名……………………………………………………………………………………

船舶编号或呼号……………………………………………………………………

船籍港…………………………………………………………………………………

登记日期………………………………………………………………………………

总吨位[①]……………………………………………………………………………

IMO 编号………………………………………………………………………………

船舶类型………………………………………………………………………………

---

① 对于IMO通过的吨位丈量临时表格所包括的船舶，总吨位为包括在“国际吨位证书(1969)”“备注”栏中的总吨位。见公约第二条第(1)(c)款。

Name and address of the shipowner[1] ....

....

This is to certify:

1. That this ship has been inspected and verified to be in compliance with the requirements of the Convention, and the provisions of the attached Declaration of Maritime Labour Compliance.

2. That the seafarers' working and living conditions specified in Appendix A5-I of the Convention were found to correspond to the abovementioned country's national requirements implementing the Convention. These national requirements are summarized in the Declaration of Maritime Labour Compliance, Part I.

This Certificate is valid until .... subject to inspections in accordance with Standards A5. 1. 3 and A5. 1. 4 of the Convention.

This Certificate is valid only when the Declaration of Maritime Labour Compliance issued at .... on .... is attached.

Completion date of the inspection on which this Certificate is based was ....

---

[1] *Shipowner* means the owner of the ship or another organization or person, such as the manager, agent or bareboat charterer, who has assumed the responsibility for the operation of the ship from the owner and who, on assuming such responsibility, has agreed to take over the duties and responsibilities imposed on shipowners in accordance with this Convention, regardless of whether any other organizations or persons fulfil certain of the duties or responsibilities on behalf of the shipowner. See Article II (1)(j) of the Convention.

船东[①]名称和地址……………………………………………………

……………………………………………………………………

兹证明：

1. 该船舶已经过检查和核实，符合《公约》的要求和所附"海事劳工符合声明"的规定。

2. 确认《公约》附录 A5-I 中具体规定的海员工作和生活条件符合上述国家实施《公约》的国内要求。这些国内要求被归纳在"海事劳工符合声明"的第 I 部分中。

本证书有效期至………………，但取决于根据《公约》标准 A5.1.3 和 A5.1.4 的检查。

只有后面附有在………………于………………签发的"海事劳工符合声明"，本证书才有效。

本证书所依据的检查的完成日期为……………………………………

① "船东"系指船舶所有人或从船舶所有人那里承担了船舶经营责任并在承担这种责任时已同意接受船东根据本公约所承担的职责和责任的另一组织或个人，如管理人、代理人或光船承租人，无论是否有任何其他组织或个人代表船东履行了某些职责或责任。见公约第二条第(1)(j)款。

Issued at .... on ....

Signature of the duly authorized official issuing the Certificate

(Seal or stamp of issuing authority, as appropriate)

Endorsements for mandatory intermediate inspection and, if required, any additional inspection

This is to certify that the ship was inspected in accordance with Standards A5. 1. 3 and A5. 1. 4 of the Convention and that the seafarers' working and living conditions specified in Appendix A5-I of the Convention were found to correspond to the abovementioned country's national requirements implementing the Convention.

Intermediate inspection:	Signed ....
(to be completed between the second and third anniversary dates)	(Signature of authorized official)
	Place ....
	Date ....
	(Seal or stamp of the authority, as appropriate)

Additional endorsements (if required)

This is to certify that the ship was the subject of an additional inspection for the purpose of verifying that the ship continued to be in compliance with the national requirements implementing the Convention, as required by Standard A3. 1, paragraph 3, of the Convention (re-registration or substantial alteration of accommodation) or for other reasons.

签发地点……………………签发日期……………………

签发此证书的正式授权官员的签字

（签发当局的钢印或印章，视情况而定）

强制性中间检查以及任何附加检查（如要求）的签注

兹证明该船已按《公约》标准 A5.1.3 和 A5.1.4 经过检查，确认《公约》附录 A5-I 具体规定的海员工作和生活条件符合上述国家实施《公约》的国内要求。

中间检查：

（需在第二个和第三个周年日之间完成）

签字……………………

（授权官员的签字）

地点……………………

日期……………………

（当局的钢印或印章，视情况而定）

附加签注（如要求）

兹证明，按《公约》标准 A3.1 第 3 款的要求（重新登记或起居舱室实质性改装）或出于其他原因，该船接受了一次附加检查以核实该船继续符合实施《公约》的国内要求。

Additional inspection: (if required)	Signed .... (Signature of authorized official) Place .... Date .... (Seal or stamp of the authority, as appropriate)
Additional inspection: (if required)	Signed .... (Signature of authorized official) Place .... Date .... (Seal or stamp of the authority, as appropriate)
Additional inspection: (if required)	Signed .... (Signature of authorized official) Place .... Date .... (Seal or stamp of the authority, as appropriate)

附加检查：
（如要求）

签字……………………………………
（授权官员的签字）

地点……………………………………
日期……………………………………
（当局的钢印或印章，视情况而定）

附加检查：
（如要求）

签字……………………………………
（授权官员的签字）

地点……………………………………
日期……………………………………
（当局的钢印或印章，视情况而定）

附加检查：
（如要求）

签字……………………………………
（授权官员的签字）

地点……………………………………
日期……………………………………
（当局的钢印或印章，视情况而定）

Maritime Labour Convention, 2006

Declaration of Maritime Labour Compliance—Part I

(Note: This Declaration must be attached to the ship's Maritime Labour Certificate)

Issued under the authority of: .... *(insert name of competent authority as defined in Article II, paragraph 1(a), of the Convention)*

With respect to the provisions of the Maritime Labour Convention, 2006, the following referenced ship:

Name of ship	IMO number	Gross tonnage

is maintained in accordance with Standard A5. 1. 3 of the Convention.

The undersigned declares, on behalf of the abovementioned competent authority, that:

(a) the provisions of the Maritime Labour Convention are fully embodied in the national requirements referred to below;

(b) these national requirements are contained in the national provisions referenced below; explanations concerning the content of those provisions are provided where necessary;

(c) the details of any substantial equivalencies under Article VI, paragraphs 3 and 4, are provided <under the corresponding national requirement listed below> <in the section provided for this purpose below> (*strike out the statement which is not applicable*);

(d) any exemptions granted by the competent authority in accordance with Title 3 are clearly indicated in the section provided for this purpose below; and

《2006年海事劳工公约》

"海事劳工符合声明"—第Ⅰ部分

（注：本声明必须附于船舶的"海事劳工证书"之后）

在……………………………（填入《公约》第二条第1(a)款界定的主管当局的名称）的授权下签发。

就《2006年海事劳工公约》的规定而言，下述船舶：

船名	IMO编号	总吨位

与《公约》标准A5.1.3保持一致。

在下签字者代表上述主管当局声明：

(a)《海事劳工公约》的规定已充分体现在下述国内要求之中；

(b) 这些国内要求载明于下文所述的国内规定中；必要时提供关于这些规定内容的解释；

(c) 根据第六条第3款和第4款的任何实质上等效的细节在＜下文所列的相应国内要求下＞＜下文为此目的而设的一节中＞（删去不适用的陈述）提供；

(d) 主管当局根据标题三所准予的任何免除在下文为此目的而设的一节中明确指出；以及

(e) any ship-type specific requirements under national legislation are also referenced under the requirements concerned.

1. Minimum age (Regulation 1.1) ....

2. Medical certification (Regulation 1.2) ....

3. Qualifications of seafarers (Regulation 1.3) ....

4. Seafarers' employment agreements (Regulation 2.1) ....

5. Use of any licensed or certified or regulated private recruitment and placement service (Regulation 1.4) ....

6. Hours of work or rest (Regulation 2.3) ....

7. Manning levels for the ship (Regulation 2.7) ....

8. Accommodation (Regulation 3.1) ....

9. On-board recreational facilities (Regulation 3.1) ....

10. Food and catering (Regulation 3.2) ....

11. Health and safety and accident prevention (Regulation 4.3) ....

12. On-board medical care (Regulation 4.1) ....

13. On-board complaint procedures (Regulation 5.1.5) ....

14. Payment of wages (Regulation 2.2) ....

Name: ....

Title: ....

Signature: ....

Place: ....

Date: ....

(Seal or stamp of the authority, as appropriate)

(e) 在有关要求中还提及了国内立法中针对任何船舶类型的具体要求。

1. 最低年龄（规则 1.1）……………………………………

2. 健康证书（规则 1.2）……………………………………

3. 海员的资格（规则 1.3）……………………………………

4. 海员就业协议(规则 2.1）……………………………………

5. 使用任何有许可证的或经发证或规范的私营招募和安置服务机构(规则 1.4）……………………………………

6. 工作或休息时间(规则 2.3）……………………………………

7. 船舶配员水平（规则 2.7）……………………………………

8. 起居舱室（规则 3.1）……………………………………

9. 船上娱乐设施（规则 3.1）……………………………………

10. 食品和膳食服务（规则 3.2）……………………………………

11. 健康和安全及事故预防（规则 4.3）……………………………………

12. 船上医护(规则 4.1）……………………………………

13. 船上投诉程序（规则 5.1.5）……………………………………

14. 工资支付（规则 2.2）……………………………………

姓名：……………………………………

职务：……………………………………

签字：……………………………………

地点：……………………………………

日期：……………………………………

（当局的钢印或印章，视情况而定）

Substantial equivalencies

(*Note*: *Strike out the statement which is not applicable*)

The following substantial equivalencies, as provided under Article VI, paragraphs 3 and 4, of the Convention, except where stated above, are noted (*insert description if applicable*):

....

....

No equivalency has been granted.

Name: ....

Title: ....

Signature: ....

Place: ....

Date: ....

(Seal or stamp of the authority, as appropriate)

Exemptions

(*Note*: *Strike out the statement which is not applicable*)

The following exemptions granted by the competent authority as provided in Title 3 of the Convention are noted:

....

....

No equivalency has been granted.

Name: ....

实质上等效

（注：删去不适用的陈述）

按《公约》第六条第3款和第4款规定的以下实质上等效，除在前面陈述外，注释如下（如适用，填入描述）：

....

....

未准许等效。

姓名：..

职务：..

签字：..

地点：..

日期：..

（当局的钢印或印章，视情况而定）

免　除

（注：删去不适用的陈述）

主管当局根据《公约》标题三的规定准许的免除注释如下：

....

....

未准许等效。

姓名：..

Title: ....

Signature: ....

Place: ....

Date: ....

(Seal or stamp of the authority, as appropriate)

职务：..............................

签字：..............................

地点：..............................

日期：..............................

（当局的钢印或印章，视情况而定）

Declaration of Maritime Labour Compliance—Part II

Measures adopted to ensure ongoing compliance between inspections

The following measures have been drawn up by the shipowner, named in the Maritime Labour Certificate to which this Declaration is attached, to ensure ongoing compliance between inspections:

(State below the measures drawn up to ensure compliance with each of the items in Part I)

1. Minimum age (Regulation 1. 1) ☐

....

2. Medical certification (Regulation 1. 2) ☐

....

3. Qualifications of seafarers (Regulation 1. 3) ☐

....

4. Seafarers' employment agreements (Regulation 2. 1) ☐

....

5. Use of any licensed or certified or regulated private recruitment and placement service (Regulation 1. 4) ☐

....

6. Hours of work or rest (Regulation 2. 3) ☐

....

7. Manning levels for the ship (Regulation 2. 7) ☐

....

8. Accommodation (Regulation 3. 1) ☐

....

9. On-board recreational facilities (Regulation 3. 1) ☐

....

10. Food and catering (Regulation 3. 2) ☐

“海事劳工符合声明”—第Ⅱ部分

为确保检查之间持续符合所采取的措施

后附本“声明”的“海事劳工证书”中具名的船东制定了以下措施来确保检查之间的持续符合：

（为确保符合第Ⅰ部分中的各项而制定的措施陈述如下）

1. 最低年龄（规则 1.1） □

....

2. 健康证书（规则 1.2） □

....

3. 海员的资格（规则 1.3） □

....

4. 海员就业协议（规则 2.1） □

....

5. 使用任何有许可证的或经发证或规范的私营招募和安置服务机构（规则 1.4） □

....

6. 工作或休息时间（规则 2.3） □

....

7. 船舶配员水平（规则 2.7） □

....

8. 起居舱室（规则 3.1） □

....

9. 船上娱乐设施（规则 3.1） □

....

10. 食品和膳食服务（规则 3.2） □

....

11. Health and safety and accident prevention (Regulation 4. 3) ☐

....

12. On-board medical care (Regulation 4. 1) ☐

....

13. On-board complaint procedures (Regulation 5. 1. 5) ☐

....

14. Payment of wages (Regulation 2. 2) ☐

....

I hereby certify that the above measures have been drawn up to ensure ongoing compliance, between inspections, with the requirements listed in Part I.

Name of shipowner:[①] ....
Company address: ....
Name of the authorized signatory: ....
Title: ....
Signature of the authorized signatory:

....
Date: ....
(Stamp or seal of the shipowner[①])

---

① *Shipowner* means the owner of the ship or another organization or person, such as the manager, agent or bareboat charterer, who has assumed the responsibility for the operation of the ship from the owner and who, on assuming such responsibility, has agreed to take over the duties and responsibilities imposed on shipowners in accordance with this Convention, regardless of whether any other organizations or persons fulfil certain of the duties or responsibilities on behalf of the shipowner. See Article II (1)(j) of the Convention.

11. 健康和安全及事故预防(规则 4.3) ☐

....

12. 船上医护(规则 4.1) ☐

....

13. 船上投诉程序(规则 5.1.5) ☐

....

14. 工资支付(规则 2.2) ☐

....

我特此证明,为确保检查之间持续符合第I部分所列的要求而制定了上述措施。

船东[①]名称:..............................

公司地址:..............................

授权签字人姓名:..............................

职务:..............................

授权签字人签字:..............................

日期:..............................

(船东[①]的印章或钢印)

---

① “船东”系指船舶所有人或从船舶所有人那里承担了船舶经营责任并在承担这种责任时已同意接受船东根据本公约所承担的职责和责任的另一组织或个人,如管理人、代理人或光船承租人,无论是否有任何其他组织或个人代表船东履行了某些职责或责任。见公约第二条第(1)(j)款。

The above measures have been reviewed by (*insert name of competent authority or duly recognized organization*) and, following inspection of the ship, have been determined as meeting the purposes set out under Standard A5. 1. 3, paragraph 10(b), regarding measures to ensure initial and ongoing compliance with the requirements set out in Part I of this Declaration.

Name: ....

Title: ....

Address: ....

Signature: ....

Place: ....

Date: ....

(Seal or stamp of the authority, as appropriate)

上述措施已经过(填入主管当局或正式认可组织的名称)审查并且在对船舶进行检查后,就确保初始并持续符合本“声明”第I部分所列要求的措施,已确定满足了标准A5.1.3第10(b)款所列的目标。

姓名:……………………………………

职务:……………………………………

地址:……………………………………

签字:……………………………………

地点:……………………………………

日期:……………………………………

(当局的钢印或印章,视情况而定)

Interim Maritime Labour Certificate

Issued under the provisions of Article V and Title 5 of the
Maritime Labour Convention, 2006
(referred to below as "the Convention")
under the authority of the Government of:

....

(full designation of the State whose flag the ship is entitled to fly)

by ....

(full designation and address of the competent authority or recognized organization duly authorized under the provisions of the Convention)

Particulars of the ship

Name of ship ....

Distinctive number or letters ....

Port of registry ....

Date of registry ....

Gross tonnage[①] ....

IMO number ....

Type of ship ....

---

① For ships covered by the tonnage measurement interim scheme adopted by the IMO, the gross tonnage is that which is included in the REMARKS column of the International Tonnage Certificate (1969). See Article II (1)(c) of the Convention.

临时海事劳工证书

根据《2006 年海事劳工公约》(以下简称“《公约》”)

第五条和标题五的规定,

经……………………政府授权

(船舶有权悬挂其旗帜的国家的全称)

由……………………签发

(主管当局或根据《公约》规定正式授权的认可组织的全称和地址)

船舶细节

船名……………………

船舶编号或呼号……………………

船籍港……………………

登记日期……………………

总吨位①……………………

IMO 编号……………………

船舶类型……………………

① 对于 IMO 通过的吨位丈量临时表格所包括的船舶,总吨位为包括在“国际吨位证书(1969)”“备注”栏中的总吨位。见公约第二条第(1)(c)款。

Name and address of the shipowner[1] ....

....

This is to certify, for the purposes of Standard A5. 1. 3, paragraph 7, of the Convention, that:

(a) this ship has been inspected, as far as reasonable and practicable, for the matters listed in Appendix A5-I to the Convention, taking into account verification of items under (b), (c) and (d) below;

(b) the shipowner has demonstrated to the competent authority or recognized organization that the ship has adequate procedures to comply with the Convention;

(c) the master is familiar with the requirements of the Convention and the responsibilities for implementation; and

(d) relevant information has been submitted to the competent authority or recognized organization to produce a Declaration of Maritime Labour Compliance.

This Certificate is valid until .... subject to inspections in accordance with Standards A5. 1. 3 and A5. 1. 4.

Completion date of the inspection referred to under (a) above was

....

---

① *Shipowner* means the owner of the ship or another organization or person, such as the manager, agent or bareboat charterer, who has assumed the responsibility for the operation of the ship from the owner and who, on assuming such responsibility, has agreed to take over the duties and responsibilities imposed on shipowners in accordance with this Convention, regardless of whether any other organizations or persons fulfil certain of the duties or responsibilities on behalf of the shipowner. See Article II (1)(j) of the Convention.

船东[①]名称和地址..

兹证明，就《公约》标准 A5.1.3 第 7 款而言：

(a) 该船已就《公约》附录 A5-I 所列事项进行过尽合理和实际可行的检查，并考虑了对下文第(b)、(c)和(d)项中项目的核实；

(b) 船东已向主管当局或认可组织表明该船有遵守《公约》的适当程序；

(c) 船长熟悉《公约》的要求以及实施的责任；以及

(d) 制作"海事劳工符合声明"的相关信息已提交给主管当局或认可组织。

本证书有效期至..，但取决于根据标准 A5.1.3 和 A5.1.4 的检查。

上述第(a)项中所述之检查的完成日期为..

---

① "船东"系指船舶所有人或从船舶所有人那里承担了船舶经营责任并在承担这种责任时已同意接受船东根据本公约所承担的职责和责任的另一组织或个人，如管理人、代理人或光船承租人，无论是否有任何其他组织或个人代表船东履行了某些职责或责任。见公约第二条第(1)(j)款。

Issued at .... on ....

Signature of the duly authorized official issuing the interim Certificate ....

(Seal or stamp of issuing authority, as appropriate)

签发地点.................................签发日期.................................

签发此临时证书的正式授权官员的签字.................................

（发证当局的钢印或印章，视情况而定）

APPENDIX A5-III

General areas that are subject to a detailed inspection by an authorized officer in a port of a Member carrying out a port State inspection pursuant to Standard A5. 2. 1:

Minimum age

Medical certification

Qualifications of seafarers

Seafarers' employment agreements

Use of any licensed or certified or regulated private recruitment and placement service

Hours of work or rest

Manning levels for the ship

Accommodation

On-board recreational facilities

Food and catering

Health and safety and accident prevention

On-board medical care

On-board complaint procedures

Payment of wages

附录 A5-III

在成员国港口内，授权官员根据标准 A5.2.1 开展港口国检查时将进行详细检查的一般领域：

最低年龄

健康证书

海员的资格

海员就业协议

使用任何有许可证的或经发证或规范的私营招募和安置服务机构

工作或休息时间

船舶配员水平

起居舱室

船上娱乐设施

食品和膳食服务

健康和安全及事故预防

船上医护

船上投诉程序

工资支付

APPENDIX B5-I—EXAMPLE OF A NATIONAL DECLARATION

See Guideline B5. 1. 3, paragraph 5

Maritime Labour Convention, 2006

Declaration of Maritime Labour Compliance—Part I

(*Note: This Declaration must be attached to the ship's Maritime Labour Certificate*)

Issued under the authority of: **The Ministry of Maritime Transport of XXXXXX**

With respect to the provisions of the Maritime Labour Convention, 2006, the following referenced ship:

Name of ship	**IMO number**	**Gross tonnage**
M. S. EXAMPLE	12345	1,000

is maintained in accordance with Standard A5. 1. 3 of the Convention.

The undersigned declares, on behalf of the abovementioned competent authority, that:

(a) the provisions of the Maritime Labour Convention are fully embodied in the national requirements referred to below;

(b) these national requirements are contained in the national provisions referenced below; explanations concerning the content of those provisions are provided where necessary;

(c) the details of any substantial equivalencies under Article VI, paragraphs 3 and 4, are provided <under the corresponding national requirement listed below> <in the section provided for

附录 B5-I—国家声明样本

见导则 B5.1.3 第 5 款

《2006 年海事劳工公约》
"海事劳工符合声明"—第 I 部分

（注：本声明必须附在船舶的"海事劳工证书"之后）

在 **XXXXXX 国海运部**的授权下签发

就《2006 年海事劳工公约》的规定而言，下述船舶：

船名	IMO 编号	总吨位
M.S. EXAMPLE	12345	1 000

与《公约》标准 A5.1.3 保持一致。

在下签字者代表上述主管当局声明：

(a)《海事劳工公约》的规定已充分体现在下述国内要求之中；

(b) 这些国内要求载明于下文所述的国内规定中；必要时提供关于这些规定内容的解释；

(c) 根据第六条第 3 款和第 4 款的任何实质上等效的细节在＜下文所列的相应国内要求下＞＜下文为此目的而设的一节中＞（删去不适用的陈述）提供；

this purpose below> (*strike out the statement which is not applicable*);

(d) any exemptions granted by the competent authority in accordance with Title 3 are clearly indicated in the section provided for this purpose below; and

(e) any ship-type specific requirements under national legislation are also referenced under the requirements concerned.

1. Minimum age (Regulation 1.1)

   Shipping Law, *No.* 123 *of* 1905, *as amended* ("*Law*"), *Chapter* X; *Shipping Regulations* ("*Regulations*"), 2006, *Rules* 1111—1222.

   Minimum ages are those referred to in the Convention.

   "*Night*" *means* 9 *p. m. to* 6 *a. m. unless the Ministry of Maritime Transport* ("*Ministry*") *approves a different period.*

   Examples of hazardous work restricted to 18-*year-olds or over are listed in Schedule A hereto. In the case of cargo ships, no one under* 18 *may work in the areas marked on the ship's plan (to be attached to this Declaration) as "hazardous area".*

2. Medical certification (Regulation 1.2)

   Law, *Chapter* XI; *Regulations*, *Rules* 1223—1233.

   Medical certificates shall conform to the STCW requirements, where applicable; in other cases, the STCW requirements are applied with any necessary adjustments.

   Qualified opticians on list approved by Ministry may issue certificates concerning eyesight.

   *Medical examinations follow the ILO/WHO Guidelines referred to in Guideline B*1. 2. 1

(d) 主管当局根据标题三所准予的任何免除在下文为此目的而设的一节中明确指出；以及

(e) 在有关要求中还提及了国内立法针对任何船舶类型的具体要求。

1. 最低年龄(规则 1.1)

经修正的《航运法》1905 年第 123 号(“《法律》”)，第十章；《2006 年航运条例》(“《条例》”)，第 1111－1222 条。

最低年龄为《公约》中所述的最低年龄。

除非海运部(“部”)批准了一个不同的时段，“夜间”系指晚 9 点至早 6 点。

限于 18 岁或以上人员的危害性工作的例子列于附表 A。对于货船而言，任何 18 岁以下的人员均不得在船舶平面图(将附在本声明之后)中被标为“危险区域”的区域内工作。

2. 健康证书(规则 1.2)

《法律》第十一章；《条例》第 1223－1233 条。

适用时，健康证书须符合《STCW 公约》的要求；在其他情况下，经过任何必要调整后适用《STCW 公约》的要求。

经部批准的清单上的合格眼科医生可以签发关于视力的证书。

按导则 B1.2.1 中所述的《ILO /WHO 指南》进行体检。

Declaration of Maritime Labour Compliance—Part II

Measures adopted to ensure ongoing compliance between inspections

The following measures have been drawn up by the shipowner, named in the Maritime Labour Certificate to which this Declaration is attached, to ensure ongoing compliance between inspections:

(*State below the measures drawn up to ensure compliance with each of the items in Part I*)

1. Minimum age (Regulation 1. 1) [X]

   Date of birth of each seafarer is noted against his/her name on the crew list.

   The list is checked at the beginning of each voyage by the master or officer acting on his or her behalf ("competent officer"), who records the date of such verification.

   Each seafarer under 18 receives, at the time of engagement, a note prohibiting him/her from performing night work or the work specifically listed as hazardous (see Part I, section 1, above) and any other hazardous work, and requiring him/her to consult the competent officer in case of doubt. A copy of the note, with the seafarer's signature under "received and read", and the date of signature, is kept by the competent officer.

2. Medical certification (Regulation 1. 2) [X]

   The medical certificates are kept in strict confidence by the competent officer, together with a list, prepared under the competent officer's responsibility and stating for each seafarer on board: the functions of the seafarer, the date of the current

“海事劳工符合声明”—第Ⅱ部分

为确保在检查之间持续符合所采取的措施

在后附本“声明”的“海事劳工证书”中具名的船东制定了以下措施以确保检查之间的持续符合：

（为确保符合第Ⅰ部分中的各项而制定的措施陈述如下）

1. 最低年龄(规则1.1) ☒

每一海员的出生日期在船员清单中的姓名旁注明。

在每次航程开始时，由船长或代表船长行事的高级船员(“主管高级船员”)对清单进行核查，并记录该类核实的日期。

在受聘时，每名18岁以下的海员收到一份禁止其从事夜间工作或从事被特别列为有害的工作(见上文第Ⅰ部分第1节)以及任何其他有害工作的通知，并要求该海员在有疑问时咨询主管高级船员。经海员在“收到并已阅”字样下面签字的一份该通知，连同签字日期，由主管高级船员保存。

2. 健康证书(规则1.2) ☒

健康证书，与主管高级船员负责下准备的、陈述船上每一海员的职能、当前健康证书的日期和有关证书上记录的海员健康状况的清单一起，由主管高级船员在严格保密的条件下保管。

medical certificate(s) and the health status noted on the certificate concerned.

In any case of possible doubt as to whether the seafarer is medically fit for a particular function or functions, the competent officer consults the seafarer's doctor or another qualified practitioner and records a summary of the practitioner's conclusions, as well as the practitioner's name and telephone number and the date of the consultation.

在对海员的身体是否适合某一特定职能或某些职能可能存在疑问的任何情况下，主管高级船员将咨询海员的医生或另一名合格的从业医生，并记录该从业医生的结论概要以及该从业医生的姓名、电话号码和咨询日期。

关于新增修正内容的说明

1998年，国际海事组织(IMO)和国际劳工组织(ILO)成立了“IMO/ILO联合特设专家工作组”，来审议有关海员在遭到遗弃及伤亡病残情况下的责任和赔偿问题。经过多轮努力，该专家工作组于2009年3月发布了有关该问题的最终报告，形成了较为完善的对《2006年海事劳工公约》“守则”相关条款的修正草案。限于当时该公约并未生效，因而无法利用该公约中的相关条款来启动修正程序。

《2006年海事劳工公约》在2006年2月通过时，限于当时对该问题的研究程度，仅在规则2.5(遣返)和规则4.2(船东的责任)中对该问题做出了较为原则性的规定，相应的守则标准和导则部分仍不完善，缺乏可操作性。

《2006年海事劳工公约》在2013年8月20日生效后，国际劳工组织理事会依据该公约第十三条设立了特别三方委员会，被指派参加该委员会的船东组代表和海员组代表向国际劳工组织总干事联合提交了有关该问题的两套修正案。国际劳工组织总干事于2013年10月4日将修正案通知给所有成员国加以评述。包括中国在内的23个成员国在规定的时间内对该修正案提出了评述和建议。

该修正案在2014年4月7日至11日召开的特别三方委员会第一次会议上通过，随后在2014年5月28日至6月12日召开的第103届国际劳工大会上得以正式通过，预计将于2017年年初生效。

特别三方委员会在通过该修正案的同时，通过了一个有关修正案过渡措施的决议。该决议强调该修正案的生效绝不会致使此前依据《2006年海事劳工公约》适当签发且仍然有效的海事劳工证书或海事劳工符合声明失效；敦促成员国确保在悬挂其旗帜的船舶上，在不迟于该修正案生效之后的第一次换证检验之日，使签发或换发的海事劳工证书和海事劳工符合声明符合经修正的《2006年海事劳工公约》的要求；明确了在实施港口国监督时，海事劳工证书和海事劳工符合声明仍依据该公约保持有效，直到该修正案生效之后的第一次换证检验。

值此重印的机会，附上该修正案的内容，供读者参考。

校译者　张铎

2014年6月

International Labour Conference

AMENDMENTS OF 2014
TO THE MARITIME LABOUR CONVENTION, 2006,
APPROVED BY THE CONFERENCE
AT ITS ONE HUNDRED AND THIRD SESSION,
GENEVA, 11 JUNE 2014

国际劳工大会

大会在其第一百零三届会议上通过的
《2006 年海事劳工公约》2014 年修正案
2014 年 6 月 11 日，日内瓦

TEXT OF THE AMENDMENTS OF 2014 TO THE MARITIME LABOUR CONVENTION, 2006

Amendments to the Code implementing Regulations 2. 5 and 4. 2 and appendices of the Maritime Labour Convention, 2006 (MLC, 2006), adopted by the Special Tripartite Committee on 11 April 2014

I. Amendments to the Code implementing Regulation 2.5—Repatriation of the MLC, 2006 (and appendices)

A. Amendments relating to Standard A2. 5

In the present heading, "Standard A2. 5—Repatriation", replace "A2. 5" by "A2. 5. 1".

Following paragraph 9 of the present Standard A2. 5, add the following heading and text:

Standard A2. 5. 2—Financial security

1. In implementation of Regulation 2. 5, paragraph 2, this Standard establishes requirements to ensure the provision of an expeditious and effective financial security system to assist seafarers in the event of their abandonment.

2. For the purposes of this Standard, a seafarer shall be deemed to have been abandoned where, in violation of the requirements of this Convention or the terms of the seafarers' employment agreement, the shipowner:

(a) fails to cover the cost of the seafarer's repatriation; or

《2006 年海事劳工公约》
2014 年修正案文本

2014 年 4 月 11 日特别三方委员会通过的对实施
规则 2.5 和 4.2 的守则及《2006 年海事劳工公约
（MLC，2006）》附录的修正案

I. 对实施 MLC，2006“规则 2.5 —遣返”的守则(及附录)的修正案

A. 关于标准 A2.5 的修正

在现有标题“**标准 A2.5—遣返**”中，将“A2.5 ”替换为“A2.5.1 ”。

在现有标准 A2.5 第 9 款之后，添加以下标题和文本：

标准 A2.5.2—财务担保

1. 在实施规则 2.5 第 2 款时，本标准做出了确保迅速和有效提供财务担保系统的要求，以便在海员被遗弃的情况下对其予以援助。

2. 就本标准而言，海员须视为已被遗弃，如果船东违反本公约的要求或海员就业协议的条款：

(a) 未支付海员的遣返费用；或

(b) has left the seafarer without the necessary maintenance and support; or

(c) has otherwise unilaterally severed their ties with the seafarer including failure to pay contractual wages for a period of at least two months.

3. Each Member shall ensure that a financial security system meeting the requirements of this Standard is in place for ships flying its flag. The financial security system may be in the form of a social security scheme or insurance or a national fund or other similar arrangements. Its form shall be determined by the Member after consultation with the shipowners' and seafarers' organizations concerned.

4. The financial security system shall provide direct access, sufficient coverage and expedited financial assistance, in accordance with this Standard, to any abandoned seafarer on a ship flying the flag of the Member.

5. For the purposes of paragraph 2(b) of this Standard, necessary maintenance and support of seafarers shall include: adequate food, accommodation, drinking water supplies, essential fuel for survival on board the ship and necessary medical care.

6. Each Member shall require that ships that fly its flag, and to which paragraph 1 or 2 of Regulation 5. 1. 3 applies, carry on board a certificate or other documentary evidence of financial security issued by the financial security provider. A copy shall be posted in a conspicuous place on board where it is available to the seafarers. Where more than one financial security provider provides cover, the document provided by each provider shall be carried on board.

(b) 未向海员提供必要的照料和扶助;或

(c) 以其他方式单方断绝其与海员的关系,包括未支付契约工资达至少两个月的时间。

3.各成员国须确保悬挂其旗帜的船舶配备了符合本标准要求的财务担保系统。财务担保系统的形式可以是社会保障体系或保险或国家基金或其他类似的安排,其形式须由成员国在与有关的船东组织和海员组织协商后决定。

4.财务担保系统须依据本标准向在悬挂成员国旗帜的船舶上被遗弃的任何海员提供直接获取的渠道、充分的覆盖范围以及快速的财务援助。

5.就本标准第2(b)款而言,对海员必要的照料和扶助须包括:充足的食品、住所、饮用水供给、在船上生存所必需的燃料以及必要的医护。

6.各成员国须要求悬挂其旗帜的且受规则5.1.3第1或2款管辖的船舶,在船上携带财务担保提供方签发的财务担保证书或其他证明文件。一份副本须张贴在船上海员能够到达的显著位置。如果不止一个财务担保提供方提供了担保,则每个提供方提供的证明须携带在船上。

7. The certificate or other documentary evidence of financial security shall contain the information required in Appendix A2-I. It shall be in English or accompanied by an English translation.

8. Assistance provided by the financial security system shall be granted promptly upon request made by the seafarer or the seafarer's nominated representative and supported by the necessary justification of entitlement inaccordance with paragraph 2 above.

9. Having regard to Regulations 2. 2 and 2. 5, assistance provided by the financial security system shall be sufficient to cover the following:

(a) outstanding wages and other entitlements due from the shipowner to the seafarer under their employment agreement, the relevant collective bargaining agreement or the national law of the flag State, limited to four months of any such outstanding wages and four months of any such outstanding entitlements;

(b) all expenses reasonably incurred by the seafarer, including the cost of repatriation referred to in paragraph 10; and

(c) the essential needs of the seafarer including such items as: adequate food, clothing where necessary, accommodation, drinking water supplies, essential fuel for survival on board the ship, necessary medicalcare and any other reasonable costs or charges from the act or omission constituting the abandonment until the seafarer's arrival at home.

10. The cost of repatriation shall cover travel by appropriate and expeditious means, normally by air, and include provision for food and accommodation of the seafarer from the time of leaving the ship until arrival at the seafarer's home, necessary medical care, passage and transport of personal effects and any other reasonable costs or

7. 财务担保证书或其他证明文件须载有附录 A2-I要求的信息，其须为英文或附有英语译文。

8. 海员或其指定的代表一经提出了请求且依据上述第 2 款有必要的正当资格来支持该请求，则须立即准予财务担保系统提供的援助。

9. 考虑到规则 2.2 和规则 2.5，财务担保系统提供的援助须足以涵盖以下各项：

(a) 依据其就业协议、相关集体谈判协议或船旗国国内法律，船东应付海员的欠付工资和其他权益，限于四个月的任何此类欠付工资和四个月的任何此类欠付权益；

(b) 海员合理发生的所有费用，包括第 10 款中所述的遣返费用；和

(c) 海员的基本需求，包括如下项目：充足的食物，必要时的衣物，住所，饮用水供给，在船上生存所必需的燃料，必要的医护，以及构成遗弃的作为或不作为所造成的任何其他合理费用或花费，直到海员到家。

10. 遣返费用须覆盖适宜和迅捷的旅行方式，通常是乘坐飞机，并包括提供从海员离船时至海员到家的食宿，必要的医护，个人物品的通行和运输以及因遗弃造成的任何其他合理费用或花费。

charges arising from the abandonment.

11. The financial security shall not cease before the end of the period of validity of the financial security unless the financial security provider has given prior notification of at least 30 days to the competent authority of the flag State.

12. If the provider of insurance or other financial security has made any payment to any seafarer in accordance with this Standard, such provider shall, up to the amount it has paid and in accordance with the applicable law, acquire by subrogation, assignment or otherwise, the rights which the seafarer would have enjoyed.

13. Nothing in this Standard shall prejudice any right of recourse of the insurer or provider of financial security against third parties.

14. The provisions in this Standard are not intended to be exclusive or to prejudice any other rights, claims or remedies that may also be available to compensate seafarers who are abandoned. National laws and regulations may provide that any amounts payable under this Standard can be offset against amounts received from other sources arising from any rights, claims or remedies that may be the subject of compensation under the present Standard.

B. Amendments relating to Guideline B2.5

At the end of the present Guideline B2.5, add the following heading and text:

11. 除非财务担保提供方提前至少 30 天通知了船旗国的主管当局，否则在财务担保有效期届满之前财务担保不得终止。

12. 如果保险或其他财务担保的提供方根据本标准已向任何海员支付任何款项,则该提供方须在其支付的金额内并依据适用的法律通过代位、转让或其他方式获得该海员本应享有的权利。

13. 本标准中的任何规定均不得损害保险人或财务担保提供方针对第三方的任何追索权。

14. 本标准的规定无意具有排他性或损害还可用于赔偿被遗弃海员的任何其他权利、索赔或救济。国内法律和条例可以规定,从其他来源收到的、源于可能是本标准项下赔偿项目的任何权利、索赔或救济的金额可冲抵本标准项下的任何应付金额。

B. 关于导则 B2. 5 的修正

在现有导则 B2. 5 的末尾处,添加以下标题和文本:

Guideline B2.5.3—Financial security

1. In implementation of paragraph 8 of Standard A2.5.2, if time is needed to check the validity of certain aspects of the request of the seafarer or the seafarer's nominated representative, this should not prevent the seafarer from immediately receiving such part of the assistance requested as is recognized as justified.

C. Amendment to include a new appendix

Before Appendix A5-I, add the following appendix:

Appendix A2-I

Evidence of financial security under Regulation 2.5, paragraph 2

The certificate or other documentary evidence referred to in Standard A2.5.2, paragraph 7, shall include the following information:

(a) name of the ship;

(b) port of registry of the ship;

(c) call sign of the ship;

(d) IMO number of the ship;

(e) name and address of the provider or providers of the financial security;

(f) contact details of the persons or entity responsible for handling seafarers' requests for relief;

(g) name of the shipowner;

导则 B2.5.3—财务担保

1.在实施标准 A2.5.2 第 8 款时，如果该海员或该海员指定代表的请求在某些方面的有效性需要时间来核实，这不应阻止该海员立即获得所请求援助中被认可为正当的部分。

C.包含一个新附录的修正

在附录 A5-I之前，添加以下附录：

附录 A2-I

规则 2.5 第 2 款下的财务担保证明

标准 A2.5.2 第 7 款所述的证书或其他证明文件须包含以下信息：

(a) 船名；

(b) 船籍港；

(c) 船舶呼号；

(d) 船舶 IMO 编号；

(e) 财务担保提供方名称和地址；

(f) 负责处理海员救济请求的人员或实体的联系详情；

(g) 船东名称；

(h) 财务担保有效期；和

(h) period of validity of the financial security; and

(i) an attestation from the financial security provider that the financial security meets the requirements of Standard A2. 5. 2.

D. Amendments relating to Appendices A5-I, A5-II and A5-III

At the end of Appendix A5-I, add the following item:

Financial security for repatriation

In Appendix A5-II, after item 14 under the heading Declaration of Maritime Labour Compliance—Part I, add the following item:

15. Financial security for repatriation (Regulation 2. 5)

In Appendix A5-II, after item 14 under the heading Declaration of Maritime Labour Compliance—Part II, add the following item:

15. Financial security for repatriation (Regulation 2. 5)

At the end of Appendix A5-III, add the following area:

Financial security for repatriation

(i) 财务担保提供方出具的财务担保符合标准 A2.5.2 要求的证明。

D. 关于附录 A5-I，A5-II 和 A5-III 的修正

在附录 A5-I 末尾处，添加以下项目：

对遣返的财务担保

在附录 A5-II 中，在“海事劳工符合声明—第 I 部分”标题下的第 14 项后添加以下项目：

15. 对遣返的财务担保（规则 2.5）

在附录 A5-II 中，在“海事劳工符合声明—第 II 部分”标题下的第 14 项后添加以下项目：

15. 对遣返的财务担保（规则 2.5）

在附录 A5-III 的末尾处，添加以下领域：

对遣返的财务担保

Ⅱ. Amendments to the Code implementing Regulation 4.2— Shipowners' liability of the MLC, 2006(and appendices)

A. Amendments relating to Standard A4.2

In the present heading, "Standard A4.2—Shipowners' liability", replace"A4.2" by "A4.2.1".

Following paragraph 7 of the present Standard A4.2, add the following text:

8. National laws and regulations shall provide that the system of financial security to assure compensation as provided by paragraph 1 (b) of this Standard for contractual claims, as defined in Standard A4.2.2, meet the following minimum requirements:

(a) the contractual compensation, where set out in the seafarer's employment agreement and without prejudice to subparagraph (c) of this paragraph, shall be paid in full and without delay;

(b) there shall be no pressure to accept a payment less than the contractual amount;

(c) where the nature of the long-term disability of a seafarer makes it difficult to assess the full compensation to which the seafarer may been titled, an interim payment or payments shall be made to the seafarer so as to avoid undue hardship;

(d) in accordance with Regulation 4.2, paragraph 2, the seafarer shall receive payment without prejudice to other legal rights, but such payment may be offset by the shipowner against any

Ⅱ.对实施 MLC, 2006“规则 4.2 —船东的责任”的守则(及附录)的修正案

A.关于标准 A4.2 的修正

在现有标题“**标准 A4.2—船东的责任**”中,将“A4.2”替换为“A4.2.1”。

在现有标准 A4.2 第 7 款之后,添加以下文本:

8.国内法律和条例须规定,确保按本标准第 1(b)款的规定来赔偿标准 A4.2.2 所界定的契约性索赔的财务担保系统符合以下最低要求:

(a) 海员就业协议中规定的且不损害本款第(c)项的契约性赔偿须毫不延迟地全额支付;

(b) 不得施压以接受低于契约金额的款项;

(c) 如果海员长期残疾的性质使得难以估算海员可能有权获得的全额赔偿,须向海员支付一笔或多笔阶段性款项以避免不应有的困难;

(d) 依据规则 4.2 第 2 款,海员接收的款项须不损害其他合法权利,但海员针对船东提出的、源于同一事件的任何其他索赔而发生的任何赔偿金可由船东来冲抵该款项;

damages resulting from any other claim made by the seafarer against the shipowner and arising from the same incident; and

(e) the claim for contractual compensation may be brought directly by the seafarer concerned, or their next of kin, or a representative of the seafarer or designated beneficiary.

9. National laws and regulations shall ensure that seafarers receive prior notification if a shipowner's financial security is to be cancelled or terminated.

10. National laws and regulations shall ensure that the competent authority of the flag State is notified by the provider of the financial security if a shipowner's financial security is cancelled or terminated.

11. Each Member shall require that ships that fly its flag carry on board a certificate or other documentary evidence of financial security issued by the financial security provider. A copy shall be posted in a conspicuous place on board where it is available to the seafarers. Where more than one financial security provider provides cover, the document provided by each provider shall be carried on board.

12. The financial security shall not cease before the end of the period of validity of the financial security unless the financial security provider has given prior notification of at least 30 days to the competent authority of the flag State.

13. The financial security shall provide for the payment of all-contractual claims covered by it which arise during the period for which the document is valid.

14. The certificate or other documentary evidence of financial security shall contain the information required in Appendix A4-I. It

(e) 对契约性赔偿的索赔可由相关海员或其最近亲属或海员的代表或指定受益人直接提出。

9.国内法律和条例须确保海员在船东的财务担保将被取消或终止时提前得到通知。

10. 国内法律和条例须确保财务担保提供方在船东的财务担保被取消或终止时通知船旗国的主管当局。

11. 各成员国须要求悬挂其旗帜的船舶在船上携带财务担保提供方签发的财务担保证书或其他证明文件。一份副本须张贴在船上海员能够到达的显著位置。如果不止一个财务担保提供方提供了担保,则每个提供方提供的证明须携带在船上。

12. 除非财务担保提供方提前至少 30 天通知了船旗国的主管当局,否则在财务担保有效期届满之前财务担保不得终止。

13.财务担保须足以支付由其担保的且发生于该证明有效期内的所有契约性索赔。

14. 财务担保证书或其他证明文件须载有附录 A4-I要求的信息,其须为英文或附有英语译文。

shall be in English or accompanied by an English translation.

Add the following heading and text following the present StandardA4.2:

Standard A4.2.2—Treatment of contractual claims

1. For the purposes of Standard A4.2.1, paragraph 8, and the present Standard, the term "contractual claim" means any claim which relates to death or long-term disability of seafarers due to an occupational injury, illness or hazard as set out in national law, the seafarers' employment agreement or collective agreement.

2. The system of financial security, as provided for in Standard A4.2.1, paragraph 1(b), may be in the form of a social security scheme or insuranceor fund or other similar arrangements. Its form shall be determined by the Member after consultation with the shipowners' and seafarers' organizations concerned.

3. National laws and regulations shall ensure that effective arrangements are in place to receive, deal with and impartially settle contractual claims relating to compensation referred to in Standard A4.2.1, paragraph 8, through expeditious and fair procedures.

B. Amendments relating to Guideline B4.2

In the present heading, "Guideline B4.2—Shipowners' liability", replace "B4.2" by "B4.2.1".

In paragraph 1 of the present Guideline B4.2, replace "Standard A4.2"by "Standard A4.2.1".

Following paragraph 3 of the present Guideline B4.2, add the following heading and text:

在现有标准 A4.2 后添加以下标题和文本：

标准 A4.2.2—契约性索赔的处理

1. 就标准 A4.2.1 第 8 款和本标准而言，“契约性索赔”一词是指相关于海员因国内法律、海员就业协议或集体协议所规定的职业伤害、疾病或危害而死亡或长期残疾的任何索赔。

2. 标准 A4.2.1 第 1(b)款规定的财务担保系统的形式可以是社会保障体系或保险或基金或其他类似的安排，其形式须由成员国在与有关的船东组织和海员组织协商后决定。

3. 国内法律和条例须确保存在有效的安排，通过快捷和公平的程序来接收、处理和公正地解决与标准 A4.2.1 第 8 款所述赔偿有关的契约性索赔。

B. 关于导则 B4.2 的修正

在现有标题“**导则 B4.2—船东的责任**”中，将“B4.2”替换为“B4.2.1”。

在现有导则 B4.2 第 1 款中，将“**标准** A4.2”替换为“**标准** A4.2.1”。

在本导则 B4.2 第 3 款之后，添加以下标题和文本：

Guideline B4.2.2——Treatment of contractual claims

1. National laws or regulations should provide that the parties to the payment of a contractual claim may use the Model Receipt and Release Form set out in Appendix B4-I.

C. Amendment to include new appendices

After Appendix A2-I, add the following appendix:

Appendix A4-I

Evidence of financial security under Regulation 4.2

The certificate or other documentary evidence of financial security required under Standard A4.2.1, paragraph 14, shall include the following information:

(a) name of the ship;

(b) port of registry of the ship;

(c) call sign of the ship;

(d) IMO number of the ship;

(e) name and address of the provider or providers of the financial security;

(f) contact details of the persons or entity responsible for handling seafarers' contractual claims;

(g) name of the shipowner;

(h) period of validity of the financial security; and

(i) an attestation from the financial security provider that the finan-

导则 B4.2.2——契约性索赔的处理

1. 国内法律或条例应规定支付契约性索赔的各方可使用附录 B4-I 列出的“收据和解除书范本”。

C. 包含一个新附录的修正

在附录 A2-I 之后,添加以下附录:

附录 A4-I

规则 4.2 下的财务担保证明

标准 A4.2.1 第 14 款要求的财务担保证书或其他证明文件须包含以下信息:

(a) 船名;

(b) 船籍港;

(c) 船舶呼号;

(d) 船舶 IMO 编号;

(e) 财务担保提供方名称和地址;

(f) 负责处理海员契约性索赔的人员或实体的联系详情;

(g) 船东名称;

(h) 财务担保有效期;和

(i) 财务担保提供方出具的财务担保符合标准 A4.2.1 要求的证明。

cial security meets the requirements of Standard A4. 2. 1.

After Appendix A4-I, add the following appendix:

Appendix B4-I

Model Receipt and Release Form
referred to in Guideline B4. 2. 2

Ship (name, port of registry and IMO number): ....

Incident (date and place): ....

Seafarer/legal heir and/or dependant: ....

Shipowner: ....

I, [Seafarer] [Seafarer's legal heir and/or dependant][1] hereby acknowledge receipt of the sum of [currency and amount] in satisfaction of the Shipowner's obligation to pay contractual compensation for personal injury and/or death under the terms and conditions of [my] [the Seafarer's][2] employment and I hereby release the Shipowner from their obligations under the said terms and conditions.

The payment is made without admission of liability of any claims and is accepted without prejudice to [my] [the Seafarer's legal heir and/or dependant's][3] right to pursue any claim at law in respect of negligence, tort, breach of statutory duty or any other legal redress available and arising out of the above incident.

---

[1] Delete as appropriate

[2] Delete as appropriate

[3] Delete as appropriate

在附录 A4-I 之后，添加以下附录：

附录 B4-I

导则 B4.2.2 所述的收据和解除书范本

船舶(船名、船籍港和 IMO 编号)：……………………………………

事件(日期和地点)：……………………………………

海员/法定继承人和/或受抚养人：……………………………………

船东：……………………………………

我，[海员][海员的法定继承人和/或受抚养人]❶在此确认收到用以履行船东义务的款项[币种和金额]，以支付[我的][海员的]❷就业条款和条件项下人身伤害和/或死亡的契约性赔偿，并且我在此解除船东在该条款和条件项下的义务。

支付款项并非承认对任何索赔负有责任，对款项的接受也不损害[我][海员的法定继承人和/或受抚养人]❸就疏忽、侵权、违反法定职责行使任何法定索赔的权利或者就任何其他可用的且源于上述事件的法律救济行使权利。

---

❶ 视情况删除

❷ 视情况删除

❸ 视情况删除

Dated: ....

Seafarer/legal heir and/or dependant: ....

Signed: ....

For acknowledgement:

Shipowner/Shipowner representative:

Signed: ....

Financial security provider:

Signed: ....

D. Amendments relating to Appendices A5-I, A5-II and A5-III

At the end of Appendix A5-I, add the following item:

Financial security relating to shipowners' liability

In Appendix A5-II, as the last item under the heading Declaration of Maritime Labour Compliance—Part I, add the following item:

16. Financial security relating to shipowners' liability (Regulation 4.2)

In Appendix A5-II, as the last item under the heading Declaration of Maritime Labour Compliance—Part II, add the following item:

16. Financial security relating to shipowners' liability (Regulation 4.2)

At the end of Appendix A5-III, add the following area:

Financial security relating to shipowners' liability

日期：..............................

海员/法定继承人和/或受抚养人：..............................

签名：..............................

确认：

船东/船东代表：

签名：..............................

财务担保提供方：

签名：..............................

D. 关于附录 A5-I，A5-II 和 A5-III 的修正

在附录 A5-I 末尾处，添加以下项目：

关于船东责任的财务担保

在附录 A5-II 中，作为“海事劳工符合声明—第 I 部分”标题下的最后一项，添加以下项目：

16. 关于船东责任的财务担保(规则 4.2)

在附录 A5-II 中，作为“海事劳工符合声明—第 II 部分”标题下的最后一项，添加以下项目：

16. 关于船东责任的财务担保(规则 4.2)

在附录 A5-III 末尾处，添加以下领域：

关于船东责任的财务担保